The Keyboard Music of
John Bull

Studies in Musicology, No. 71

George Buelow, Series Editor

Professor of Music
Indiana University

Other Titles in This Series

The Keyboard Music of
John Bull

by
Walker Cunningham

UMI RESEARCH PRESS

Ann Arbor, Michigan

Produced and distributed by
UMI Research Press
an imprint of
University Microfilms International
Ann Arbor, Michigan 48106

Library of Congress Cataloging in Publication Data

Cunningham, Walker.
    The keyboard music of John Bull.

    (Studies in musicology ; no. 71)
    Revision of thesis (Ph.D.)–University of California–
Berkeley, 1981.
    Bibliography: p.
    Includes index.
    1. Bull, John, d. 1628. Keyboard music. I. Title.
II. Series.

ML410.B93C8 1984   786.1'092'4   84-59
ISBN 0-8357-1466-7

42,303

The human understanding of its own nature easily supposes there to be more order and uniformity in things than it finds. . . .

Francis Bacon, *Novum Organum* (1620)
Book I, Aphorism XLV

Contents

List of Tables

List of Abbreviations

BW   The Byrd Edition
17. *Consort Music,* ed. K. Elliot
(London, 1971).

CK   *Pieter Cornet: Collected Keyboard
Works,* ed. W. Apel, *Corpus of Early
Keyboard Music,* voL 26 (1969).

DVB   *The Dublin Virginal Manuscript,* ed.
J. Ward (Wellesley, Mass., 1954).

EECM   *Early English Church Music*
6. *Early Tudor Organ Music I: Music
for the Office,* ed. J. Caldwell (London, 1965).
10. *Early Tudor Organ Music II: Music for the Mass,* ed. D. Stevens
(London, 1967).

FK   *Girolamo Frescobaldi: Orgel- und
Klavierwerke,* ed. P. Pidoux, 5 vols.
(Kassel: 1949–54).

FVB   *The Fitzwilliam Virginal Book,* ed.
J. A. Fuller-Maitland and W. Barclay
Squire, 2 vols. (1899; New York,
1963).

MB   *Musica Britannica*
1. *The Mulliner Book,* ed. D. Stevens, 2nd rev. ed. (London, 1954).
5. *Thomas Tomkins: Keyboard Music,* ed. S. Tuttle, 2d rev. ed. (London, 1964).
9. *Jacobean Consort Music,* ed. T. Dart and W. Coates, 2d rev. ed. (London, 1962).
14. *John Bull: Keyboard Music I,* ed. J. Steele and F. Cameron, 2d rev. ed. (London, 1967).
18. *Music at the Court of Henry VIII,* ed. J. Stevens, 2d rev. ed. (London, 1969).
19. *John Bull: Keyboard Music II,* ed. T. Dart, 2d rev. ed. (London, 1970).
20. *Orlando Gibbons: Keyboard Music,* ed. G. Hendrie, 2d rev. ed. (London, 1967).
24. *Giles and Richard Farnaby: Keyboard Music,* ed. R. Marlow (London, 1965).
27. and 28. *William Byrd: Keyboard Music,* ed. A. Brown, 2d rev. ed. (London, 1976).
44. *Elizabethan Consort Music: I,* ed. Paul Doe (London, 1979).

MK   *Thomas Morley: Keyboard Works,* ed. T. Dart, 2 Vols. (London, 1959).

MMB   *Monumenta Musicae Belgicae*
4. *Charles Guillet, Giovanni (de) Macque, Carolus Luyton: Werken voor orgel of voor vier speeltuigen,* ed. J. Watelet (Antwerp, 1938).

MMN   *Monumenta Musica Nederlandica*
3. *Dutch Keyboard Music of the 16th and 17th Centuries,* ed. A. Curtis (Amsterdam, 1961, rev. ed. forthcoming).

SK   *J. P. Sweelinck: The Instrumental Works,* Opera Omnia, vol. 1 (Amsterdam, 1968).
1. Fantasias and Toccatas, ed. G. Leonhardt
2. Settings of Sacred Melodies, ed. Alfons Annegarn
3. Settings of Secular Melodies and Dances, ed. Frits Noske

TK   *Thomas Tallis: Complete Keyboard Works,* ed. D. Stevens (New York, 1953).

The abbreviations Add. MS, Roy. App. and RML refer respectively to manuscripts in the Additional, Royal Appendix and Royal Music Library collections of the British Library, London. Manuscripts in the library of Christ Church College, Oxford are designated ChCh. Sigla for the manuscript and printed sources of Bull's keyboard music are given in Appendix I.

Foreword

In the early music movement, which has played so important a role in this half-century, the music of John Bull has not been ignored. Nearly all the music that can be ascribed to Bull has recently been made available in new editions,[1] a good sampling of keyboard music is available on phonograph recordings, and favorite pieces are frequently heard in concert alongside virginal music of Byrd, Gibbons, Farnaby, and Tomkins. The fashion for early keyboard music and early music in general has not only manifested itself in editions, sound recordings, and concert performances of music before Bach, but has also made its influence felt on music written in our own time. Yet the revival of interest in early music has brought with it no study of Bull such as it has of his peers Byrd and Sweelinck. It is significant that the most intelligent modern discussions of Bull's keyboard music are found in Alan Curtis's *Sweelinck's Keyboard Music* (Leiden and London, 1969) and in Oliver Neighbour's *The Consort and Keyboard Music of William Byrd* (London, Berkeley, and Los Angeles, 1978). To the extent that these studies make reference to the keyboard music of Bull, the surface has been scratched. Yet a consideration of the wider literature—a few weak articles and some brief, descriptive passages in survey books—leaves little doubt that Bull's music has in general been poorly understood and inadequately appraised.[2]

Until recently hopes for a comprehensive critical appraisal of Bull's music remained understandably dim, for the sources had not been collated, good texts had not been established, and all the music had not been printed. While these obstacles were largely removed with the issue of the complete edition *MB* (*Musica Britannica*) 14 and 19, this landmark publication created certain problems of its own. Some of its texts are less than sound (particularly those in the earlier volume) and many of the works included are either dubiously or incorrectly attributed to Bull. It is particularly this lack of a reasonably definitive canon of authentic works that stands in the way of serious criticism. The same deficiency frustrates efforts to establish a chronology, a situation which is exacerbated by the lack of firm dates for many of the sources. Thus it becomes clear that close study of the music itself is needed to find answers to the outstanding critical questions and to set forth a relative, but not absolute, chronology of Bull's works. The task of the present work is therefore a triple one: first, to establish which works may best be considered authentic and, as a corollary of this scrutiny, to suggest where necessary how the texts printed in *MB* may be improved; second, to examine the music from a critical point of view with the purpose of defining Bull's place within the two musical cultures which his life spanned—the one English and Renaissance, the other Continental and Baroque; and third, to determine how Bull's style evolved over the course of his compositional career and to date the music insofar as possible.

Acknowledgments

Foremost gratitude is due faculty members of the University of California at Berkeley, where this work originated. The idea for the topic came out of discussions with Alan Curtis, who enthusiastically supported the project from the beginning. Philip Brett gave exceptionally close attention to the critical aspect of my writing and encouraged its pursuit at every point; and Leonard Johnson effectively edited the text with a stringent eye toward simplifying my prose. I am also indebted to Lawrence Moe for the continuing interest he has shown in my work and to Alan Nelson for his counsel in matters of paleography.

In the early stages of my research, Mssrs. William Oxenbury and Allen Percival, executors of the estate of Thurston Dart, gave their generous permission to examine the papers of the late musicologist. Professor Brian Trowell of King's College, University of London, insured my access to the materials, and a Haskell Fellowship from Oberlin College provided the necessary funds for the work, as well as for manuscript research in England and France. While in England I was shown every kindness by Susi Jeans, who helped shed light on several biographical questions. Mr. Oliver Neighbour, whose profound work on the instrumental music of William Byrd has been an ever-present example, scrutinized the final text and made many invaluable suggestions. When advice was needed on the identity of handwritings, Anthony Petti of the University of Calgary and Pamela Willets, Deputy Keeper of the Department of Manuscripts, British Library, took time to give their expert opinions. Friendly assistance has been given everywhere I have worked. I am especially grateful to the staff of the New York Public Library, the Bibliothèque Nationale in Paris, and the libraries of the Universities of California at Berkeley, Cambridge University, Christ Church College, Oxford, the Royal College of Music, King's College, University of London, as well as the Public Record Office in Chancery Lane.

I owe great appreciation to my friend and colleague Davitt Moroney both for his moral support and for his observations on music of the period.

Brad Chames prepared the typescript and Richard Turnquist copied the musical examples. Finally, the role played by my family and close friends must not go unnoticed, for their love and advocacy have lightened tasks that otherwise would have seemed impossible.

Music examples from printed editions incorporated into the text are used with kind permission of the following: Stainer and Bell, for extracts from *Musica Britannica,* vols. 1, 14, 19, 20, 27, 28, *Early English Church Music,* vols. 6 and 10, the *Byrd Edition,* vol. 17, and Morley's *Keyboard Works*; Vereniging voor Nederlandse Muziekgeschiedenis (Drift 21, Utrecht), for extracts from Sweelinck's *Keyboard Works*; American Institute of Musicology, for extracts from Cornet's *Collected Keyboard Works*; Bärenreiter-Verlag, for an extract from Frescobaldi's *Orgel- und Klavierwerke,* vol. 3; A–R Editions, for an extract from Tye's *Instrumental Music*; Editions du Centre National de la Recherche Scientifique, for an extract from *Oeuvres de Nicolas Vallet pour luth seul*; and Oxford University Press, for an extract from *Six Seventeenth-Century Carols from the Netherlands*.

1

Introduction

Bull's Life

There is scarcely a composer whose life has been clouded with more legend and fantasy than Bull's. Responsible for this situation are both the apparent paucity of documentation for those periods of his life around which speculation has grown up (chiefly his very origins, his first trip to the Continent, his flight to the Spanish Netherlands, and his conjectured encounter with Sweelinck) and the nature of the music itself, which is awesome in both stylistic range and technical demands. The height of popular rumination was Leigh Henry's well-known *John Bull* (London, 1937), a "biography" in which a handful of facts is expanded to some 300 pages, leaving the reader with a certain impression of the composer but with little reliable information. Yet Henry was not creating in a vacuum. Early historians such as Mattheson, Hawkins, and Burney, and lexicographers such as Walther and Gerber had pieced together miniature biographies based on the sketchy and often unreliable accounts in the *Fasti* of Anthony à Wood's *Athenae Oxoniensis* (London, 1691) and on John Ward's *The Lives of the Professors of Gresham College* (London, 1740).[1] In 1886 the most complete biography to date was published by William Barclay Squire in the *Dictionary of National Biography*. Later, Seiffert added to existing accounts by suggesting that Bull and Sweelinck had been in close contact on the Continent and in doing so began the process of filling in with speculation the gaps left between facts.[2] The state of scholarship represented by Edward Rimbault and William Barclay Squire's entry in *Grove 2* (1904; except for the addition of a "Catalogue of Virginal Pieces," the same article that appeared in *Grove 5,* 1954) remained the status quo until Thurston Dart began his archival researches after World War II.

Dart's work on Bull's life culminated in 1960 with the publication of a "Calendar of the Life of John Bull" in the prefatory material to the first volume of the keyboard music. Containing many hitherto unknown pieces of evidence, Dart's "Calendar" began to clear the murky waters surrounding Bull's life. It was updated in the second edition of the volume (1967) and is the basis of Paul Chappell's short biography, *A Portrait of John Bull* (Hereford Cathedral, 1970). After Dart's untimely death in 1971, Susi Jeans resumed the task of researching Bull's life. Working with British archivist John Guy, she discovered several new and pertinent documents. Facts brought to life through these discoveries are reflected in her article on Bull in *Grove 6* and are promised further elaboration in her projected book on Bull's life, his anthems, and canons.

We know that Bull was born about 1563.[3] In Dart's 1952 entry for *Die Musik in Geschichte und Gegenwart* he presumes that Bull's family originated in Somerset, where it is possible that Bull was born. The story that the composer was related to the Bulls of Peglich, Somerset originated with Anthony à Wood and does not figure in Dart's 1959 article for the *New York Times,* where he writes that Bull was "probably the son of a London goldsmith. . . ."[4] In the first edition of the "Calendar" Dart states a third possibility: that the composer "may have been connected with the John Bull for whom Daman composed *The Psalmes of David in English Meter* (London, 1579)." More recent evidence concerning Bull's origins, cited in the second edition of the "Calendar," seems to indicate that the composer's family came from Hereford, where Bull became a choirboy at the Cathedral in 1573. Finally, Susi Jeans has attempted to settle the matter by claiming that Bull's place of birth was Radnorshire. Though her evidence appears sound, no birth records have been discovered.

At about 11 years of age Bull entered the Chapel Royal, of which Thomas Tallis and William Byrd were then the organists. After being apprenticed to the Merchant Taylors' Company in 1577–78, Bull received in 1582 his first appointment, as organist of Hereford Cathedral, and shortly thereafter became Master of the Children.[5] Bull seems to have maintained his post at Hereford, at least in name and despite temporary suspensions, for some time after he became involved with musical life at the court. He was sworn a Gentleman of the Chapel Royal in 1585–86 and eventually assumed the position of organist alongside his teacher John Blitheman. Blitheman, whose tombstone bore an epitaph claiming Bull as his pupil, had succeeded Tallis upon his death in 1585. Bull attained the degree of B.Mus. from Oxford in 1586, then Mus.D. from Cambridge in 1589, and a second doctorate, from Oxford by incorporation, in 1592. By this time Bull was chief organist in the Chapel Royal, having replaced Blitheman, who died the previous year.

Upon the founding of Gresham College in London in 1596, Bull was appointed to the position of Reader in Music. His initial colleagues there were Anthony Wotton (divinity), Edward Brerewood (astronomy), Henry

Briggs (geometry), Henry Mowtlow (law), Caleb Willis (rhetoric) and
Matthew Gwinne (physic, ie., medicine.)[6] The text of the opening of
Bull's inaugural lecture at Gresham College on 6 October 1597 has been
reconstructed by Alex Hyatt King:

> It is written, Right worshipful, that the Eagle onely soaring aloft into the clouds,
> looketh with open eye upon the Sun: such a quick sighted bird should now bee in this
> place who flying thro' heaven might fetch [?] Apollo's harp and sound unto you the
> prayse of the heavenlie Musick. My Master liueth and long [may he] lyve, and I his
> scholar not worthy in yours & his present to speak of this Art and Science. Bear, I
> pray you, with all my defects of knowledge, and you shall finde that dilegence shall
> recompense the [three words illegible]. One starre is not so light as another, yet as by
> a faint light you may see your way, so by my simple knowledge may you in some form
> [?] learn this Science: & although I am not, as it were, winged to flye to the hill
> Parnassus, there to sing with the Muses a part in the praise of Musick, yet give me
> leave, I pray you, first [two words illegible] to shew you the foundation and
> foundress. . . .[7]

Dart observed in the "Calendar" that it seems to be William Byrd whom
Bull reveres here as his teacher and whose presence at the lecture is
acknowledged. Furthermore, he noted, Byrd's son Thomas deputized for
Bull at Gresham during Bull's absence in 1601–2. Though there is written
record only for Blitheman's having taught Bull, the connection with Byrd
is probably stronger than heretofore recognized. Musical evidence in several keyboard works of Bull and Byrd point toward a close exchange of
ideas between the two composers lasting up to Bull's final departure from
England in 1613.

In 1601–2 Bull took leave of England for a sojourn of about 18
months on the Continent. His trip was ostensibly for reasons of health
but has in fact never been fully and satisfactorily explained.[8] In a *New
York Times* article Dart flatly stated that Bull travelled "in fact as a kind
of Spy Extraordinary for the Queen's private intelligence service," yet
Dart produced no evidence in support of his conjecture.[9] The theory was
probably suggested by drawing parallels between Bull and two of his
contemporaries, Alfonso Ferrabosco I and Thomas Morley, who acted as
spies for the Queen. Still more mysterious than the reasons for Bull's trip
to the Continent are his whereabouts while there. Dart's suggestion that
Bull travelled to Paris is based on a presumed connection between the
English composer and Jacques Champion, a connection which is, however, completely insupportable (see p. 17ff.). He may have visited Wolfenbüttel, for Bull dedicated pieces to the Duke and Duchess of Brunswick.
The dramatist and Duke, Heinrich Julius, was known for his patronage
of English theater and foreign musicians, especially lute and keyboard
players.[10] There is, however, no evidence of Bull's actual presence in

Wolfenbüttel; and the pieces in question could have been commissioned as gifts to Heinrich Julius and his wife (James I's sister-in-law), possibly on the occasion of a visit from the Duke's son, Friederich Ulrich, to Prince Henry in April, 1610.[11] Anthony à Wood has Bull in St. Omer, among other places, yet the historian's account rings distinctly apocryphal. Telling a story of Bull's having added 40 more parts to a 40-part "lesson or song" while at St. Omer, Wood then compounds legend by adding that he "was so much admired for his dextrous hand on the Organ, that many thought that there was more than Man in him.[12]

That Bull's trip of 1601–2 was the occasion of a visit to Amsterdam was also postulated by Dart. Bull's presence at some point in Amsterdam is needed to explain his supposed acquaintance with Sweelinck, itself a rumor founded on no documentary evidence but a connection that has seemed an obvious one to almost all commentators since Seiffert. The inclusion of a canon inscribed "Doctor Bull fecit" in Sweelinck's treatise on composition, a fantasy by Bull "op de fuge van M. Jan pieterss:" dated the year of the Amsterdam organist's death, and the possibility that Sweelinck made a new ending for Bull's *God Save the King,* have been cited as evidence for close contact between the two composers. Still more convincing are stylistic affinities, for Sweelinck consciously emulated the English keyboard style most characteristically represented by Bull, and Bull's own style underwent changes that appear to reflect Sweelinck's influence. There is no record of Bull's presence in Amsterdam, yet the 1601–2 trip remains the strongest possibility for an encounter between the two composers, since their paths appear never to have crossed after Bull's permanent settlement in the Spanish Netherlands.[13] Brussels alone can be established with any certainty as one of Bull's places of sojourn, for he received a letter there from Queen Elizabeth charging him to return home. While in Brussels Bull came to be on friendly terms with the Spanish Archduke whose organist, the English recusant Peter Philips, had left England in 1582. When Bull himself later quit England for good, his ties with Brussels proved useful in establishing himself in his adopted land.

Bull's chief duties under Elizabeth were as Gentleman and Organist of the Chapel Royal. He was not the Queen's official virginalist, who is said to have been Walter Earle, but he evidently wrote some pieces (the "Chromatic" Pavan and Galliard and the "Regina" Galliard) for her. After Queen Elizabeth's death in 1603, however, Bull's ties with the reigning family became stronger. Under James I he was music teacher to the royal children and became head of Prince Henry's household musicians. In the latter position he naturally was associated with others whom the illustrious Prince employed or otherwise patronized, such as George

Chapman and Salomon de Caus, the remarkable French engineer, architect, inventor, and musician.[14]

On 16 July 1607 Bull was admitted, along with Nathaniel Giles, into the Livery of the Merchant Taylors. Prior to his admission, Bull played the organ for an occasion of the Merchant Taylors in honor of James I. The event is recounted in John Nichols's *The Progresses, Processions, and Magnificent Festivities of King James the First,* quoted there from the company's records:

> At the upper end of the Hall there was set a chair of Estate, where his Majesty sat and viewed the Hall; and a very proper child, well spoken, being clothed like an Angel of gladness, with a taper of frankincense burning in his hand, delivered a short Speech, containing 18 verses, devised by Mr. Ben Jonson, which pleased his Majesty marvelously well; and upon either side of the Hall, in the windows near the upper end, were galleries or seats, made for music, in either of which were seven singular choice musicians playing on their lutes, and in the ship, which did hang aloft in the Hall, three rare men, and very skilful, who song to his Majesty; and over the King, sonnetts and loude musique, wherein it is to be remembered, that the multitude and noyse was so great, that the lutes nor songs could hardly be heard or understood, and then his Majesty went up into the King's chamber, where he dined alone at a table which was provided only for his Majesty and the Queen (but the Queen came not), in which chamber were placed a very rich pair of organs, whereupon Mr. John Bull, Doctor of Music, and a Brother of this Company, did play all the dinner-time. . . .[15]

In the same year Bull was married and consequently resigned the Gresham Readership in music. His wife, Elizabeth Walter, bore him a daughter. In late 1612 or early 1613, just before leaving England for good, Bull published seven keyboard pieces in the collection of Byrd, Bull, and Gibbons, *Parthenia.* The original issue of this historic volume, "The Maydenhead of the first musicke that ever was printed for the Virginalls," was dedicated to James I's daughter and Bull's pupil, Princess Elizabeth, and to Prince Frederick V, Elector Palatine of the Rhine. The young couple was married, after a period of lavish public and private celebrations, in a ceremony at Whitehall on 14 February 1612/13. For the occasion, which is described in detail in the *Old Cheque-Book,* Bull himself wrote an anthem, *God the Father, God the Son,* but no copy of the piece survives.[16]

On 6 November 1612, in the midst of joyful preparations for the mythically tinged Protestant union of Elizabeth and Frederick, Bull's patron suddenly died. The immediate impact of Henry's death on Bull's personal and professional life is not known, though James I did grant the composer a pension of 40 pounds a year for two years. Yet on 24 September 1613 Bull entered the service of the Archduke Albert in Brussels. The circumstances surrounding his flight from England are shrouded in mystery, even from the earliest sources. Charles Burney had the following opinion:

> Dr. Bull has been censured for quitting his establishment in England; but it is probable that the increase of health and wealth was the cause and consequence. Indeed, he seems to have been praised at home, more than rewarded; and it is no uncommon thing for one age to let an artist starve, to whom the next would willingly erect statues.[17]

In fact, however, Bull's appointment with Archduke Albert lasted barely a year, being terminated as a result of pressures on the Archduke from James I.[18] He had to resort to asking for alms from the city of Antwerp before ever receiving the appointment there as organist of the Cathedral. Bull's financial situation had at any rate been a reasonable one before he left England (irrespective of the death of his patron); and if improving that situation was the "cause" for his leaving, it most certainly was not the immediate "consequence."

Various theories have been put forward to explain Bull's sudden and secretive departure, but none has received much support. Writers have generally shied away from accepting at face value William Trumbull's letter of 31 March 1614, first printed in William Barclay Squire's account of Bull's life for the *Dictionary of National Biography*. In it Trumbull, Ambassador in Brussels, informs the King:

> I told him [the Archduke] that I had charge from your Majestie to acquaint him that your Majestie upon knowledge of his receiving Dr. Bull your Majesties organist and sworne servant into his chappel, without your Majesties permission or consent, or once so much as speaking thereof to me, that am resyding here for your Majesties affairs: that your Majesty did justly find it strange as you were his friend and ally, and had never used the like proceeding either towards him or any other foreign prince; adding, that the like course was not practized among private persons, much less among others of greater place and dignity. And I told him plainly, that it was notorious to all the world, the said Bull did not leave your Majesties service for any wrong done unto him, or for matter of religion, under which fained pretext he now sought to wrong the reputation of your Majesties justice, but did in that dishonest manner steal out of England through the guilt of a corrupt conscience, to escape the punishment, which notoriously he had deserved, and was designed to have been inflicted on him by the hand of justice, for his incontinence, fornication, adultery, and other grievious crimes.[19]

While it seems unlikely that such an outburst from a public official would lack basis in fact, it has been thought until very recently that the accusations had little or no foundation. In 1960 Dart discussed in an article for *Acta Musicologica* a letter from Bull to the city officials at Antwerp in which Bull asked for employment. The letter seems to support the theory that Bull left England for religious reasons:

> Be it humbly known that John Bull, organist, was in the service of the King of England; and how, in the month of October in the year 1613 he was forced to take flight thence hither, since information had been laid against him that he was of the Catholic faith, and that he could not acknowledge his Majesty as head of the Church. Which is a capital offence there.[20]

Yet the wording of this letter is of note: Bull does not pointedly profess Catholicism, despite the fact he is eyeing a post at a Catholic cathedral, but rather claims that such accusations have been made against him. Recusancy was the reason many English musicians found themselves self-exiled to the Continent at this time. Might this not have been a convenient excuse for escaping the wages of the less reputable "crimes" alleged by Trumbull? A letter from William Abbot, Archbishop of Canterbury, to Trumbull affirms this interpretation. Published already in 1940, it was only brought to the attention of music historians in 1977:

> Concerning Dr. Bull, when I first understood of his departure, I advertised it by letter to one now about the king, who was somewhere abroad, and then I did not mention from whom I received it. But upon his Maj. returning his saying that he marvelled that you wrote not so much unto him, I told his Maj. that I had received that advertisement from you. But yet do you now take knowledge of the reason of this wise man's departure. There were articles put against him in the High Commission Court, whereunto he took his oath to answer, but before he was examined, he fled over the seas. The accusation was for notable and impudent adultery. Himself and his wife lay in the upper bed, and in a truckle bed under him lay two of his maid servants. Bull, in a summer morning when it was very light, riseth from his wife's side, goeth to the other bed, raising up one of his maidens, biddeth her to lie by her mistress, he taking her place committeth adultery with the other, which the maid beholding awaketh her mistress, and biddeth her see what her master is doing. His wife beholdeth it and telleth her servant that this was no news to her, for her husband had long and often been a dealer that way; which indeed is since verified by common report. Again he was charged to come into a church a little before the beginning of prayer, and there as the minister was entering into service, in the sight of the congregation Bull pulled him violently out of his seat and despitefully entreated him. . . . The man hath more music than honesty and is as famous for marring virginity as he is for fingering of organs and virginals.[21]

Unfortunately, we have little information regarding Bull's activities at Antwerp.[22] As successor to Raymond Waelrant, he was organist of the Antwerp Cathedral and retained the post until his death. Although his music was widely disseminated in German-speaking countries by mid-century, he apparently did not attract pupils from afar, as did Sweelinck; and only one organist in Antwerp itself, Guglielmus à Messaus, appears to have been connected with him. Bull did not travel widely, as many English musicians on the Continent did.[23] His presence outside of Antwerp is only once recorded, on the occasion of an organ inspection in 's-Hertogenbosch. On 15 March 1628 Bull died and was buried in the cemetery next to the Cathedral, an area called the "Groenplats." The whereabouts of his will are not known, and in recent years his tomb has been excavated, along with the rest of the Groenplats cemetery, to make room for a new underground station.

The Sources of the Music

There are 30 known extant sources for Bull's keyboard music, including manuscripts and prints. About 80 percent of the pieces are found in four manuscript collections: *Bu, Ant, Tr* and *Vi*.[24] (The relationship by common repertoire is shown in Table 1). The remaining pieces are scattered among the other sources, which also contain texts of many pieces found in the four main manuscripts. For the purposes of our discussion, these four scores will be considered fundamental: they transmit the greatest share of the music and preserve what are in most cases the earliest and best texts.

Paris, Bibliothèque Nationale, Fonds du Conservatoire, Rés. 1185 (Bu)

As Table 1 shows, *Bu* provides the greatest number of pieces and the largest number of unique texts. Its contents, together with that of *Ant,* comprise two-thirds of the known keyboard works of Bull. The collection is bound with an exemplum of *Parthenia* (Rés. 1184) in modern leather, using remnants of the original tooled and gilt leather binding and stamped with the initials "MW". There are 348 pages of music written on paper of folio format (trimmed to approximately 29.5 × 19.2 cm) with four systems of six-line keyboard staves per page. Two main hands have copied the music, with a third interrupting the second for one piece only (f. 172'–75), a pavan of Gibbons. There are five watermarks.[25]

Bu consists of two layers, an earlier and a later, corresponding to hands I and II. These layers are intermixed in the first part of the manuscript (up to f. 172), for hand II has restored and augmented the earlier texts by recopying parts of pieces and adding other pieces, sometimes as substitutes for existing ones in either hand I or II. With the exception of the Gibbons pavan, the second part of the manuscript was written entirely by hand II and, like the additions and substitutions in the first part, consists of music by Gibbons and mid-seventeenth century English and French composers.[26] A single exception is the "Melancholy" Pavan, which was removed from its original place, preceding the first piece in the existing order, and recopied on f. 176'–77'.

Table 1. Relationship by Common Repertoire
among the Four Main Sources

Sources	Unique Pieces*	No. of Pieces Also in				Total No. of Pieces
		Bu	Ant	Tr	Vi	
Bu	43	—	2	32	1	75
Ant	34	2	—	3	0	37
Tr	15	32	3	—	2	49
Vi	8	1	0	2	—	10

*among these sources

NOTE: The count of pieces in this table includes all those in *MB* 14 and 19, a number of which may be erroneously attributed to Bull. The two pieces common to *Bu* and *Ant* and the one piece common to *Bu* and *Vi* are also in *Tr*; thus (line 1) 43 + 32 = 75, and (line 2) 34 + 3 = 37. Conversely, two of the three pieces common to *Tr* and *Ant* and one of the two pieces common to *Tr* and *Vi* are also in *Bu,* so that (line 3) 15 + 32 + 1 + 1 = 49, and (line 4) 8 + 1 + 1 = 10.

The earliest record in the history of *Bu* is provided by the index, which is dated 1652 and signed by Benjamin Cosyn. The hand of the index is the same as that which added missing titles to many of the pieces in hand I and is also identical with the hand that wrote the index of *Co,* signed and dated 1920. Thus it was Benjamin Cosyn, 32 years after he made an anthology of works by himself, Bull, and Gibbons, who repaired and added to a large existing manuscript of Bull's music.[27] Only two pieces ascribed to Bull in *Co* (Fantasy d3 and Pavan g1) are not to be found in *Bu* at all; they were either copied from another source or from *Bu* itself before several repairs and changes were made. For example, the Prelude F also appears not to be in *Bu,* yet it can be discerned as the original piece of f. 172 before a pasteover covered it. (Underneath the other pasteovers, f. 112, 147', and 175, Cosyn's own hand can be read, indicating two stages in his manipulation of the collection.) Changes such as the substitution of new paper for old (f. 36–37' and 107–8') may also be accountable for the loss of concordances.

Of principal concern is the repeated speculation that hand I might be Bull's. The possibility that the earlier layer of *Bu* is holograph rests on the exceptional size of the collection, the fact that it contains works mostly by one composer, and the lack of identification of the hand. No conclusive argument has ever been brought to bear on the question, which has been disputed since the early 1930s.[28] The absence of ascriptions in hand I, along with the fact that a good number of the pieces can be established through concordance to be Bull's has been taken as evidence that the collection was made by the composer, who naturally knew which pieces were his and which were not. We cannot be sure, however, that there was not at one time an index giving ascriptions in hand I; and it would be a mistake to assume that the absence of a composer's name in hand I ensures either that the collection is autograph or that it was intended to represent entirely the work of one composer. The beginning of the manuscript is missing and could have contained the original index, a situation which may have also been the case in *Ant.* Cosyn, in fact, must have had access to some index, for several pieces are more precisely identified by him ("The Lord Lumnies Pavin," for instance, for "paven") in both his index to *Bu* and in *Co* than they are by hand I.

The concordance of two pieces with a mid-sixteenth century manuscript is also noteworthy, yet offers little more help in the matter. Two hymn verses on f. 164–164' are found in a collection containing mostly liturgical organ music from the middle of the sixteenth century, Add. MS 29996 (earliest layer, ca. 1547–49). The music of Redford, Preston, Philip ap Rhys, Nicholas Carleton, Byrd, Parsons, and others is represented. This manuscript was owned and expanded in the seventeenth century by Thomas Tomkins. The section in which the two hymn verses are found is written not in the first hand, which may be that of Philip ap Rhys, but in the same one that copied side-by-side keyboard transcriptions of In Nomines by Byrd and Parsons. The verses belong to a set of 20 hymn cycles of two to five verses each. They were meant for alternatim practice, and are based not on the chants themselves, but on their faburdens.[29] Such features, along with the style of the pieces, date them from well before Bull's earliest compositions and probably before Byrd's In Nomine. Though the composer has never positively identified, Preston has recently been accorded tentative credit for the compositions.[30] The composers in the second layer of the manuscript (Byrd and Parsons) and the hand responsible for the third layer (Thomas Tomkins) strongly suggest an association with the Chapel Royal, beginning in the last quarter of the sixteenth century. Since none of the anonymous hymn verses appears anywhere else, it is very likely that they were copied into *Bu* by someone who had access to this private manuscript. Whether it was Bull who copied them directly while at the Chapel Royal cannot be inferred from the fact of this unique concordance. It merely suggests that there is some connection between our collection and the milieu of the Chapel Royal.

A set of recently discovered documents thought to be in Bull's hand also fails to shed light on the handwriting matter.[31] In the State Papers, Miscellaneous Supplement (SP 46/162 and SP 46/126) of the Public Records Office, London, there are four half-folios comprising four of the original five parts of a short instrumental piece. The piece has not been identified, nor can anything of its function be determined from the location of the sheets in the miscellany, which is not always in chronological order. Three of the four sheets are signed: two "finis John Bull" and one, the secondus part, "finis JBull."[32] This third signature appears to be a kind of monogram, incorporating the "J" into the "B". It seems that such a personal idiosyncracy is unlikely to have been used by other than an autographer and, in fact, is a feature of the 1606 signatures of Bull in the Old Cheque Book of the Chapel Royal.[33] If, on the basis of this hand-print, the SP parts may be tentatively judged holograph, what comparison can be made between the writing in them and that of hand I in *Bu*? Here the murky waters of handwriting scrutiny are further clouded by the absence of a signature in *Bu*. In addition, the writing in both sources is italic-based and, as such, is a poor indicator of individual hands. Bull's name does appear once in hand I, in the title of "Bulls Goodnighte" (f. 71'), but a comparison of it with the signatures in the SP papers produces no noteworthy results. Other verbal notations in the SP papers, the part names, reveal by contrast to those in *Bu* only the superficial resemblances that many italic hands of the period bear to one another. A comparison of the music calligraphy is of little addition help.[34]

More important than the autograph question is the matter of textual quality. *Bu* and *Tr,* the two sources having the largest common repertoire and giving the most reliable readings, both contain the early Fantasy d1. The differences between the two sources are remarkable. Although *Bu* (like all contemporary sources) is not entirely consistent in its use of accidentals, it is superior to *Tr. Bu* provides greater melodic and harmonic clarity through better delineation between natural and melodic versions of the scale, a feature of some importance in this piece. The harmony of one entire bar is different in the two sources: *Bu* maintains the major mode from b. 57 to 60 (*MB*'s barring) rather than needlessly interrupting the modality with the g-minor harmony of b. 58. Where contrast *is* needed, *Bu* again gives the better text. The two-semibreve melodic segment beginning at b. 61 is sequenced literally, a fifth higher, in b. 63–64. When it is again sequenced in the following bar, the segment is pointedly altered so that it contains a minor, not a major, third. The detail is not explicit in *Tr.* In matters of notes and rhythms, *Bu* typically offers the more attractive choices. The variants in b. 105 (see *MB* 14, p. 162) clearly show the difference between the composer's vigorous, serpentine, and unpredictable melodic conception and Tregian's patterned delivery. The two extra f'-sharps and the rhythm of the left hand in the penultimate bar make better linear sense, as does the top f'-sharp, not a', of the final bar.

Bu does contain errors, including occasional wrong notes and gaps in the text. In five instances (f. 30', 76, 92, 98', and 149) a bar or part of a bar has been left out and later inserted above, below, or at the end of the system to which it belongs. Once an extra bar of cantus firmus was crossed out (f. 38). Whole numbers of bars are missing in several other pieces: Alman G2 (f. 79') lacks the first half of the second-strain reprise found in *El*; a similar situation exists in the galliard on f. 159, which has no concordance; the Welch Dance (f. 162') has a first strain and reprise of four bars in this source, of six bars in *Pl*; finally, Miserere 1 (f. 34) is missing five bars in the second section. Although these imperfections cannot totally discount the holograph theory, they are sufficient to weaken it considerably. The overall good quality of the texts, the large number of unique texts, and the few, but glaring, errors and ommissions together best support the assumption that *Bu* is the work of a diligent, if fallible, copyist who probably had access to Bull's own scores.

In the light of this assumption and the fact of Cosyn's recopyings, additions and attributions, two questions remain. What is the date of the earlier layer? Which pieces in the manuscript are Bull's? The likelihood that the copyist of the earlier layer was working from Bull's own scores strongly suggests that the date of the collection could be no later than 1613, when Bull left England. The two pieces common to *Bu* and *Parthenia*, which was published in 1612/13 seem to support this. Versions of Bull's prelude (*Bu*, f. 83, *Pa*, no. 9) and of Gibbons's fantasy (*Bu*, f. 86, *Pa*, no. 17) both show evidence of having undergone change from one source to the other. The changes may be noted in the printed editions and critical notes to these pieces (*MB* 19:117 and *MB* 20:12). The *Parthenia* text of Gibbons's piece is the more intricate of the two and may represent a rethinking of the piece for harpsichord rather than organ. The *Pa* text of Bull's prelude differs from that of *Bu* chiefly in figuration, and in the ornamentation of the final cadence. Though it would be difficult to prove that *Pa* gives later versions in both cases, one would at least assume them to be more nearly identical if they dated from around the same time. Certainly, if *Bu* had been copied after *Pa* was published, the manuscript version could be expected to follow that of the printed edition.

Few of the pieces in *Bu* can be dated with any certainty, but for certain of them a *terminus ad quem* can be established. Cosyn includes the "paven chromatique" in his own collection of 1620 and lists it in the index as "Queene Elizabeths pavin" (a2). The piece presumably dates from no later than 1603, when Elizabeth I died. Pavan and Galliard G6 are also found in *Co* and *Tr*. Both the titles in *Tr* and in Cosyn's indices to *Co* and *Bu* dedicate the pieces to Lord Lumley (or "Lumnie"). The death of John, Lord Lumley in 1609 likewise provides a terminal date for that work.[35] Falling halfway between the latest datable piece and the publication of *Parthenia*, Dart's suggested date of 1611 for *Bu* appears to be a reasonable one.[36]

With regard to the question of attributions, most of the pieces in Cosyn's hand can be eliminated from discussion since they are in a much later style and cannot be Bull's. The absence of ascriptions in hand I, however, leaves the authorship of many pieces in the earlier layer open to question. Three are certainly not by Bull: the fantasy of Gibbons and the two anonymous hymn verses. The fourth, a galliard on f. 127', is ascribed to Ferdinando Richardson in *We*. It can be established through concordance that most of the remaining pieces are by Bull. However, pieces which have no concordance, have conflicting attributions, or have concordances with anonymous texts leave room for doubt. The conflicting attributions of *Bonny Sweet Robin* seem to owe to a rewriting of Bull's piece by Farnaby (Byrd is excluded on grounds of style), while the authorship of Alman G1 is less clear. Remaining questionable are two pieces entitled "Dorick Musique," a pavan and galliard (*MB* 109a and b), a single galliard (*MB* 19, p. 223, incipit) and a beautiful setting of *Aurora lucis rutilat*. The archaic style of this last piece and its contiguity with the "Preston" hymn verses identifies it with an older repertoire.[37]

The "Fitzwilliam Virginal Book" (*Tr*)

The second largest source of Bull's music and one of the most important collections of keyboard music from any period, the 220 folios of *Tr* contain nearly 300 compositions, representing most of the important English composers of the period. (Gibbons is the only one slighted.) In addition, the collection includes works of some earlier composers such as Blitheman and Tallis, and gives a small but choice sampling of the work of Sweelinck.

The book was copied by Francis Tregian, who also wrote two other large collections. One of these contains madrigals and motets (NYPL, Drexel 4302), and one contains vocal and instrumental music (BL, Egerton, 3665).[38] Tregian was convicted in 1608–9 in connection with some financial dealings and was subsequently imprisoned in the Fleet. The first record of his incarceration is from 1614; yet considering the quantity of music Tregian is believed to have copied while in the Fleet, an earlier date seems more plausible as a *terminus a quo* for the virginal book. The latest date in the manuscript is 1612, affixed to Sweelinck's hexachord fantasy. Neither the Drexel nor Egerton collection contains music that seems later than about 1612. If, as would seem possible, Tregian was working from scores already in his possession rather than from new sources to which he had access during his imprisonment, it is likely that he began copying about 1612. Such a starting date would allow six years in which Tregian would have copied around 2000 pieces, or very roughly a piece a day. A slightly later date of 1614 has been proffered,[39] but it is probably too late, at least as a cut-off point for Tregian's sources. The fastidious, unhurried appearance of all three sources accords well with the 1612 commencement; and two pieces common to *Parthenia* and *Tr* (nos. 36 and [185]) appear not to have been copied from the print. In any event, none of Bull's music in *Tr* can postdate the middle of 1613, since Bull left England in that year and there is no evidence that any of his music reached England once he was exiled in the Spanish Netherlands.

In fact, however, *Tr* (like *Bu*) contains no pieces that on external evidence require a dating later than 1609, the probable *terminus ad quem* for Pavan and Galliard G6. Despite the large common repertoire of *Bu* and *Tr*, evidence suggests that Tregian's sources may actually predate *Bu*, which was almost certainly copied first. The chronology is most clear in Tregian's versions of the Quadran Pavan and in the Galliard "St. Thomas Wake," which are superseded respectively by texts in *Bu* and *Pa*. The situation is sometimes less straightforward, as in *My Jewel* 1 dealt with below in chapter 5, yet it is useful to remember that lost, intermediate sources may often account for apparent chronological anomalies.

In general, a circumspect attitude toward the texts in *Tr* is well advised. Incoherent accidental practice, significant variants from the more solid texts of *Bu*, rewritten or added final chords—any of these may be due either to the vicissitudes of Tregian's supply of sources or to his own proclivity for altering details at his pleasure. Tregian's texts are certainly not debased; they are in fact among the best, and in any case provide a good number of works that are to be had nowhere else. Yet one is led inevitably to the suspicion that many texts have been somewhat weakened under Tregian's pen.

In the matter of attribution, Tregian has proved quite reliable, at least so far as Bull's works go. In only one instance (a galliard—*Tr*, no. 48), has a conflicting ascription shown itself to be more convincing. Cosyn, in his 1620 collection, attributes the piece to himself; the ascription is far more credible than Tregian's in view of the quality of the piece, particularly the weak third strain. The anonymous *Veni Redemptor gentium* 2 and "Dalling" Alman were included in *MB*; neither presents any particular problem, as their styles are appropriate for Bull. The former comes in *Tr* between two pieces ascribed there to Bull, and the latter is found in *Bu* and in *El*, ascribed to Bull. Two pieces ascribed by Tregian to G. Farnaby, Alman G1 and *Bonny Sweet Robin* have been mentioned in connection with *Bu*; a third, *Rosasolis*, is also given to Farnaby by Tregian, but appears in *Ant* as the work of Bull. Finally, a prelude given anonymously in *Tr* (no. [177]), is probably Bull's; its candidacy for reattribution is discussed in chapter 3.

British Library, Add. MS 23623 (Ant)

This collection is second in importance only to *Bu* as a source of unique texts for Bull's music, and is of special value in that it gives a good number of works from Bull's late, Continental period. The volume is in a nearly square format (23.1 × 19.5 cm) and consists of 22 full gatherings of four to five bifolios, with two missing from the front and as many as five from the back. The music is written in black (faded) and red ink, three systems per page, by one main and two secondary hands (f. 33–36').[40] It is preceded by a title page written in the late eighteenth century bearing a drawing with the caption "Eliza-Bohemia"; at the end there is an index which, though it predates the title page and has the same watermark, is not original with the music manuscript. Copying dates of a number of pieces are given, testifying that the collection was made between 1627 and 1629. Other dates indicate when the pieces were composed: e.g., Fantasy a1, "van Doctor Bull quod fecit 30 meÿ 1622" and the fantasy on a theme of Sweelinck, dated 1621, the year of the Amsterdam organist's death.

Pepusch, according to the catalogue of Bull's works in John Ward's *Lives of the Professors of Gresham College,* owned the volume in 1740. Where and when Pepusch initially acquired the manuscript is difficult to know, but it seems that *Ant* never travelled in musical circles before coming into Pepusch's hands: the pieces in the collection believed to be by Bull appear, with three exceptions (all in *Tr*), in no other sources.[41]

The earliest information about *Ant* is found in Ward's *Lives,* where the manuscript can be identified as no. 18, vol. 2 in Pepusch's catalogue.[42] Dart held that *Ant* was written by Guglielmus à Messaus, thought to be a student of Bull's in Antwerp.[43] Unfortunately, little is known of Messaus. St. Walpurgis, the church where he was succentor, was destroyed by fire along with its archives. Since none of his manuscripts survive, no comparison of hands is possible. Pepusch's transcription of the index to *Pe 16* gives a number of titles in Dutch, and has at the end the inscription, "Incepit 6 Apr. 1628, finivit 20 Oct. 1628. Scribebat Guglielmus à Messaus, Divae Walburgis Antwerpiensis phonascus." The next manuscript listed by Ward, *Pe 18,1,* contains pieces with English, French, and Dutch titles, with the Dutch ones in the majority. Then follows no. 18, vol. 2 (*Ant*) with its predominantly Dutch titles. It was perhaps on the basis of the common language that Dart assumed vol. 16 and the two manuscripts of vol. 18 to have been written by the same person. Though no known hand suggests itself, there is no sound evidence to connect *Ant* with Messaus. It also cannot be in Bull's hand, as Hans Redlich thought, since the composer died before the latest date was entered in the manuscript, 16 November 1628.[44]

Of the pieces ascribed to Bull (all save six in the collection), six prove not to be by Bull and a much greater number are highly questionable. Since the provenance of the collection is assumed to be Antwerp, it is

Bull's own papers that have been taken by recent commentators to be the source. Why, though, if the copyist was working from the composer's autographs, should there be so many incorrect ascriptions? Dart casually put forward the suggestion that the copyist, assumed to be Messaus, was a loyal student of Bull's and therefore enthusiastically attributed almost everything to him. The theory makes little sense. The only thing a copyist would have had to gain by attributing others' works to Bull, a composer of local fame, would be through publishing them under his name. The manuscript is not, though, a fair copy destined for printing, but a finished product. Furthermore, if the copyist had wanted to make a collection exclusively of Bull's music, he would have ascribed no works in it to others; yet there is one piece ascribed to "Hieronimo Ferabosco" (Ex. 1–1), whoever that may have been, and several others that are left anonymous. These anonymous pieces, with the possible exception of Fantasy C1, are in a style that anyone close to Bull would have immediately recognized as uncharacteristic. The falsely attributed pieces, however, would have seemed very much like Bull's to a Netherlander unfamiliar with the subtler individualities of current English composers. It seems most probable, then, that all the pieces not otherwise identified were assumed by the copyist to be by Bull, the person who had in fact composed the majority of the pieces.

On the whole, the copyist of *Ant* appears to be more reliable in his delivery of texts than in his attributions. Although the lack of concord-

Ex. 1-1   "Toccata Di Roma Sexti Toni: Di hieronimo ferabosco" (*Ant,* f. 23')

ances prevents comparison, the texts have the straightforward appearance of a faithful copy and lack the capricious touches characteristic of many scribes. Occasionally contradictory accidentals and the confusing placement of organ registrations in *Laet ons met herten reijne* may indicate that the copyist himself was not a player and, as such, less likely to tamper with the texts than he otherwise might have been.

However, the problems of attribution are many. Besides *Bonny Sweet Robin* and *Rosasolis,* with their conflicting ascriptions to Farnaby, elsewhere there are six pieces ascribed more convincingly to other composers: two to Gibbons, and one each to Byrd, Macque, du Caurroy, and Tallis. Aside from those in later hands (which cannot be Bull's), at least 30 other pieces (a good three-quarters of the repertoire) pose stylistic problems of a greater or lesser degree. These are best taken up one by one in the course of this study, but a notable exception in the conformity of the index with the titles in the manuscript deserves special mention. Nos. 17–20 are listed in the "Register" as follows:

> Fantas: de Chappel
> Pauana simphoni^e de Chappel
> Gaillarde de Chappelle
> Het Joweel voor cappelle 1621

Here the compiler of the index identified four pieces with a person not mentioned in the music text; in order to do so, he must have either known the pieces from another source, or had access to an earlier index containing the references to "Chappel." This situation, the fact that the added pieces on f. 33–36 are not found in the index and that at least some of the pieces missing from the ends of the manuscript *are* listed there, suggest a dating of the "Register" from roughly the middle of the seventeenth century. Who, then, was this "Chappel"? Dart constructed a theory by which he identified this name with Jacques Champion, father of Chambonnières. On the basis of his theory, he attributed nos. 17–19, the fantasy, pavan, and galliard, to Champion and no. 20 to Bull as a piece dedicated to Champion.[45]

Dart argued that since many of the ascriptions in the text of *Ant* are incorrect on external grounds, those of the index must be more accurate. In it are found three pieces ascribed to a composer whom Dart identified as the famous harpsichordist, known also as "sieur de la Chappelle." Dart assumed that Bull probably met Champion in Paris on his first trip to the Continent and could have continued to exchange pieces with him throughout his life. Since there is not a single other piece, however, that is ascribed differently in the index than in the music text, Dart's reasoning was circular. The superiority of the index's ascriptions over those of the music text was based solely on the four titles which he accorded the greater authority.

The individual to which the index makes reference is mentioned in two other sources. One is *Pe 18, 1,* which contained a piece "door Dr. Bull gemacht, ter eeren Van Goduart Van Kappell." Is this not the same person mentioned in the title of a (lost) piece at the end of the index to *Ant,* "Fuga per g. van Cappel"? Dart thought not, and commented about it in a footnote to his article on the subject:

> The Dutch Christian name and particle suggest to me that we are dealing with an entirely different person or persons, perhaps connected with the family from whose stock was later to spring Arnold Joost van Keppel, first Earl of Albermarle.[46]

Dart has equated "Chappel" (or "Chappelle," or "Cappelle") with Jacques Champion without any special evidence from the index. To then reject Goduart van Kappell as the same person is really only to say that Goduart is not Champion; it is not to say that Goduart may not be identical to "Chappel." As far as the particle is concerned, there is no consistency whatever in spelling or usage in the index. "Van" and "de" were one and the same to its compiler. "Chappel," "Goduart van Kappell," and "g. van Cappel," therefore, are the same person. His name also appears in the titles of four other pieces in *Pe 18, 1,* two courantes, an allemande, and a galliard (see Ward's list in Appendix II).

Another source thought to contain a reference to this mysterious individual is a tablature from ca. 1662 in the Bomann-Museum, Celle.[47] The piece in question is an allemande with three variations called "Allemande de Chapelle" and bears the inscription "M. Jean Piterson" at the beginning and "M.G.P.S." at the end of the piece. Both nos. 17–19 in *Ant* and the allemande in the Celle tablature were at one time accepted as the work of Bull and Sweelinck, respectively.[48] Dart's argument that the *Ant* pieces were Champion's prevented their being included in *MB,* though their exclusion was never supported by stylistic evidence. Scrutiny of the allemande by Frits Noske and Alan Curtis demonstrated beyond reasonable doubt that the piece was not by Sweelinck.[49] It therefore found no place in the new complete works edition published in 1968. In fact, the Celle piece probably has no connection with the ones under question in *Ant* (a proposition supported by the stylistic gulf that separates them). The "Alemande de Chapelle" is a setting of a tune called "Almande Chapelle" in the songbook *Druyven-Tros der Amoureusheyt* (1602), also known as "Almande c'est pour vous belle dame" in Adriaenssen's *Pratum Musicum* (Antwerp, 1600) and as "Almande la Isapelle" in the

Thysius Lute-Book (ca. 1600).[50] This last title proffers a plausible explanation of the designation "Chapelle" in this instance, i.e., a corruption of "la Isapelle," presumably a reference to the daughter of Phillip II of Spain and archduchess of the Netherlands.

Dart's attribution of the *Ant* pieces to Champion, already on shaky grounds, further loses credibility with the slightest examination of the style and quality of the works. The two dances are distinctly Anglo-Dutch, both in style and structure. They have little to do with any French music of the period. It is equally difficult to imagine the Netherlandish fantasy being the work of a French composer, though we have admittedly little with which to compare it.[51] Certainly, the ensemble character of the fantasies in the Paris publications of Eustache du Caurroy (1610), Claude le Jeune (1612) or Charles Guillet (1610) bears no resemblance to the piece in question.[52] Guillaume Costeley's single surviving fantasy, which has come down to us only in a manuscript copy, is an exception to the above in that it appears to have been conceived for keyboard.[53] The style, however, is that of a vocal intabulation. From this period Charles Raquet's fantasy alone, printed by Mersenne, encourages a connection between the styles of France and the north.[54] The date of the piece is yet not known; but since it was published only in 1636, it may be too late to have any relevance for Champion's style.

Can the pieces be by Bull? Probably not, for their uneven quality suggests a composer who is less sure of himself than Bull, even if the fantasy does approach the style of Bull's late works. "Het Jowell voor cappelle" is another matter, however, and is probably authentic, perhaps even made for someone name "Cappelle." In any event, the pieces are almost certainly not by Champion, and furthermore appear unrelated to the "Alemande de Chapelle" ascribed to Sweelinck in the Celle tablature.

Vienna, Oesterreichische Nationalbibliothek, Cod. 17771 (Vi)

The fourth of the chief sources of Bull's keyboard music, *Vi,* is important for the number of unique texts from Bull's late period which it provides. It is an unusually small manuscript, 9 × 16 cm, consisting of 221 folios, almost a third of which are blank. It has been trimmed by the binder to such an extent that parts of some pieces have been lost. Written in German organ tablature, the keyboard portions of the manuscript contain 10 complete pieces, one from which the first page is missing (the chromatic hexachord fantasy), and a fragment, the "Fantasia" begining of f. 18' and having no continuation. Following the first section of the manuscript, f. 7'–21, 127 canons have been entered in mensural notation. The third section consists of two more keyboard pieces which, judging from the less faded ink, are later additions and probably in a different hand from the first section. The first section of the manuscript uses five to six lines per page, the third only four. All the music in *Vi* is ascribed to Bull.[55]

The collection opens with a piece headed "fantasia. doctor Johan Bull. Organist zu Anwerben. Anno 1621." The ascription is repeated at the end of the piece. This is in fact the chromatic fantasy ascribed in two of its other sources to Sweelinck and given here in a weak text.[56] There can be little doubt that this famous piece is Sweelinck's, not Bull's. Why, then, does it appear here ascribed to the English composer? The exact provenance of the manuscript is unknown, but titles and ascriptions in it indicate that the copyist was German-speaking. The date of Sweelinck's piece, 1621, may represent the date of copying: due to the paucity of concordances for the pieces of Bull's there is no evidence against this. However, it could also be a date transcribed by the copyist from his source. When the copyist came across the chromatic fantasy, dated the year of Sweelinck's death, he copied it as a piece of the English composer. The fantasy which follows it, based on the ascending chromatic fourth, or the inversion of Sweelinck's theme, would have made the attribution obvious in the mind of the copyist.

The misattribution of Sweelinck's fantasy naturally opens to question the authenticity of other pieces in *Vi*. Four pieces are found in other sources, where they are given as the work of Bull,[57] and all but one of the rest, Fantasy d4, exhibit no stylistic anomalies. This last piece raises doubts, as there are no known works of Bull similar to it, and because it seems to be a somewhat later piece.

Vi is best characterized as a "sampler" of Bull's music, keyboard and ensemble, earlier and later, and in a variety of genres. Besides the above-mentioned fantasies, there is the chromatic hexachord fantasy, a piece conceived for viols and probably preserved by Bull in Antwerp in its keyboard transcription. Both English and Continental plainsong settings are represented by the bicinium on *Miserere* and two sets of verses, designed for liturgical use, on the *Salve Regina* antiphon. Prelude g called by the copyist "fantasia," most probably dates from Bull's English period, as it is closely related to a prelude by Gibbons. *Revenant*, Bull's variations on "More Palatino," exemplifies the composer's later, more austere approach to variation so different from that of the earlier *Walsingham*. The "Prince's" Galliard, one of Bull's most individual dance movements, and *The King's Hunt* demonstrate the English secular style at its most effusive. *Vi* gives a cross-section of the composer's work, including fantasies, plainsong settings, a prelude, a variation set, a dance, a programmatic piece, and a large number of canons. It is the sort of sampling that would have been made by a foreign musician—or musicians—who hadn't the occasion to make a large anthology of the English composer's music but was able to cull a few representative works.

Since none of the sources giving concordances with pieces in *Vi* could have served as its source, a judgment on the quality of texts using comparative techniques is impossible. The unusual degree of inconsistency in the notation of accidentals for a German tablature source may be due to the scribe's relative unfamiliarity with the conventions of Anglo-Dutch keyboard notation (this is particularly true in the first section of the manuscript). Potential mistranscriptions in the rhythmic values of several bars of Fantasy d4 are discussed in chapter 3. The text given by *Vi* for the chromatic hexachord fantasy is at little variance with that of *Tr*; but its text for *The King's Hunt,* also in *Tr,* is outshone by that of *Bu.* The "Prince's" Galliard has considerable variants with respect to the other source, *D2,* that appear to represent slightly different versions of the piece. As with *Ant,* the paucity of concordances leaves little choice but to accept the texts at face value. If the weak text of Sweelinck's fantasy is indicative, however, other works in the collection may also have undergone similar degrees of corruption.

2

Plainsong Settings

The plainsong-based compositions listed below are discussed in this chapter and are considered authentic works of Bull. Uppercase letters are used to designate major mode, lowercase minor mode.

Included in the list is a setting of an unidentified plainsong omitted from *MB* 14, but nevertheless probably by Bull. It is found in *To* (between In Nomines 3 and 4, "Kyri Eleyson," listed along with Bull's In Nomines in Tomkins's index); in *El,* p. 143 (no title, ascribed to Gibbons); in *Co,* f. 100 ("In nomine," ascribed to Gibbons); in *Tu,* f. 45 ("Voluntary. 2 parts on a plainsong," ascribed to Gibbons); in *P1,* f. 87 (no title, anonymous); and in *P2,* p. 42 (no title, anonymous, imperfect copy). Tomkins is the most reliable in the matter of attribution, and all ascriptions to Gibbons may well rest upon Cosyn.

Christe Redemptor omnium	*MB* 14:33
Miserere 1	14:34
Miserere 2	14:35
Miserere 3	14:36
Salvator mundi 1	14:37
Salvator mundi 2	14:38
Salve Regina 1, 5 verses	14:40
Salve Regina 2, 2 verses	14:41
Veni Redemptor gentium 1	14:42
Veni Redemptor gentium 2	14:43, 2
"Upon a plainsong"	20:48
In Nomine a1	14:20
In Nomine a2	14:21
In Nomine a3	14:22
In Nomine a4	14:23
In Nomine a5	14:24
In Nomine a6	14:25

In Nomine a7	14:26
In Nomine a8	14:27
In Nomine a9	14:28
In Nomine a10	14:29
In Nomine a11	14:30, 2
In Nomine d	14:31

Owing to the many problems of authorship and dating they pose, the following hymn verses and Alleluias in *Ant* are treated separately at the end of the present chapter:

Aeterne rerum, 3 verses	*MB* 14:47, 3–5
Aurora lucis rutilat, 3 verses	14:47, 1, 6, 7
Jam lucis orto sidere 1	14:45, 1
Jam lucis orto sidere 2	14:45, 2
Salvator mundi 3	14:39
Te lucis ante terminum	14:46
Telluris ingens conditor	14:47, 2
Vexilla regis prodeunt, 4 verses	14:44
Alleluia: Per te, Dei genetrix	14:48
Alleluia: Post partum, Virgo inviolata permanisti	14:49

Settings in Two Parts

In 1559 the Act of Uniformity eliminated the organ's liturgical role from both the Mass and office. Yet works such as Tallis's *Felix namque* settings, dated 1562 and 1564 by Tregian, many plainsong settings in the *Mulliner Book* (excluding those of Redford, who died in 1547) and Byrd's essays in the genre must have been composed during the Protestant decades of the century.

This repertoire belongs to a common practice of the period in which composers continued to set certain hymn and antiphon melodies—for either keyboard or consort—despite the fact that there was no liturgical need for such settings. While Byrd foresook early the strictures of plainsong composition and turned to other means of building larger forms, the younger composer Bull embraced the tradition with an enthusiasm that was unrivaled by his English contemporaries or successors. Plainsong setting appealed to Bull as an exercise in itself, providing the composer with a vehicle for his rich imagination in the invention of keyboard devices. Yet it also furnished his guiding principles in other genres: in the course of Bull's life nearly every facet of his compositional thinking was influenced by his experience with English plainsong setting.

The simple means of building a piece on a plainsong involving an unadorned melody in the upper voice and divisions against it in the lower voice apparently did not appeal to English composers in the first half of the sixteenth century as much as might be expected. The manner preferred by Redford and his contemporaries for two-voice settings was that of placing the decorated plainsong (or its faburden) in the bass with a free melodic part above it. Only two bicinium compositions survive in any source predating the *Mulliner Book,* and one in a source roughly contemporary with it.[1] Mulliner, however, copied no less than six examples of the genre: two bicinia probably by Redford, two by Blitheman with a third apparently by him as well, and one by Carleton.[2] That the bicinium held less interest for earlier composers than other textures can be seen in the paucity of imagination in pieces of that genre compared to Redford's preferred melodic style. Yet it was this simplified approach to counterpoint that appealed to Mulliner, for he included settings that other compilers must have ignored (nos. 7 and 8, if they are Redford's, cannot be contemporary with the *Mulliner Book*); and he omitted other settings in the older, melodic style.[3] That the starker two-voice style was a current one in the 1560s is evidenced not only by the number of these settings in the *Mulliner Book* but also by the fact that around this time one was undertaken by Byrd, a composer otherwise more interested in melody than in the figurations per se implicit in bicinium style. His *Salvator mundi*[4] is clearly related to the bicinium flowering as an offspring of Blitheman's second *Gloria tibi Trinitas.*[5]

In addition to reflecting a certain currency of the genre, the bicinia in the *Mulliner Book* also show a new approach to it being taken by younger composers. Two *Miserere* settings and an *Agnus Dei* by Redford in Add. MS 29996 which Mulliner copied demonstrate the two existing types of bicinia: one involves a continuous lower-voice motion, the other a motion interrupted by rests or notes of longer value (which articulate motivic units). The possibilities that Blitheman saw in the two-part style can be observed in his second *Gloria tibi Trinitas,* which had interested Byrd, and in the *Christe Redemptor omnium,* which Blitheman presumably also composed. In the first piece the composer begins with the anacrustic left-hand figure that characterizes the opening of Redford's bicinia and continues to spin out eight notes to the semibreve, but for only less than a quarter of the piece's duration. The ensuing increase in motion from eight to 12 springs from the restlessness of the opening. Contrast is heightened by the introduction of a new motivic idea; and at the midpoint of the piece a third voice joins into the play of the left hand, resulting in the characteristic celebration of thirds and sixths. Calculated changes of rhythmic proportion and motive are here responsible for advancing the continuous-motion bicinium over that of the first of the two

Miserere. In the other piece Blitheman's style resembles more that of Redford's *Agnus Dei,* in which the left hand falls into longer or shorter phrases set off by brief halts in the motion. This is a more schematic approach, one in which the sequencing of the small melodic unit creates a sense of motive and the change of figuration a sense of period. The greater differentiation ensures that the piece can continue without major contrast for a longer time than can the continuous-motion type of piece. Accordingly, Blitheman calls in tripla and a third voice at the last moment.[6]

Bull succeeded in further developing this latter type of bicinium in pieces such as the Hexachord Fantasy 2, Fantasy G2, *God Save the King* and *Salvator mundi* 1—works in which the technique and its spirit are in the service of a larger structure. Yet in his two plainsong settings that rely exclusively upon this technique, *Miserere* 2 and *Veni Redemptor gentium* 2, Bull takes after the continuous-motion type of setting, missing the point made by Blitheman that repetition and contrast weigh delicately against one another. In *Miserere* 2 continuous left-hand motion and extremely short units of figuration (never long enough to constitute a motive) combine to create a stultifying effect. The composer may have attempted to give a virtuosic impetus by increasing the number of notes against the cantus firmus to 16, rather than the usual eight or 12, and may have sought to provide variety by an alternation of scalar and "Alberti" passagework (cf. Blitheman's *Christe Redemptor omnium*). However, his efforts are not sufficient to compensate for the lack of differentiation. In one piece where the repetition of the cantus firmus note would appear to require special attention to contrast, Bull simply repeats the same accompanying figure a fourth lower (b. 23–24); and his single attempt at rhythmic articulation (b. 6) is without consequent, falling dead on the music.

Veni Redemptor gentium 2 is given anonymously by Tregian, whose copy of the piece is the only surviving one. It lies between two of his pieces in the manuscript, and the style is like Bull's. Here Bull demonstrates a more conscientious approach to melodic organization within the confines of the continuous-motion type of piece. Ascending and descending scales are used as the basic device, creating wave forms whose compression yields rhythmic ambiguities. Such cross-rhythms, metrically contrary patterns imposed on the existing order, could have come from either Blitheman or Tallis (Ex. 2-1).[7] A semblance of melodic forethought, occasional chromatic inflections, and the calmer 12:1 proportion might have given this piece a sense of motivation that is lacking in *Miserere* 2. Yet the persistent lack of rhythmically organizing elements is wearing, and the introduction of the tripla comes too near the end to serve as a contrast of any structure import. The rhythmic articulation in b. 18 is apparently intentional, if incongruous, and is not an error in transcription as is suggested by the editor's footnote; it comes between the third and fourth phrases of the hymn melody and has the same abrupt effect as that noted in b. 6 of *Miserere* 2.

Bull does excel in the bicinium when he abandons the scale of Blitheman's pieces and replaces their goal of balance and restraint with one of maintaining energy over a longer period of time through a few clearly delineated ideas. In the opening sections of *Salvator mundi* 1 and *God Save the King,* the distinctive style emerges which must have made a strong impression on Continental composers. In the former piece a kind of expanded Redfordian scheme is used: one motive at a time is developed, but the motives change frequently enough and are sufficiently distinguished from one another in rhythm and shape to avoid any monotony.

Ex. 2-1   Bull, *Veni Redemptor gentium* 2, b. 12

Blitheman, *Gloria tibi Trinitas* 2, b. 7 (*MB* 1:92)

Tallis, *Felix Namque* 1, b. 79 (*FVB* no. [109])

(This much, at least, he must have learned from Blitheman, though the transition from motive to motive here is a much less organic one than in his teacher's work.) In the latter piece, Bull begins the bicinium in two-voice imitation, an idea he also used for Hexachord Fantasy 2 and Fantasy G2. From this opening the values gradually decrease and cellular shapes—not really motives—spill out in dizzying fashion, producing an effect of great freedom, of a cogent virtuosity. Both the idea and spirit of these pieces figure in works of Sweelinck, such as the Fantasy in G and the variations on Psalm 140, where athletic bicinia are used as part of large, continuous compositions.[8]

Some perspective on the relationship of Bull and Blitheman is gained by an examination of their approaches in bicinium settings. That Blitheman was Bull's teacher is often pointed to in order to explain stylistic affinities between the two composers, yet upon closer examination many of these affinities turn out to be superficial copying. Bull may take over the idea of a cross-rhythm or of an "Alberti" pattern, but he never combines them with Blitheman's musical thinking. Nor can we be sure that it was from Blitheman that Bull always drew such ideas, for both the cross-rhythm and "Alberti" patterns are found in Tallis's *Felix namque* 1. The most that can be said in this regard is that Bull does follow Blitheman's lead—which was, again, that of Tallis's two *Felix namque*—in treating melody and figuration separately. The opposite attitude, which Byrd adopted, reconnects with Redford. In doing so it sets Byrd forever apart from Bull and, eventually, from the ensuing developments in plainsong setting. That Byrd's single preserved effort in bicinium is more like Blitheman than anything of Bull's is ironic. However, it demonstrates both how far Byrd was willing to go in trying a style he would come to reject and, by contrast with Bull's bicinia, how far Bull would have to veer from Blitheman's approach is order to achieve a new identity in the genre.

English Setting in Three and Four Parts

The majority of Bull's longer plainsong settings are cast in three voices, with the cantus firmus most often in the tenor or cantus but occasionally in the bass. The three-voice plainsong setting with unadorned cantus firmus is a tradition that can be traced back to the first half of the century. Like the bicinium, this procedure was exceptional for earlier composers. For Bull, however, it was the rule.

Behind the immediate precedents of Bull's three- and four-voice plainsong settings was a fundamental change in the manner of representing the chant. Redford and his contemporaries had occasionally used an unadorned cantus firmus in the cantus or in the bass, though a plainsong placed in an outer voice was usually ornamented. In a style which apparently held more attraction for Redford's contemporaries and successors than for Redford himself, a cantus firmus in long notes allowed for free roaming of the other two voices in imitation or figuration. The forces at work in pieces such as the two anonymous *Felix namque* settings in Royal Appendix 56 (ca. 1530) would eventually subordinate the plainsong to a purely skeletal role.[9] The counterpoint of these pieces was then free to evolve independently of the melodic structure of the plainsong. Preston and composers of his generation followed this line alongside that of the established textures of Redford in pieces that developed either the imitative or figurative aspect. In pieces in which figuration ruled, the cantus firmus appeared in dotted semibreves. In four-voice imitative textures, which Preston pursued more ardently than Redford had, the cantus firmus was in breves.[10] Preston's first *Felix namque* in Add. MS 29996 and Farrant's *Felix namque* in Mulliner exemplify the former procedure; Preston's second setting of the tune in the same source is representative of the latter.[11]

Once the practice of the unadorned plainsong had been established by mid-century composers, concurrent with consort In Nomines which employ the same technique, there remained two further developments which would define the manner of plainsong setting inherited by Bull. Both of these are observable in Tallis's *Felix namque* settings. The first was to lay out the cantus firmus of a setting reliant largely upon figuration not in dotted semibreves, but in breves (or two semibreves per plainsong note). In both *Felix namque* settings Tallis uses this procedure with the result that the pieces are enormously expanded from within. The origin of this development may well be a practical rather than a musical one if, as Neighbour suggests, these pieces were intended for an occasion where an unusually long offertory was required.[12] In his pieces in the *Mulliner Book*, Blitheman confines himself to the semibreve, which had also become an option for figural settings, thereby keeping his dimensions compact. But Bull, intrigued by Tallis's adventuresome approach, or else required to write pieces of similar length, prefers to retain the cantus firmus in breves. (*Miserere* 1 and *Salvator mundi* 1 are important exceptions to this pattern.)

The second development concerns the placement of the cantus firmus. In the mid-century style a plainsong-carrying tenor was never undecorated, but had to participate to some extent in the melodic movement of the outer voices. It was the later generations of Tallis and Blitheman who changed this state of affairs by freezing the inner-voice cantus firmus. This then allowed the outer parts to engage fully in the dialogue occasionally implicit in the earlier three-voice pieces, such as that found in the second verse of Redford's *Deus Creator omnium* (Ex. 2-2a). An early suggestion of the technique as it later envolved can be found in the third verse of an anonymous setting of *Iste confessor* in Add. MS 29996 (Ex. 2-2b); and two very tentative settings of the *Miserere* employ a cantus firmus in equal values in the tenor, though without allowing an outer-voice movement faster than double that of the plainsong.[13] The style which immediately precedes Bull appears for the first time in the 1560s—even Blitheman's earlier works in Mulliner do not use it—and is signaled by Tallis's *Felix namque* 2 and the fourth and fifth settings of Blitheman's *Gloria tibi Trinitas*. Elaborate surface and extended length generated by stripping the plainsong of any decoration in order to free the accompanying parts, and slowing down the movement of the cantus firmus to allow more divisions per plainsong-note are the essential ingredients of the majority of Bull's larger plainsong settings.

In *Miserere* 3 the typical pattern of three-voice settings with unadorned tenor cantus firmus is seen: two closely related parts weave in imitation at short intervals around a central voice in long notes. Here the cantus firmus is in breves, not merely semibreves or dotted semibreves, but the setting owes little to the vocal-imitative textures of Preston. Rather, Bull's texture is derived through Tallis from one popular in mid-century consort music, particularly that of Parsons and White (Ex. 2-3).[14] In Parsons's famous five-part In Nomine, which appears in keyboard transcriptions in Add. MS 29996, *Fo* and *Tr*, the outer parts are equalized and detached from the cantus firmus voice, creating a rapid dialogue far terser

Ex. 2-2a   Redford, *Deus Creator omnium*, vs. 2 (*EECM* 6:42II)

Ex. 2-2b   Anon., *Iste confessor*, vs. 3 (*EECM* 6:46III)

Ex. 2-3 Parsons, In Nomine, b. 49- (*FVB* no. [140])

Tallis, *Felix Namque* 2, b. 53- (*FVB* no. [110])

Bull, *Miserere* 3, b. 9-

than that found in contemporary keyboard music. The fact that Parsons's piece was well-circulated in keyboard transcriptions, and the extent to which its effects surface in the music of Tallis, Bull, and others, leave little doubt that this device held a strong attraction for keyboard as well as consort and vocal composers.[15]

The prominent features of this and similar textures (see Bull's *Christe Redemptor omnium*) are short third-derived motives, allowing of a relatively slow harmonic rhythm, and stretto imitation that is conceived as rhythmic rather than melodic. The sum is a static, oscillating effect that has many parallels in vocal music where a short, rhythmically defined motive is imitated in stretto over a very slow harmonic rhythm. A cantus firmus A–D–G–C could be provided for Tallis's passage in Ex. 2-4 without doing violence to its intent. Yet it is not for reason of a cantus firmus that the harmonic rhythm is slow: Tallis is responding to a contemplative moment in his text. In his *Felix namque,* on the other hand, the harmonic rhythm results from the obedience of the polar voices to the dicta of the cantus firmus. Thus the harmony only changes if the plainsong note changes. While this procedure goes far back into the history of plainsong settings, the harmonic aspect is one which may have been inspired by

Ex. 2-4   Tallis, *Derelinquat impius,* b. 4- (*TCM* 6, p. 189)

vocal textures, then implemented by appropriately constructed motives to surround the central cantus firmus.

Beginning a piece in the manner of Bull's *Miserere* 3 (and other pieces) is yet a different matter from beginning with imitative points and working around to this kind of texture. The latter invites the listener in the manner of the rhetorical *exordium* (see p. 98ff.) into the piece's frame of mind. The former, however, plunges him immediately into a trancelike world out of which the true animation of the piece eventually emerges. Bull drew from Tallis the specific technique needed to produce this effect, but then used it in characteristically different fashion. It functioned not as a special internal event, but as a means of initiating a composition, recalling the opening of Parsons's In Nomine itself. From this point of departure the building process for the composition is largely sequence. Predicating the movement of the free voice on that of the plainsong is a technique as old as English plainsong setting itself (Ex. 2-5), yet extensive use of this technique could engender aimlessness. In *Miserere* 3 this weakness is exacerbated by a lack of melodic organization: motives are little more than isolated, matter-of-fact events. The problem is one inherent in

Ex. 2-5   Burton, *Te Deum,* b. 11- (*EECM* 6:1)

cantus firmus setting with paired free voices (as opposed to Redford's melodic approach with decorated plainsong). Bull solved it in certain pieces, notably his In Nomines, through ensuring that motives evolve logically from one another and through establishing a web of interrelationships among the motives. The techniques for alleviating this weakness in *Miserere* 3 are less refined, yet fundamental. Two of the techniques, pacing the changes in figuration and pacing the rhythmic rate, are common in Bull's music; one, articulating structure through regularly placed cadences, is less common.

Miserere 3 opens with four divisions to the semibreve; a scalar motive advances the motion from four to eight divisions, then to 16, accompanied by slower values in the left hand. The rhythm finally retracts and the scales dissolve into a version of the opening pattern. Such rhythmic structuring, absent from the short bicinium settings, is characteristic of Bull's larger plainsong settings, and is, of course, related to the changing of the figuration itself. The present version, speeding up then slowing down for the end, is less common than continually speeding up, or speeding up through stages that are punctuated by passages in slower values. The idea, again, is not new with Bull. In a *Felix namque* in Royal Appendix 56 the increase in motion, achieved through both decreasing values and a proportional change, is continuous up to the resolution of the duple-triple conflict, where the movement proceeds in a more relaxed manner to the end.[16] On the other hand, increasing rate of motion may be punctuated by periodic retractions as in Preston's *Felix namque* I in Add. MS 29996.[17] It is this type that Tallis, Blitheman, and Bull are following when they introduce subcycles of longer note values within the larger plan of increasing motion.

Two consort settings of Byrd, In Nomines 5/4 and 5/5, also exhibit the tendency to increase in speed gradually through the reduction of note values.[18] Considered by Neighbour to be Byrd's finest and, presumably, last In Nomines before turning to other types of consort writing, they are not alone among string music as regards this structural feature. The flourishing of the attitude toward building a piece through increasing its motion is a point of contact between keyboard and consort music, one which is indicative of the concern for finding ways of building ever larger instrumental compositions without the aid of a text. Whereas Byrd was to abandon the cantus firmus in his search, Bull stuck by it and sought ways to make it work, using rhythmic impetus as a structural means.

Changes in rhythmic rate and changes in figuration are separate but related phenomena: the motive may change without increasing or decreasing the rate of speed, but a change in the rate of speed rarely takes place without an accompanying change of motive. Tallis had impressed with the breadth of his ideas in his two *Felix namque* settings, yet he failed to find a way of exerting convincing structural controls over the morass of small events. Lacking the guidance of a text and strapped by the limited power of his modal harmony to articulate cadences, he could only set one section of music apart from the next by altering the substance of the texture. This amounted to changes in figuration and rate of motion that were only sometimes accompanied by a cadence. Bull and others must have sensed the crisis inherent here, for they avoided both this particularly long plainsong and settings of this length in general. (In Nomine a9 is an exception which Bull either undertook as an experiment or felt he deserved, having found ways to organize such a big work.) Bull's advantage 20 years later was in wielding the powerful tool of the V-I cadence as a device of structural articulation. As long as the rhythmic values of the plainsong were variable, or as long as the plainsong could be broken, the harmony of the metrical unit was not strictly confined to what the note of the plainsong could allow. A problem arose, however, when the long, equal values in the plainsong caused one harmony per plainsong-note to rule, leaving only the variety of figuration to give life and shape to the music. Imposing a larger metrical organization on the kind of undifferentiated surface invented by Tallis was a task Bull undertook in *Miserere* 3 by using V–I to tonicize either the plainsong-note or a note of melodic arrival in one of the other voices. Yet this was an exceptional procedure for him. The structuring of freely composed instrumental music—i.e., music not modelled directly on preexisting pieces—through a periodic organization appears to have been a natural consequence of the growth of abstract instrumental music from vocal and dance genres. Byrd recognized and used this principle, whereas Bull more often relies upon control of the surface of the music to make structural sense of large, textless compositions.

In *Miserere* 3 downbeats, mainly defined by cadential articulations, occur in units of eight and six semibreves, sometimes coinciding with rhythmic-motivic changes (b. 31 and 45), sometimes overlapping with them (v. 23 and 39):

bar:	1–8	9–22	23–30	31–38	39–44	45–53	54–60
unit of semibreves:	8	14(8+6)	8	8	6	8	8

The importance of this scheme lies in its relative regularity. Structural articulations at erratic intervals have little organizing power, but are often found in Bull's plainsong settings. In such cases changes in rhythmic rate may take precedence over harmonic events. The setting of an unidentified plainsong ascribed variously to Bull and Gibbons, "Upon a plainsong," begins with an initial paragraph of 14 bars, defined by both an arrival on v and by a rhythmic retraction. This is followed by a paragraph of 12 bars in the new steady-quarters motion, which closes with a return to the tonic and the introduction of a new motive (b. 27). The next change in motion, at b. 31, fails to coincide with a strong harmonic articulation and, conversely, the reaffirmation of the tonic at b. 35 (as well as the return to the minor dominant at b. 44) prescribes neither a different motive nor a new rhythmic rate. Sections of 14, 12, eight, and nine bars—followed by no perceptible downbeats before the end, 26 bars (or 30 in *El*) later—give little sense of prosody. Periodic changes of rhythmic rate at intervals of 14, 16, 28 (or twice 14), and 12 bars are perhaps of greater significance as landmarks in the piece than the cadences themselves, only one of which corresponds to a rhythmic-motivic change.

The longer the plainsong, the greater becomes the problem of maintaining structural coherence. To this end Bull uses in *Christe Redemptor omnium*, a setting related to *Miserere* 3, not a regular metrical scheme but a psychological, or rhetorical, organization. The piece opens with the familiar oscillating figure in a paragraph of 10 semibreves. A cadence at b. 6 is followed by an extension of the material for six more semibreves, during which the motion picks up. At b. 9 there is a sense of return, or rounding off, achieved through a cadence and changes of motive and motion—the three factors that unite in defining the opening paragraphs of *Miserere* 3 and "Upon a plainsong." This much established, the piece then wanders with barely any articulation up to b. 29, where goal-oriented scales are introduced, creating short periods. At b. 36 the turning point of the piece is reached. A return to the static notion of the beginning is suggested (in values twice as fast) as a replacement for the tonicizing scales, and is treated in a ten-semibreve unit which both recalls the opening metrical unit and reverses the foregoing process of shortening periods. From here to the end the articulations become stronger through the coincidence of changes in figuration with cadences. The last step of the rhythmic progression is then accomplished by introducing 16 notes to the semibreve. Finally, Bull chooses a plainsong-note harmonizing with the piece's opening tonality as the point of retraction (at b. 48) into the tripla that slow the piece's momentum before its out-of-key close.

The considerable rhythmic variety concentrated into the last one-third of the piece (with the notable exception of the redundant b. 38), and its straightforward correlation of changes in figuration with cadences, contrast markedly with the bewildering picture of the first two-thirds of the piece. If the earlier part is not succinct, it yet has its role to play in the piece as a whole. Regression from a cogent opening into aimless figuration is halted by a return to the mood of that opening—signaled in part by the driving effect of the scales—and any expectation that the whole process may recycle after b. 36 is foiled by the orderly progress of the remainder of the piece. The sense that things may have gone, or may be about to go, too far before a dramatic change in the music occurs is here, as elsewhere in Bull's music, an important psychological dimension of the structure. Presence or absence of larger metrical units and progress of figuration and rhythmic rate are the controlling factors of such a structure. The techniques can be found in the music Bull knew—especially that of Tallis—but the application of them was a new and personal one. Care should be taken in performance of *Christe Redemptor omnium* to restore two details that have been altered in *MB* 14: b. 38, last note of the bass should be B, not f sharp; and the rhythm of the bass, b. 49, should read ♩ ♩ ♩. as noted in the textual commentary.[19]

Veni Redemptor gentium 1 and *Salvator mundi* 2 both exploit the principle of uninterrupted rhythmic acceleration growing out of a vocal-imitative opening. Their initial points—stated first in the bass, beginning from c against g in the tenor, and answered by the cantus—mirror one another's melodic shape. The type of opening here, as in "Upon a plain-song," is Tallis's traditional way of starting (Ex. 2-6), not the headlong

Ex. 2-6   Tallis, *Iam lucis orto sidere* (*MB* 1:86)

Bull, *Veni Redemptor gentium* 1

way of Bull in *Miserere* 3 and *Christe Redemptor omnium*[20] Both pieces evolve gradually and convincingly into the figural style, the one relying upon scales and the other upon a broken-chord figure. The ensuing rhythmic progression is characterized in *Salvator mundi* 2 by short motives that pass easily from hand to hand and conform in their multiples to the minim and semibreve. In *Veni Redemptor gentium* 1 this progression is accomplished through longer, less distinct figures, which maintain their vitality through nonconformity to the tactus. The comparatively plastic treatment of *Veni Redemptor gentium* 1 is obviously a more interesting way of proceeding, yet the sharper motives of the other piece lend it greater immediacy. A progression from two to 24 divisions to the semibreve, greater than even Bull normally uses, enhances the effect. No retraction, or even reminiscence, can occur in this kind of piece.

Motivic contrast, greater in *Salvator mundi* 2 than in *Veni Redemptor gentium* 1, and rhythmic acceleration, common to both, are the determinants of these settings. Neither has an underlying metrical scheme to help organize the profusive surface. Although the triplet figure of *Salvator mundi* 2 will likely be perceived in larger metrical units, there is yet no apparent attempt at periodicity. The piece has to stand on its impetus alone. In *Veni Redemptor gentium* 1, on the other hand, one might expect contrast in the length of the motives with the unit of the plainsong, or the quality of the figuration itself, to sustain interest. Neither, however, suffices at every stage of the rhythmic progression. Expectation of the next faster level tends to set in before the present one is exhausted, and suspense turns to tedium.

Tregian included one from each of the preceding pairs of plainsong settings in his keyboard anthology: the bicinium *Veni Redemptor gentium* 2; *Veni Redemptor gentium* 1; and *Miserere* 3. In doing so he represented Bull in the simple two-voice type of setting, and in the two distinct approaches to the larger figural setting, one with initial imitative points and one without. Another approach was exemplified by two pieces in *Tr, Miserere* 1 and *Salvator mundi* 1. These five pieces, taken with the 11/4 In Nomine, reflect the virtual gamut of Bull's English plainsong technique.

Miserere 1 and *Salvator mundi* 1 are based on the principle of continuous variation. That Tregian included not one but two examples of this minor species of setting may indicate an intrigue with it and, further, a desire to record contrasting versions of it. Continuous variations on a melody are not unknown in exclusively secular keyboard music or in consort music, but they are unprecedented in keyboard plainsong settings.[21] The technique is related to the ground, and was used by Stonings in his consort *Miserere* found in Add. MS 31390. There the melody appears five times, once in each part. In Bull's two continuous settings he once keeps the melody in the cantus for two statements, changing it to the tenor for the third, and once retains it for all three statements in the cantus. Continuous variations appealed to Bull, yet he rarely made rotating the theme's position in the texture a part of his process.

Besides the short bicinia, *Miserere* 1 and *Salvator mundi* 1 are Bull's only settings using the semibreve as the unit of the cantus firmus. In both settings the plainsong need only be stated in semibreves, for the threefold repetition of the tune is sufficient to obtain the desired length. In *Miserere* 1 the first and second statements are contrasted by an increase of motion in the lower voices; the second and third statements in turn are contrasted by a rearrangement of the texture so that the running movement of the bass is transferred to the cantus. *Salvator mundi* 1 is less rigid in its rhythmic scheme, in spite of the fact that the tune is cemented in the treble. Bull must have found an allowance of greater flexibility in the fixed cantus firmus, for this piece exploits a much wider variety of technical means than does *Miserere* 1. The same could be said of the second Hexachord Fantasy, *God Save the King* and *Walsingham,* all works in which Bull chose never to vary from a treble melody.

The rhythmically stratified texture which opens *Miserere* 1 is characterized by a repeated-note figure often found in Bull's settings of secular tunes, such as *Walsingham,* var. 8, or in pieces where a special effect is desired, such as Pavan G5 and *The King's Hunt.* The idea was one that appealed to both Farnaby and Sweelinck (Ex. 2-7) in particular, but is common in keyboard music of all periods. Bull seems to have not so much discovered as rediscovered the device of repeated notes, freely using it out of the context of battle and hunt pieces with which it had been associated since the *caccia* of the fourteenth century. Bull doubles the motion of the two free voices in the second statement of *Miserere* 1 and in doing so creates the proportional relationship among the three that is maintained for the rest of the piece. This is the same texture and vertical rhythmic relationship as that which begins the second variation of *Salvator mundi* 1, and of *God Save the King,* b. 85–106. The transformation of a rhythmically heirarchical texture through a proportional increase resulted, of course, from the rhythmic progress built into the plan of the piece. It was another of Bull's mechanical devices that also shows up in Sweelinck.[22] The third variation, which maintains the same rhythmic levels but in different vertical arrangement, creates a texture that Farnaby and Sweelinck again found useful (Ex. 2-8). Sweelinck even includes repeated notes for an effect remarkably similar to Bull's. The single concluding event of *Miserere* 1 is a reinstatement of the fastest values to the left hand at the penultimate bar.

Abounding in typical features, *Miserere* 1 gives the impression of a school book example, and is reminiscent of Morley's doctrinare instructions for writing divisions against a cantus firmus. *Salvator mundi* 1 is a more advanced effort at setting a plainsong in the manner of continuous variations. The idea of opening with a bicinium, then increasing to three and four voices in varied textures of frequently changing figuration, is one Bull used for *God Save the King* and Hexachord Fantasy 2, and one that Sweelinck used for about half of his chorale settings. The final outcome of Sweelinck's pieces is, however, marked by less bravura and more restraint. Sweelinck's settings, like Bull's *Salvator mundi* 1, are only partially continuous, one or more variations being separable from their surrounding ones. This is the type of piece which seems to interact most closely with Sweelinck's style of chorale setting, not the more elusive

Ex. 2-7 Farnaby, *Spagnioletta,* b. 41- (*FVB* no. 54)

Sweelinck, *Da pacem Domine,* b. 39- (*SK* 2:4)

Ex. 2-8 Farnaby, *Ground,* var. 8 (*FVB* no. [240])

Sweelinck, *Da pacem Domine,* b. 72-

pieces such as *Christe Redemptor omnium* or the In Nomines. Swee-linck's temperament allowed for assimilation of certain details from those kinds of pieces, but their point-to-point procedure must have been too obscure, not schematic enough for his purposes.

The complexity of the bicinium which opens *Salvator mundi* 1 stems from the pacing of changes in figuration—they are never allowed to stagnate—and from the avoidance of effecting such changes, or cadences, in conjunction with phrases of the hymn tune. (The fourth phrase, b. 35, is the exception: as noted, Bull gave similar attention to the fourth phrase in his bicinium on *Veni Redemptor gentium*.) The texture which initiates the second variation allows for little periodic articulation since there is no real sense of motive to lend organization, and the continuousness of the movement undercuts any feeling of arrival when a cadence is implied. All the same, when the figuration first changes, at b. 72, it occurs in the middle of a phrase of the hymn; and the single correspondence between changes of figuration and hymn phrase is again reserved for the beginning of the final phrase, at b. 82. Even this is not straightforward, for a strong cadence occurs one bar later.

The third variation introduces imitation for the first time. A filled-in fourth, later expanded to the octave, is treated in parallel thirds and sixths in the manner of the third variation of *Walsingham*. The resulting faburden effect is then broken down into an alternation of root-position chords (b. 115–27) made possible by the unusual four-voice texture. The triplum of Tye's In Nomine "Rounde" shows the affinity of this texture to consort music, where the fashion for note-against-note style and the presence of several real voices made its realization obvious.[23] Tallis uses both the parallel faburden and the angular juxtaposition of root-position chords in his *Felix namque* 1, while Blitheman's imitation of the effect is limited to two active voices (Ex. 2-9).

The return to duple divisions for the last phrase of the hymn, again setting it apart from the others, corresponds with a major change of figuration which banishes imitation for the remainder of the work. Reverting to duple meter after having once left it is a device Bull expands into an alteration between the two in his second Hexachord Fantasy, a piece which is similar to this one in design and figuration. Bull finishes his plainsong variation with a toccatalike flourish, the alternative to a grave, imitative ending such as in Hexachord Fantasy 2 and *God Save the King*. With the exception of the bicinium section, this piece—along with its lesser counterpart, *Miserere 1*—exhibits more similarities with Bull's style in settings of secular tunes than with other plainsong settings. Indeed the very inspiration for the continuous-variation type seems to have come

Ex. 2-9   Tallis, *Felix Namque* 1, b. 104-

Ibid., b. 146-

Blitheman, *Gloria tibi Trinitas* 2, b. 26-

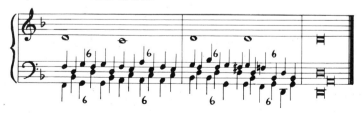

from secular music. Although these works were without precedents in the keyboard repertoire, they were of consequence for the future of keyboard variations through their link with Sweelinck's style.

Bull and the In Nomine Tradition

The keyboard In Nomine came directly on the heels of the mid-century consort In Nomine tradition, which seems to have begun losing impetus around the mid-1570s.[24] Byrd's contributions to the consort In Nomine date from the 1560s, according to Neighbour, after which there was a decline in the popularity of the genre until early in the next century when Jacobean composers revived the viol tradition.[25] Though the manuscript collections from the late sixteenth and early seventeenth centuries indicate that such pieces were still in demand—mostly by their inclusion of copies of earlier composers' works—the number of new settings is greatly reduced.[26] When the works of Byrd's younger contemporaries—Lupo, Ferrabosco II, Coprario, Gibbons, Weelkes, Ward, and Bull—begin appearing in collections of consort music, settings of the In Nomine represent a small percentage of the total repertoire, which is itself a less homogenous one. The change is due to the presence of a large number of pieces that reflect the new taste of the last two decades: the taste for dances and song settings, and for freely composed fantasies. On the one hand, the fashion for lighter forms and the sound of the broken consort, itself too heterogenous for the more vocal ideal of the plainsong setting, gradually pushed exercises like the In Nomine out of the picture.[27] On the other hand, the fantasy tended to replace it, as that which Morley called "the principal and chiefest kind of music which is made without a ditty."[28]

At the same time that the practice of setting the In Nomine was beginning to decline in popularity among composers for consort, another genre, the *Felix namque* setting, was losing interest for keyboard composers. This offertory for the Lady Mass, of which no fewer than 13 settings figure in manuscripts from mid-century and earlier,[29] makes only three appearances in the *Mulliner Book*. Its popularity with Redford, Preston, and composers of their generations diminishes with their successors, finally vanishing all but completely.[30] The latest settings, along with those of Blitheman, Farrant, and Shelbye in *Mulliner,* are the two of Tallis from 1562 and 1564. They must have signaled the last trumpet for this venerable tradition, both to Bull (who learned so much from them), and to others who took the trouble to copy the lengthy pieces 30 years or more after they were written.[31]

Table 2.   In Nomines in the Mulliner Book

Composer	Mulliner's No.	Concordances
Blitheman	91	ChCh 1142A, f. 20'
Blitheman	92	*We*, f. 58'; Add. MS 31403, v. 8'
Blitheman	93	*Tr*, no. 50; *D2*, p. 108
Blitheman	94	
Blitheman	95	
Blitheman	96	
Carleton	3	
Johnston	45	Bodley D. 212–216, no. 20; Add. MS 31390, f. 53
Taverner	35	ornamented version in ChCh 371, f. 6* (*Altenglische Orgelmusik*, ed. Denis Stevens [Kassel, 1953], p. 12)
White	87	Bodley D. 212–216, no. 6; Add. MS 22597, f. 54'

*There are seven additional keyboard and consort concordances; see *MB* 1, p. 93.

Table 3.   Other Sixteenth-Century Keyboard In Nomines

Composer	Sources
Alwood*	*We*, no. 34 (*Early English Organ Music*, ed. Margaret Glyn [London, 1939], p. 22)
Alwood	*We*, no. 40 (*Early English Organ Music*, p. 23)
Byrd	*To*, p. 36 (*MB* 28:50)
Byrd	Add. MS 29996, f. 69 (transcription of his consort In Nomine 5/5)
Parsons	Add. MS 29996, f. 68; *Fo*, p. 272; *Tr*, no. [140] (Transcriptions of his consort In Nomine 5/1 [Neighbour's numbering]; *MB* 28:51 is the text from *Fo*, the transcription attributed with reservation to Byrd.)
Strogers	ChCh 371, f. 22'
Strogers	ChCh 371, f. 23' (*Altenglische Orgelmusik*, p. 11)
[Strogers]	ChCh 371, f. 25 (incomplete, at end of ms.)
Tallis	ChCh 371, f. 14 (*TK*, p. 32)

*Alwood's "In Nomine" in *Mulliner* is not based on the *Gloria tibi Trinitas* antiphon, but on the cantus firmus of the *Sanctus* of his Mass *Praise Him Praiseworthy*, in *Early Tudor Masses: I*, transcr. and ed. John D. Bergsagel (London, 1963), p. 37.

The late sixteenth-century keyboard In Nomine may be regarded as both inheritor of a consort tradition, that of the In Nomine itself, and successor to the *Felix namque* keyboard tradition. Signs of this transition are readily perceptible in the *Mulliner Book*, which contains four single In Nomines plus Blitheman's set of six. These settings, given in Table 2, plus those listed in Table 3 comprise the surviving keyboard In Nomines which are likely to have existed at the time Bull began writing his own.[32] Of these pieces, about one-fourth are transcriptions of consort In

Nomines. Keyboard versions of the Parsons setting were still famous enough in the seventeenth century for both Tregian's and Forster's inclusion of the work in their anthologies. (Along with Tallis's two *Felix namque,* it is among the earliest pieces in *Tr.*) The fact of such transcriptions co-existent with new settings for keyboard suggests that the latter evolved out of the former, probably as a result of some need on the part of keyboard players to have this music for their own use. Furthermore, they must have wanted to play it on the organ, which suits the slow sustained manner of string and vocal writing, rather than on the harpsichord or virginals. The locations of these pieces, and of the In Nomines in *Mulliner* in particular, may also indicate what motivated this transfer of medium. Add. MS 29996 has a long association, in all of its layers, with the Chapel Royal. In it the Byrd and Parsons transcriptions come in the midst of a group of hymn verses for liturgical use. The *Mulliner Book,* though multipurpose, is layered according to pieces for church use—whether liturgical or incidental—and pieces of a secular nature; all the In Nomines are found with the former. ChCh 371, though a varied source, is comprised chiefly of liturgical organ music and contains In Nomines of Tallis, Taverner, and Strogers. The decline of the *Felix namque* (concurrent with the appearance of the first keyboard In Nomines) and the location of these pieces within sources of liturgical organ music seem to indicate that the keyboard In Nomine gradually took a place alongside—and eventually outlived—the *Felix namque* as a favored genre of plainsong setting for incidental service use.[33]

Even in its restricted role of the late sixteenth century, the organ continued to play at certain times during the service, especially at the offertory.[34] As the *Felix namque* fell out of style, plainsongs of appropriate length would have been chosen as the basis for offertories during the period before freely composed fantasies and voluntaries became the rule. It is therefore not surprising to find Alwood's In Nomines in the midst of fantasies by the younger composers Harding and Ferrabosco I in *We.* In view of its connection with the Mass, the *Gloria tibi Trinitas* antiphon was a logical choice of plainsong; yet through consort settings it had lost any unsavory popish associations. The sudden disappearance of the *Felix namque* may have been the result of a change in attitude after the death of Mary toward music suitable for the church. However, it is difficult to imagine strong objections—at least in Elizabeth's chapel—to a traditional tune which is itself associated with the Virgin.[35] Neighbour has even suggested that Tallis's big settings may themselves have been written for a special occasion of the queen.[36] Rather, the decline of the *Felix namque* is a symptom of the disappearance of liturgical organ music in general around this time. In the last quarter of the sixteenth century, settings of Mass portions, Magnificats, antiphons, and office hymns wane in favor of settings of those few plainsongs which had through secular and didactic practice lost their liturgical associations—the *Miserere* and *In nomine* in particular—and the newer fantasy and voluntary. Were it not for its unwieldy length, the *Felix namque* might have retained its position rather than yielding to other cantus firmi.

Though the origin of the keyboard In Nomine is to be seen in the transcription of consort settings, very likely for incidental service use, such transcriptions can only partially account for the sizeable pieces which Bull wrote. There is both a direct and an indirect continuity from the consort style to Bull's keyboard style through works like Tallis's *Felix namque* settings. Yet the consort style leaves little room for elaboration; it is musically self-sufficient and does not lend itself to ornamentation as did the chanson and madrigal.[37] Only one keyboard arrangement ornaments its model, Taverner's In Nomine in ChCh 371, but here it is a vocal, not instrumental, setting that serves as the point of departure. Such settings apparently were of little interest to Bull. Tallis's and Byrd's single settings and the first of Strogers's three would have had equally small impact: the two-voice melodic style in which they were written was obsolescent. They are isolated attempts to transfer the In Nomine tradition to the keyboard using an old keyboard idiom, without reference to consort style. Alwood's approach, with its broken plainsong and monothematicism, is equally old-fashioned. The beginnings of a more modern attitude are depicted in Carleton's use of the bicinium and in the three-part textures of Strogers's second and third settings. Only Blitheman's settings, however, evidence the independence of thought necessary to bridge the gap between the style of the transcriptions and that of Bull's settings. A keyboard In Nomine had to be a discreet and synthetic piece which drew upon both keyboard and consort styles, not simply an arrangement or emulation of existing models. It must have been Blitheman's set of six In Nomines that provided Bull with the impetus to compose idiomatic settings on a large scale.

Inspired by his teacher, Bull proceeded to develop the genre along highly individual lines that are a combination of the inherited styles of Blitheman and Tallis and the consort style. Though it could still serve where incidental music was needed, the expansion of the genre both in length and range of idiom resulted in a vehicle which went beyond the limitations of function or medium.[38] As conceived by Bull and imitated by Lugge and Tomkins, keyboard In Nomines were not merely *Gebrauchsmusik,* but abstract keyboard display works equally suitable to organ or harpsichord. Furthermore, they were works of impressive ambition, exhibiting a lively involvement with the Elizabethan spirit of vying upon a plainsong.[39]

Bull proceeds in his In Nomines as he does in the three-voice plainsong settings such as *Christe Redemptor omnium*. The cantus firmus is set in long notes and the accompanying voices move in relation to one another through imitation at short intervals. He places the cantus firmus in the tenor and cantus, as usual, but also experiments with it in the bass (a1, a4, and a9) as Blitheman does in two settings.[40] Regardless of whether the cantus firmus was in divided breves, semibreves (occupying the value of the dotted semibreve), or composite values (a9), the free voices could participate fully in the figuration. Never are they made subservient to the kind of democratic texture of Blitheman's one setting which pays homage to the consort style. Both Blitheman's texture, reduced from five to four voices, and motive recall Tye's monothematic In Nomine "Beleve me" (Ex. 2-10).

Levels of rhythmic speed are again at work as a function of structure in Bull's In Nomines. The phenomenon of accelerating note values can be traced through vocal music back to the fifteenth century, where its short-term application corresponds with the "drive to the cadence." In the organ music of the next century, levels of increasing speed began to play a structural role through their alliance with motivic changes. The progression of a composition through decreasing note values, sometimes accompanied by a metrical change, can also be seen in consort music such as Byrd's In Nomines 5/4 and 5/5.

With the exception of the a8 setting, Bull's In Nomines begin in either

Ex. 2-10   Tye, In Nomine "Beleve Me" (*Instrumental Works*, p. 42)

Blitheman, *Gloria tibi Trinitas* 6 (*MB* 1:96)

Tallis's invitatory manner—which Bull had used in two other settings—
or in his own manner: *in medias res*. The figures that are then used to
build the piece around its cantus firmus are no longer merely enumerated,
but emerge smoothly from one another, each successive one derived from
the contour or rhythm of the preceding. Blitheman's limited range of
melodic ideas and the motivic thinking manifested by current consort
music are influences felt here in the control and direction of the figuration.

The kind of construction represented by pieces such as *Salvator
mundi* 2 and Tallis's work from which it comes may be compared to a
certain stage in the development of the consort style as seen in In Nomines by Parsley, Stonings, Strogers, and others.[41] There, contrast is
achieved through motives deployed in short intervals of imitation. In *Salvator mundi* 2, figures are similarly contrasted, but without the aid of
thoroughgoing imitation. The thinking is analogous despite the different
effects. Use of successive contrasting points of imitation has greater significance for the development of the fantasy than for the In Nomine,
which takes a different direction in the works of White and Byrd. Related
ideas of low contrast growing from a single theme in the In Nomines of
these composers is the alternative to Tye's monothematicism or the high
sectional contrast of Stonings and Strogers. Similarly close relationships
between succeeding points can be seen in White's first or third In Nomine, and in Byrd's 5/1 (Ex. 2-11). In Byrd's piece the opening point, characterized by an ascending fifth, is soon given a sense of urgency through
a minor rhythmic alteration, yielding an anacrusis. The fifth is subsequently contracted to a fourth and filled in, its syncopated rhythmic figure
then becoming the link to the next point which restores the fifth in inversion. Finally, a derivation of this short motive serves as the basis for
the triplum. Though Bull was obviously taken with Blitheman's more
illusory, less systematic way of working, he was also aware of Byrd's
process. This is evident in the unfolding of his motivic vocabulary.

Blitheman works once with this technique in his sixth setting, the
only one in consort style; but his most significant contribution is a different one. He manages to create sectional contrast by juxtaposing ideas
of different shape, rhythmic character, and speed, giving a coherence to
the whole through an associative process, yet without making close motivic derivations. The set of six must be taken together in order to realize
the logic inherent in the sequence of events.[42] A rising motive that en-
compasses the hexachord begins nos. 2 and 5, and is contrasted in both
cases by a falling triplet using a repeated note. The emphasis on B flat
here is confirmed in the narrower motive of the third setting, then relieved
in the fourth. Its opening motive is again an anacrusis figure, but as motion

Ex. 2-11   Byrd, In Nomine 5/1, cantus (*BW* 17:18)

increases it begins to resemble the faster motive of nos. 2 and 5. In the sixth setting, the B flat is again stressed.

Such thinking does not count on the close derivation of successive ideas, as in Byrd's 5/1, yet it provides a unity to the motivic invention by allowing the development of melodic units out of deeper shapes. That is, Blitheman is not working from an *Urform* as Byrd does, but from an *Urgestalt* which provides the melodic parameters and rhythmic vocabulary that generate the surface. That Bull adopts this method can be seen in the continual emergence of figures that are related by intervalic association. Never is there such an orderly motivic development as there is with Byrd. However, Bull does take from this way of working the capacity to fuse successive figures by allowing the rhythm of one to suggest that of the following, even if the melodic content changes. This process of rhythmic imitation is one which has roots deep into the Tudor tradition (Ex. 2-12); and one which played a major role in Byrd's consort and vocal writing alike.[43] The stylistic maturity of the majority of the In Nomines relative to pieces such as *Salvator mundi* 2 can be accounted for by this dual assimilation of elements from Blitheman and from consort music, which itself drew upon vocal styles.

Ex. 2-12   Taverner, *The Western Wynde* Mass, Agnus Dei (*TCM* 6, p. 23)

The Twelve In Nomines

The disposition of Bull's In Nomines in the sources is suggestive of groupings (see Table 4). *Bu* gives nos. a1–a3 as a set of three with a4–a6 following on singly. *To* and *El* adopt the grouping, though *El* reverses a1–a3
and a4–a6. *Bu* also provides for the formation of a third set, using a9 with
a1 and a3, the latter two having been recopied for this purpose. The exact

concordance between *Bu* and *El* is suggestive of the derivation of the latter. *To*, on the other hand, omits a9 and includes three other settings not found in other sources, making a numbered set from two of them and In Nomine d. It was undoubtedly the practice of making variation sets in multiples of three that accounts for the third "set" in *Bu* and the still different one in *To*. There is nothing in the latter case, however, to support grouping the early In Nomine d with a7 and a8.

The form of the *Gloria tibi Trinitas* antiphon on which Taverner based his Mass of the same name is given in Ex. 2-13 (arrows indicate where an extra value was inserted).[44] In the *Dona nobis pacem* and *Benedictus* Taverner chose, in contrast to other parts of the Mass, a monorhythmic cantus firmus. It was the more open, four-voice texture of the *Benedictus* which was transcribed for consort and used as a model by imitators. Bull followed tradition in using the plainsong as Taverner did. Also, in half his settings he added a third extra note (n. 23', Ex. 2-14), which is found in Blitheman's first setting, two of Byrd's consort settings, and a few others.[45]

Table 4.   The Sources of Bull's In Nomines

Setting	Bu	To	El	Tr
a1	p. 134 & 166	p. 50	p. 173	
a2	139	53	176	
a3	143 & 175	55	179	
a4	146	60	165	
a5	151	62	167	
a6	156	66	171	
a7		43		
a8		45		
a9	159		181	no. 119
a10		29		
a11		68		44
d		41		37

As attested by the early style of In Nomine d, Bull started out composing In Nomines in the key his teacher had used, the key of Taverner's original, and that most commonly used for consort settings. But the old key put up an obstacle to Bull's penchant for the new tenor cantus firmus technique: it placed the plainsong in the wrong register. Blitheman had only once tried the plainsong in the tenor, with the result that the bass and treble were too widely spaced for the kind of active dialogue between outer parts that Bull liked. Transposed up a fifth the plainsong worked well in the cantus or bass—both Blitheman and Bull began their sets with a bass cantus firmus—allowing room in which the free parts could move;

as a tenor cantus firmus it permitted the outer parts to stay close together while still occupying their natural registers. Only in the alto would the transposition not work well. Except for his consort setting (itself in d), Bull never used that placement.

In the first six In Nomines, Bull treats four, a1–a3 and a5, in the manner of *Christe Redemptor omnium:* an exercise in figuration, advancing in rhythmic values. In the sixth, he chooses a constant over an advancing rhythmic motion and actually retracts slightly at the tripla, ending on a calmer note; in the fourth he begins with an imitative point in the manner of *Salvator mundi* 2 and *Veni Redemptor gentium* 1, subsequently maintaining a faster but constant motion to the end. In Nomine a9 belongs to the category of nos. a1, a2, a3, and a5, though the metrically additive arrangement of its cantus firmus, four-voice texture and somewhat more systematic use of imitation at the outset are exceptional. All the In Nomines except the one in d share a community of motives that grow from the first interval of the plainsong, the minor third. Both Byrd and Tallis refer to this interval while paraphrasing the plainsong at the opening of their two-voice settings. In Bull's settings the minor third likewise mirrors the head of the chant and serves as the background from which a cohesive corpus of figures is projected. (The interval is also heard at the outset of In Nomine d, but the figures of that setting are not related to those of the others.) The interrelationship of melodic units derived by this process and the lack of frequent and regular cadences frustrate any attempt to discover periodic thinking behind the effusive surface. The long sections of which

Ex. 2-13 Antiphon, *Gloria tibi Trinitas*

Ex. 2-14 Antiphon melody, transposed

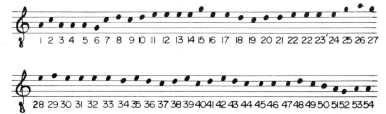

the pieces are comprised are knit together by their common motivic background; and the sections distinguish themselves from one another through rhythmic changes. Periodic metrical structure, which occasionally influenced Bull as it did Byrd in his plainsong settings, is not at work here.[46]

The pattern for the position of the cantus firmus in the group of six settings is bass–tenor–cantus, bass–tenor–cantus. Another plan, that of rhythmic rate, is also at work in the relationship among the members of the sets. In Nomines a1 and a2 advance by a factor of three and a3 by one and one-half (from four to twelve and six to nine per semibreve, respectively). The fourth setting achieves a ratio or eight to one between its fastest and slowest values (excluding b. 1–2), but checks the sixteenths at the end for an overall ratio of four to one. In Nomine a5 also advances by a factor of four, while a6 retracts (x 3/4). This retraction has more to do with the way the piece begins, however, then with the way it ends: if Bull had not set up the perpetual motion rhythm at the outset, he would probably have started with six to the semibreve, as in a3, and ended with the same relationship of one to one and one-half.

The plan of the first three settings is similar in that each progresses through a series of related ideas in decreasing rhythmic values before breaking into sesquialtera proportion. This final section itself then speeds up, though the acceleration is constrained in the third setting, as it is in the sixth. The structural principle here, already seen in other plainsong settings, is that of a series of sections differentiated by changes in rate of movement and corresponding changes of motive:

a1: bar no: 1–23 / 24–37 / 38–71
    length of section: 23   14   17   (34 in *MB*)

a2: bar no: 1–18 / 19–40 / 41–55
    length of section: 18   22   15

a3: bar no: 1–23 / 24–40 / 41–55
    length of section: 23   17   15

The opening figure of In Nomine a1 contains the essential motivic elements found in the related settings: an ascending minor sixth enclosing a minor third is reciprocated by a stepwise descent in rhythmic suspension (Ex. 2-15a). Figures built around ascending and descending minor thirds, and around the scale, comprise the bulk of Bull's motivic vocabulary in the In Nomines. For example, the second idea (Ex. 2-15b) serves as an answer to the first by inverting its contour and moving the dotted rhythm to a different part of the measure. In b. 9, the descending fifth and dotted rhythm are extracted and combined in a chasing figure. The shift from one idea to the next is accomplished through such subtle redisposing of a few melodic and rhythmic germs, recalling the melodic transformation of a rhythmic idea as used by composers from Taverner through Byrd. Figures relate not only within the piece by this transformational process, but also among pieces by identification or association. Thus while the motive which initiates the final section derives from the filled-in third in dotted rhythm, the idea also figures in the central section of In Nomine a2; and the syncopated triadic figure of a1, b. 32, cantus, is not immediately developed, but takes a major role in a4 (b. 53ff.) and a5 (b. 24ff.).

In Nomine a2 begins by isolating the minor third, then answers it with the descending scale. The resulting shape is analogous to that of the opening of a1. The second section of the piece extracts the implicit sixth-leap, again answering with a stepwise descent. As slower motion gives way to faster motion in each section, disjunct motives yield to scales: that which is contained in the cell (Ex. 2-15a) is projected to the whole. The final section then relies primarily upon scalar figuration punctuated by the dotted gigue rhythm of a1 and its variants.

The initial motive of In Nomine a3 fills in the minor third rather than enclosing it. It assumes a role of major importance in the ensuing figurations, which extrapolate it both melodically and harmonically (Ex. 2-16). Of major interest in the first section of the piece is the motive first heard in b. 9 which, like the opening motive, is imitated in stretto. This is again an idea which Bull further develops elsewhere (Ex. 2-21b). Sesquialtera proportion yields the accustomed gigue rhythm in the last section of the piece, supplemented here with an offset pattern in the left hand. It begins

Ex. 2-15a   Bull, In Nomine a1, b. 1

Ex. 2-15b   Ibid., b. 6

Ibid., b. 9

Ex. 2-16   Bull, In Nomine a3, b. 11 and 16

its measure four consecutive times on the second quarter value rather than the first, giving a metrical asperity which is compressed in b. 45, then resolved in b. 47. A smoother flow then recalls the texture and figures of corresponding sections in the previous settings, and prepares for the striking registral contrast which brings the piece to a close.[47]

The motion which should characterize this setting is similar to that of In Nomine d. In the only source for that piece that cantus firmus is represented as $o \; d$ in each bar. *Bu* gives the cantus firmus for a3 in the same way. The editors of *MB* 14, in following Tomkins's consolidation into (dotted) semibreves, have weakened both the effect of the rhythm and the intended contrast with a6, the other triple-meter setting of the set, where full (dotted) semibreves are used. The fault is easily remedied by reading $d \; d$ in the cantus for b. 1–40, and $d. \; d.$ thereafter (omitting the a' in the last bar).

In a comparison of the texts from *Bu* and *To* it is clear that the later source rarely offers improvements. In his copy of In Nomine a2 Tomkins introduces faster values at the opening of the triple-meter section in place of *Bu*'s more deliberate motion, while at the same time overlooking the dotted rhythm important to the imitation (Ex. 2-17). Likewise, the eighth-note motion of the tripla, In Nomine a3, b. 51–52, has been mitigated by both copies in *Bu* through a mixture of faster and slower values. *To*, however, opts for continuous eighths throughout (Ex. 2-18). Tomkins's preference for more continuous motion can again be seen in In Nomine a1, the other piece *Bu* gives in two texts. There *To* follows the second text in filling out passages of slower motion with running eighths and sixteenths. Behind this tendency was the mind of a composer who, judging as well from his own works, was virtually obsessed with fast note values. As an editor, he was unhappy leaving Bull's calculated rhythmic contrasts alone.

Predictable differences between the two *Bu* texts of In Nomines a1 and a3 include ornamentation and accidentals, while other variants appear to represent more serious differences of intent: five bars (b. 15, 53, 56, 59 and 61) of In Nomine a1 differ from the first to the second copy. The

Ex. 2-17   Bull, In Nomine a2, b. 41- (*Bu*)

Ibid., (*To*)

Ex. 2-18   Bull, In Nomine a3, b. 50- (*Bu*, first copy)

Ibid. (*Bu*, second copy)

Ibid. (*To*)

Ex. 2-19   Bull, In Nomine a1, b. 15 *Bu*, first copy   *Bu*, second copy

differences are in relatively small details, yet the second copy consistently aims toward a faster, more filled-in motion (Ex. 2-19). Some of those in In Nomine a3 (Ex. 2-18), however, represent rewritings that go beyond the usual corruptions and changes of detail from one source to another. There has been a rethinking that is hard to accept as the work of a copyist alone. The changes appear to be those of the composer, whether he wrote the manuscript himself or simply provided the texts for it.

Overall rhythmic drive appears to take precedent over calculated changes of pace in In Nomines a4–a6. Even so, rhythmic changes define the asymmetrical bipartite constructions which contrast with the tripartite ones obtained in nos. a1–a3.

a4:	bar no:	1-33 /	34–60
	length of section:	33	27
a5:	bar no:	1–34 /	35–54
	length of section:	34	20
a6:	bar no:	1–36 /	37–53
	length of section:	36	17

In Nomine a4 is a major exception in the group of six in that it prepares the entry of the cantus firmus with an imitative point. As if to return swiftly to his established melodic world, Bull quotes from a1 as soon as the three voices have entered (Ex. 2-20). The quotation serves to establish the importance of the sixth, which generates the accented neighbor (or passing) tone first heard in b. 10. The sixth above the bass resolving to the fifth, itself a very conservative sound, had already made an appearance b. 18 and 19 of In Nomine a1. It continues to have significance as the values decrease in a4, b. 19–20, then disappears in favor of a less harmonically determined figuration, but one which continues to involve sixth-spans. The structural point at b. 34 is made by the introduction of a long–short–short motive that recalls the movement of a3. Bar 40 introduces an angular configuration of the sixth, inverted, that assumes motivic importance in this piece and the next. Bull has apparently worked himself around to stock figures here and in the central section of In Nomine a2, judging from the rather routine occurence of the two ideas as the third and second points, respectively, of Morley's Fantasy (Ex. 2-21). The maximum speed in this setting, reached in b. 51–53, is shunned for the final bars in favor of the syncopated triadic figure whose rhythm is assiduously pursued in the following setting.

The text of *Bu* at b. 51 is eccentric but, typically, more interesting than that of *To*, which has been followed in the *MB* reading. *To* banishes

Ex. 2-20 Bull, In Nomine a4, b. 6-, cantus

Ex. 2-21 Bull, In Nomine a2, b. 32   Morley, Fantasy, b. 17
                                            (*FVB* no. [124])

Bull, In Nomine a4, b. 40   Morley, Fantasy, b. 33

Ex. 2-22 Bull, In Nomine a4, b. 51 (*Bu*)

* Ms. reads c.

the group of six and the harmonic asperities of the second and third quarter-beats. *El,* as usual, follows *Bu* more closely than does *To*[48] (Ex. 2-22).

In Nomine a5 brings back a motive from the second section of a2, imitating its inversion in stretto. This sets the pattern for the piece, which is one of extremely close interaction between outer voices. The broken descending sixth first heard in a4, b. 40, is produced in stretto from b. 11. The motion is advanced through a figure that incurs typical conflicts with the established meter beginning with b. 21. *MB* 14 rebeams the figure from its original fours in accordance with this aspect of the rhythm, a confusing practice that obscures the true meaning of the rhythm rather than highlighting it. Furthermore, the cantus of b. 27 is given by *Bu* with a beaming that indicates it is to be thought of as an imitation of the bass, not merely a syncopation (Ex. 2-23). The major structural articulation of the piece occurs at b. 35, very nearly the Golden Section,[49] where a strong mediant cadence introduces the scalar figurations that carry the piece to its conclusion.

The texture of In Nomine a6 is close kin to that of a3, a feature which further underlines the parallelism of the two groups. A treble cantus firmus with two free voices always yields for Bull a certain kind of texture, such as that of In Nomine d. Yet the relationship between In Nomines a3 and a6 is a particularly clear one, owing to the use of similar figuration (Ex. 2-24). Groups of threes-in-four (b. 20–21) are a point of contact with the previous setting, while the closing section is a reworking of that of a3. The ending to In Nomine a6 provided by Tomkins demonstrates another of his proclivities as a copyist. Tomkins has extended the tonic by a full bar and replaced the e in the bass on the second beat of *Bu*'s penultimate bar with an A (Ex. 2-25). The effect of this, along with the

Ex. 2-23   Bull, In Nomine a5, b. 24, cantus

Ex. 2-24   Bull, In Nomine a3, b. 18   In Nomine a6, b. 18

In Nomine a3, b. 14   In Nomine a6, b. 35

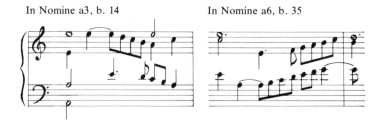

ornamentation of the final chord, is redundant and tiresome by contrast to the direct approach of the *Bu* cadence. Players may further note in *Bu* (and *El*) that the inner voice in b. 8 should rhyme with the analogous spot in b. 10; staff divisions indicate that the parallel sixths stay in the left hand throughout that bar (Ex. 2-26).

The most unusual and intense of the In Nomines is a9. Its power lies in its extraordinary length, derived from an exceptionally long rhythmic ostinato coupled with a leisurely procession of well-developed ideas. Compared to In Nomine a9, Bull's other settings will appear dry and didactic, for here the composer unleashes the full powers of his imagination. Both the length of the piece and the proportions of its structure are dependent upon the isorhythm of the cantus firmus: when each note of the plainsong occupies 11 rather than eight beats, the overall length will be almost half again the usual one; the proportions of the piece's sections, which are approximately 4:2:1, correspond to the halving of

Ex. 2-25   Bull, In Nomine a6, final bars (*Bu*)

Ibid., (*To*)

Ex. 2-26   Bull, In Nomine a6, b. 8 and 10 (*Bu*)

values implicit in the latter two-thirds of the isorhythm. Thus $\circ \downarrow \downarrow$ = 4:2:1, which translates roughly into the three sections of the setting:

bar no.   1–96 / 97–138 / 139–160
notes of c.f.   32   14   8   (last isorhythmic
                                                unit incomplete)

There is the sense here, as there is in Bull's other two settings with bass cantus firmus, that the piece is built from the ground up. Movement of the bass line usually predicates a root-position harmony, and the effect is intensified by the solidity of a four-voice texture. Phrase lengths, though they tend to depend somewhat on the 11-beat unit, are irregular enough to maintain tension with the bass, an important and long-standing feature of the English cantus firmus tradition. Cadences at bars 57 and 60, for instance, occur not with but against the isorhythmic unit as a result of a slight breaking of the plainsong.

The idea of an isorhythmic cantus firmus combining duple and triple metrical units was known in keyboard music at least from the time of the anonymous *Felix namque* of Royal Appendix 56, which lays out the plainsong in dotted semibreves of five beats each.[50] Quintuple meter was used by Richard Alwood in the *Agnus Dei* in his Mass *Praise Him Praiseworthy,* and in consort In Nomines by Tye ("Trust") and Nicholas Strogers.[51] The inspiration for an 11-beat isorhythm, however, may have come from a 5-part *Miserere* by Mallorie in which each note of the plainsong is given $\downarrow \downarrow \downarrow \downarrow \downarrow \downarrow$.[52] A connection between this piece and Bull's setting becomes more probable in view of the fact that *Bu* (and *El*) give the cantus firmus in this rhythm, rather than in the consolidated values of *Tr.* The thumping, droning effect of the former is quite unlike Tregian's version, which is adopted by *MB* 14.

The opening motive of the piece is a variant of that of In Nomine a1, a disjunct ascent followed by a conjunct descent with rhythmic suspensions (cf. Byrd's In Nomine 4/1). The texture of the first section is generated from this motive by the same logical unfolding process that characterizes the other settings, yet the result resembles more closely than any others the consort sound. Smooth motion, thoroughgoing imitation, and a four-voice texture contribute to a rich keyboard sound that imitates the consort in a manner which foreshadows the emulation of special ensemble effects by much of later Baroque keyboard music. Also remarkable, as in In Nomine a4, is Bull's frequent recourse to the 6–5 melodic progression (in effect on every third bar from b. 3–14), itself perhaps inspired by the stately consort sound he sought to imitate.

The second section abandons this texture for a more customary and idomatic one. The initial figure, at b. 97, seems to derive from the ornamental one of b. 70–77, and eventually generates perpetual 16th-notes. Here Bull's purpose is to build momentum, then retract from it through the long harmonic stasis provided by the three C's of the cantus firmus (b. 130–41). A metrical shift articulating the third section then reawakens a livelier motion, which remains constant to the end.

The plan for this work rests on the same principle as do Bull's plainsong settings in general: a multisectional scheme articulated by changes of rhythmic rate and motive. Thirty-three divisions per note of the plainsong versus 11 at the outset preserves the ratio of a2, which this setting in effect replaces in *Bu*'s optional third set. In Nomine a9 yet stands apart from the others by virtue of its striking proportions, based on those of the isorhythm. Exact proportions 4:2:1 cannot be worked from the plainsong as Bull normally uses it, since it is not divisible by seven. If Bull had retained n. 24' and added one note after n. 48 (see Ex. 2-14), the plainsong would have divided perfectly into segments of 32, 16 and 8. This however would have meant interrupting somewhere the dramatic bass descent of the triple-meter section. The uniquely late placement of the tripla (n. 47) with respect to other settings is designed as a comformity to the structural macrocosm of the isorhythm and as the most immediate route to the tonic.

Of the remaining settings, all except In Nomine d are related through common motives to a1–a6 and a9. Like the first three, In Nomine a7 has a tripartite scheme:

bar no:	1–30 / 31–47 / 48–55		
length of section:	30	17	8

These proportions, resulting from the abrupt rhythmic change at b. 31 and the introduction of the cadenzalike scales at b. 48, are similar to those of a9. (In the second section of this piece Bull also hints more strongly at the consort style than anywhere outside of the 11/4 setting.) The motive at b. 8 is reminiscent of b. 4 of In Nomine a4, with which it shares an imitative opening; b. 31 again recalls a4, b. 40, as well as a5, b. 11; b. 18 relates equally to the opening of a5 and to the material of the central section of a2. In short, the plan and substance of the work are not remarkably different from the other settings discussed thus far.

In Nomine a8 is unlike the rest in several regards:

1) It opens in neither of Bull's usual ways, but with a prelude into which the first four notes of the plainsong are incorporated;

2) it uses a four-voice texture in a rigorously imitative manner unlike that of a9, the only other In Nomine in four voices;
3) it avoids both tripla and rapid motion at the end;
4) it is organized in four sections, three of which end with full stops, instead of the usual two or three. (The double bars marking off these sections may be Tomkins's addition, but his is the only source for the piece.)

Despite these anomalies, the style is still Bull's and many motives seem to connect with others of his In Nomines. The motive introduced at b. 9 is similar to that of b. 18 in the previous setting (and its relatives in other settings), and a filled-in third from b. 61 assumes the same rhythm as that of the opening of a6. The textures at the opening, and at b. 77ff., are in the same class with those in a3 at b. 19–23 and 9ff., respectively. In view of such common features as these, and taking into account Tomkins's usual reliability in the matter of attribution, any serious doubt concerning the authorship of this setting must be reserved.

In Nomine a10 is in the spirit of a3. Both are figural settings in triple meter and underlie the treble cantus firmus with triple subdivisions (*proportio sesquialtera*) for the closing section. In addition, the same shuffling, ambiguous texture of a3, b. 46, is produced in this setting at b. 35. This is the only setting that attains a symmetrical bipartite structure, resulting here from the early placement of the tripla:

bar no.:   1–27 / 28–54
length of section: 27   27

Cadences in the second section incline toward seven-measure periods with unusual regularity. The final measure is weak and resembles suspiciously Tomkins's ending to a6.

In Nomine 11[53] follows the plan of a10 and a3 as regard meter and position of cantus firmus. The surface is more varied than a10, however, and increase of rhythmic rate more intense. In contrast to a10, this setting falls easily into three sections whose proportions are much like those of no. a3:

bar no.:   1–24 / 25–40 / 41–55
length of section: 24   16   15

Dynamism is heightened by following the fastest values (b. 32–40) with conflicting duple and triple divisions. The persistence of the triple over the duple releases even motion at b. 46ff. Tregian's reconciliation of the bass voice at this point (in *MB*) undercuts the effect, preserved by Tomkins (Ex. 2-27).

In Nomine d contains but one figure which connects it with other settings, the parallel thirds of b. 36, 45, etc. Otherwise, the texture is a simpler one, not unlike that of Preston's *Diffusa est gratia* in Add. MS 29996,[54] and less concerned with imitation of successive short ideas than the other settings. Yet Bull at this stage had already thought of beginning with a minor-third motive, pursued with all the fanaticism of a young student, and sought to set off sections through progressive motion. The sectional structure resulting from first the increase in motion of the bass, then of the middle voice, is a tripartite one which maintains a consistent rhythmic heirarchy among the three voices:

bar no.:   1–18 / 19–31 / 32–58
length of section: 18   13   27

These proportions, which are unlike those of Bull's later settings, are the result in part of the addition of four values to the end of the plainsong. These extra values are needed in order to allow the four-beat pattern introduced on the penultimate note of the plainsong (b. 53) to be repeated three times, thus bringing it back into conformity with the tactus (Ex. 2-28). Sections distinguished by vertical rhythmic hierarchy (as in *Miserere* 1) as well as by motive, choice of final, and the long tonic extension are features Bull chose never again to use in his In Nomines. Four measures in the edition of *MB* 14 must be given attention in performance: The second note of the bass, b. 14, reads c natural in both sources. In b. 24, the eighth note of the bass should be A, not F, and in b. 27, the first two notes should be f, d, not d, B-flat, both in accordance with *Tr.* Finally, both *Tr* and *To* give the more piquant a, not g, for the eighth note of the middle voice, b. 51. The preceding note ought to be f-sharp.

Ranging from the taut and earthy In Nomine d to the boldly expansive 11/4 work, the 12 In Nomines find Bull at his most ambitious in plainsong setting. He brought the achievements of his other plainsong-

Ex. 2-27   Bull, In Nomine a11, b. 47 (*To*)

Ex. 2-28   Bull, In Nomine d, b. 53

based compositions to bear on the consort tradition with the example of
Blitheman's fine set of six as background. While it is probable that Bull's
In Nomines a1–a6 were written to some extent in imitation of or in tribute
to Blitheman, neither the goals nor the results of the two men were the
same. In his English maturity, which the six surely represent, Bull had
to confront the necessity of formalizing an almost uncontrollable enthusiasm for keyboard figuration. Blitheman's achievement, which was to
develop a cohesive figural language, helped Bull to organize his own
thoughts to some extent. When Bull gave free rein to his imagination,
however, neither Blitheman's model nor that of other keyboard and consort music provided sufficient guidelines. As a result, Bull's process remained an elusive one which sometimes suceeded and sometimes faltered.
Compared to the prodigious longevity of the In Nomine tradition, which
continued with few interruptions from Taverner through Purcell, the keyboard In Nomine itself had a relatively brief flowering. Its very center
was Bull, followed by his admirers, Lugge and Tomkins. The latter composers' attempts to sustain the keyboard In Nomine failed under the
weight of excess, and by the end of their generation the tradition was
forgotten.

Salve Regina Verses

Very little of the music Bull must have written while in Brussels and
Antwerp survives, and much of the contents of the contemporary Continental sources (*Ant* and *Vi*) dates from before 1613, when he left England.[55] A five-verse setting and an incomplete two-verse setting of the
Salve Regina in *Vi* are, however, in an unmistakably new style, evidencing
strong interaction with contemporary Continental organ music.[56] Based
on the Marian votive antiphon and set in verses for alternatim use, they
were most probably written for the Antwerp Cathedral, where votive
masses took place daily.[57]

From the organist-composers whom Bull knew in Brussels and Antwerp, few precedents survive to account for the drastic style changes
encountered in the *Salve Regina* verses. We have no keyboard music from

Gheri Gersem, Joachin Zacharias, or Vincenzio Guami, Bull's lesser colleagues in Brussels, or from Raymond Waelrant, whom Bull succeeded at Antwerp.[58] The extant keyboard music of Philips, Master of the Royal Chapel in Brussels, is of little relevance as a point of contact with the style of Bull's *Salve Regina* verses, for none of his pieces appear to be plainsong settings. A *Benedicam Dominum* in *El* (pp. 251–53) may be a vocal intabulation, and a *Veni Creator Spiritus* in ChCh 89 is based on no known tune for this hymn.[59] All 10 verses of the latter are set, a fact which excludes them from alternatim practice; and the short verses have the character of strophic variations in the Spanish style. From Cornet survive a five-verse *Salve Regina,* useful for comparison with Bull's settings, and a single *Tantum ergo.*[60]

Of considerable interest, however, are the large number of anonymous organ pieces for Roman use in ChCh 89. Thurston Dart postulated that this manuscript was written around 1620 by Richard Dering, organist of the Convent of English Benedictine Nuns in Brussels.[61] The anonymous pieces may or may not be Dering's—their style certainly suggests a Continental composer more strongly than an English one. However, the majority of the manuscript's contents are liturgically relevant; and the locus of the only named composers, "Guil. Brouno",[62] Philips, and Cornet, argue for a provenance from the area in which Bull lived and worked for the last years of his life.

ChCh 89 contains organ masses and magnificats, hymns, sequences, antiphons (including two sets of five verses each on the *Salve Regina*), preludes, toccatas, and fantasies. The settings of hymns and antiphons show four fundamental approaches which may be described as follows:

I. Motet Style

    a. Opens with a regular series of points derived from the head of the tune; the cantus is usually the last voice to enter. Faster motion, derived from the continuation of the countersubject, eventually proliferates and a single voice may break away as an independent solo voice. The process is one of a four-voice *Vorimitation* texture which, once established, is more prone toward the development of figuration.

    b. Begins with two simultaneous subjects, one based on the chant, of contrasting rhythmic rates. Imitation may occur successively in the third, then the fourth voice—which is sometimes delayed—or it may occur in the third and fourth voices as a pair. The faster of the two subjects assumes the role of figuration when all voices have entered.

II.   Cantus Firmus Style

   a.   A four-voice texture is heard from the outset with the tune
in the cantus, usually unadorned at the beginning, then ornamented and brought into rhythmic play with the other
voices. Imitation is incidental, just enough to articulate the
homophony. This texture can temporarily dissolve into tir-
ades, or it can evolve into IIb.

   b.   The tune, stated in the cantus, tenor or bass, is accompanied by parallel figures or short, imitative points. The cantus firmus voice may retain the tune intact and
unornamented, or it may eventually engage in the figuration
of the other voices. This procedure is the closest of all to
that used by Bull in his English plainsong settings.

These are typologies derived from the considerable variety in manner
of setting manifested, not categories into which all the hymns and antiphons of the collection neatly fit. As fundamental approaches, they can
be seen in the *Salve Regina* settings of Cornet and Bull as well. Bull must
have come to adopt a Continental approach because the methods of plainsong setting he had brought with him from England were unworkable in
his new situation. The older verse style of English plainsong setting was
musically archaic, and the practice of broken plainsong was unfamiliar
to his audience. The style he was accustomed to using in his large settings, on the other hand, was inappropriate for alternatim use. A comparison in Table 5 of Bull's two *Salve Regina* settings with the two in
ChCh 89[63] and the one of Cornet show that they share the above procedures, and that Bull drew upon the first of them in particular.

Table 5.   Five Salve Regina Settings

Bull 1	Bull 2	ChCh 89, 1	ChCh 89, 2	Cornet
1: Ia	1:Ia	1:Ia	1:IIa	1: Ia
2: Ia (treble solo)	2: Ia (bass solo)	2:Ia	2: Ib	2: Ia
3: Ia (bass solo)	—	3: Ia	3: Ia (bass solo)	3: Ib
4: bicinium	—	4: Ia	4: IIb	4: IIb
5: Ia	—	5: IIb	5: Ia	5: Ib

Essential to all these procedures, but especially important to Ia, is
the freedom with which any voice may break from the rhythmic con-

straints of the texture and become a solo line. This tendency is strong in the settings from ChCh 89 and those of Cornet, but it is the scalar coloration in the former that is closer to Bull's style of melodic ornamentation than Cornet's more patterned, mechanical figures (Ex. 2-29). Rhythmic values range no further in Bull's settings than in the comparable ones, yet faster values are more explicitly used in the coloration: compare, in Ex. 2-30, analogous passages from Bull's *Salve Regina* 1, verse 1 and Cornet's first verse, where the treble rises to speak. Even so, Bull—in the midst of embracing the Continental style of coloration—occasionally unmasks his English side. This may be seen in the treble ostinato in verse 4, so reminiscent of Redford.

Where Cornet will give variety by altering his subject or by using two subjects, as in his fifth verse, Bull effects a greater intensity through monothematicism and melodic emphasis. The colored melodic voice of *Salve Regina* 1, verse 5 emerges from an opening compacted by stretto, and attains its melodic peak through a typical melodic figure (Ex. 2-31), one which predominates in these settings. From a brief flowering of ornamental melody in this verse, imitation reasserts itself with a new subject and is combined with the faster values. By contrast, the colored voice takes over entirely in *Salve Regina* 2, verse 1, rhapsodizing as before, but here to the exclusion of any real activity in the other voices. The closing figure could only have been used by a composer familiar with the virginalistic idiom (Ex. 2-32).

That the soloistic aspect of Continental organ music interested Bull is strongly evident in *Salve Regina* 1, verses 2 and 3, and 2, verse 2. These are true solo pieces—for treble, bass, and bass, respectively— likely intended for execution on a two-manual instrument at Bull's disposal.[64] (One setting, *Salve Regina* 2, verse 2, can however be played as a bass solo on an instrument with registers divided at c'–c'-sharp.) Cornet never uses this texture, though the bass line is occasionally melodically independent. Both treble and bass solos, however, are to be found in ChCh 89. In three treble solos—two *Tu solus altissimus* and one fantasy for the Elevation—the registration "per le cornetti" is indicated.[65] The use of the treble solo may have been suggested by the word "altissimus" and the act of the Elevation. Perhaps it was the word "clamamus" which prompted Bull to use a solo "voice"—once in the treble and once in the bass—for the second verse of each set. The third verse of the first set then balances it with a bass solo. Might the third verse of the second set have been, by analogy, a treble solo?

In one verse of the second *Salve Regina* set and in several hymn verses in ChCh 89, the bass voice is set apart for the entire piece. The consistently higher level of rhythmic activity than is usually encountered

Ex. 2-29 Anon., [*Dulcis Virgo*] (ChCh 89)

Cornet, *Eia ergo* (*CK*, p. 62)

Ex. 2-30 Cornet, [*Salve Regina*] (*CK*, p. 58)

Bull, *Salve Regina, 1,1*

in the bass suggests that the clarity of a reed stop may have been called for (Ex. 2-33).

The principle of treble and bass solos as used by Bull and the anonymous composer of ChCh 89 is that of Ia. Thus there is the usual imitative point followed (in the case of Bull's *Salve Regina* 1, verse 2) by a second, then a third which is not however presented by the other voices. The procedures for *Salve Regina* 1, verse 3 and 2, verse 2 are progressively less schematic, the relationship between melodic invention and chant becoming more obscure as the coloration becomes more lavish. The pieces

Ex. 2-31   Bull, *Salve Regina,* 1,5

Ex. 2-32   Bull, *Salve Regina* 2,1

Ex. 2-33   Anon., *Eia ergo* a 3 (ChCh 89)

begin with what will come to be known as *Vorimitation,* and end by in-
dulging in the freest sort of melodic coloration.

It is remarkable that Bull, who apparently paid no attention to the
English melodic tradition of plainsong elaboration which interested Byrd,
should have turned to a form of it later in life. Such a transition in style
is unthinkable without the confluence of Bull's music with that of Continental composers. In view of Bull's use of bicinium, his more advanced
use of solo textures, more extensive use of smaller rhythmic values, and
tighter contrapuntal approach relative to Cornet, J. H. van deer Meer's
evaluation of the situation is difficult to accept:

Only an Englishman could have created this type. If therefore a 'Salve Regina' by Bull's Brussels colleague Cornet . . . has the same structure it is Bull who influenced Cornet and not vice versa.[66]

If Cornet knew Bull's *Salve Regina* settings, prior to composing his own he could have been little more than superficially impressed by them, for Cornet followed none of Bull's more striking procedures. With the exception of a tentative beginning in the figural manner of IIb and a mild use of English figuration throughout, Cornet seems not to have been influenced by English style in these pieces. If, on the other hand, Bull knew Cornet's settings, it was with a considerably larger stylistic frame of reference than Cornet's that he undertook to write his own.

The Hymn Verses and Alleluias in Add. MS. 23623

Of all the works ascribed to Bull in *Ant,* the most problematic are 17 short hymn verses and two Alleluias. These pieces are, for the most part, not based on tunes like the *Miserere* and the *In Nomine,* which fueled the imagination of the composer as he strove toward the development of independent instrumental forms. Rather, they are founded on office hymns and Alleluia verses whose alternatim practice should have been extinguished with the Act of Uniformity. Since the verse structure of the pieces seems to indicate liturgical use, the question has arisen whether they might be late works of Bull, written for Brussels or Antwerp. The tunes, however, are among those commonly set by composers in the mid-sixteenth century for the Sarum Rite, not those used by composers in the first half of the seventeenth century for the Roman Rite. (*Vexilla regis prodeunt* is the single possible exception; settings of the tune are found in ChCh 371 and ChCh 89.) Furthermore, the works (aside from *Vexilla regis,* verse 1) are neither in the style of Bull's authentic English plainsong settings nor in the style of his late *Salve Regina* verses.[67]

The idea has also been put forward that this repertoire may be the work of Tallis. One of the hymns in *Ant* (excluded from *MB* 14) is a *Veni Redemptor gentium* ascribed to Tallis by Mulliner.[68] On the strength of Mulliner's ascription, Margaret Glyn suggested that others of the hymns in *Ant* could also be by Tallis.[69] In response to Glyn's suggestion, Oliver Neighbour had the following to say:

The music . . . gives no support to Tallis's authorship. Quite apart from questions of musical quality, three characteristics of the pieces in the Mulliner book will serve as mechanical tests: (1) their monothematicism, (2) their dissonant harmony, (3) the special care expended on the close of each piece (cf. Tallis's *Gloria tibi trinitas,* his short *Point,* and his untitled 3-part organ piece). Of the pieces attributed questionably to Bull by Messaus none answers to (1), only the antiphon *Alleluia Post partum* to (2) (except where recalcitrant canons are being forced into place), and only one or two to (3). The harmonic style in any case suggests a somewhat younger man.[70]

It is true that the pieces do not hold up to the test of Tallis's style, yet they withstand with equal frailty the scrutiny of Bull's style. Fourteen of the 19 pieces under consideration are in four parts. Bull used four-part textures in his plainsong settings either to evoke a consort or vocal texture, or to create a bravura effect. The first section of In Nomine a9 and parts of In Nomine a8 emulate the viol consort in homogenous, broadly spaced textures of unusually regular imitations and melodic, unmechanical figurations. On the other hand, *Salvator mundi* 1, var. 3, uses the four-part texture in a fashion idiomatic to the keyboard, exploiting a wide variety of figurations to animate the homophony. With the exception of *Telluris ingens conditor,* which resembles the consort texture, the four-voice verses of *Ant* do not belong in these stylistic categories: their polyphony is taut, slow-moving and oriented toward treble melody. Although *Telluris ingens conditor* exhibits some of the mechanical features characteristic of Bull's English settings, it also remains exceptional by its use of a broken plainsong. Bull came to adopt the Continental type of four-voice texture related to the motet in his settings of the *Salve Regina.* But in that piece rhythmic activity is higher than in the *Ant* pieces, and the polyphony never remains intact for a whole verse; rather, it breaks into a simplified texture of colored melody supported by two or three accompanying voices.

The textures of the three-voice settings save one, *Vexilla regis prodeunt,* verse 1, are also unusual. Instead of an unadorned cantus firmus against a pair of free voices, we typically find a broken plainsong accompanied by two parts that maintain a minimum of rhythmic contrast with the plainsong voice. The treble-melodic emphasis again appears anachronistic, suggestive of some mid-century organ music.[71] Yet the more modern harmonic range of most of the examples, absence of two-voice settings, and lack of florid rhythms obstruct any serious attempt to date the pieces from that period, where they seem to belong in function.

Two links to the repertoire in question may be cited. One is Fantasy g, ascribed to Bull in its only source (*El*); the other is his In Nomine d. The fantasy is a three-voice piece unlike any of the other fantasies. Its unusual texture has prompted the suggestion that it may be a setting of an unidentified broken plainsong.[72] Many of the stylistic criteria of the three- and four-voice settings in *Ant* are met here: nonmonothematicism and low dissonance (relative to Tallis), predilection for treble melody, and close polyphonic motion with an avoidance of faster note values. In addition, a tendency can be seen in this piece toward the parallel movement of the outer voices which is evident in *Vexilla regis prodeunt,* verses 2, 3, 4, and *Jam lucis orto sidere* 1 and 2. In the third verse of the former, the pairing off of voices results in a splitting of the texture so that it is in dialogue with itself. The same effect is attained in three voices in *Aurora lucis rutilat,* verse 3. Though these resemblances are suggestive, the link to Fantasy g remains a weak one, for the authorship of the fantasy itself comes into question. As far as we know, Bull wrote no other fantasies like it, and the copyist's attribution was made some 30 years after Bull had left England.

In Nomine d uses its plainsong as the basis for a duo between two lower voices which progressively increase in speed. The same is true of *Vexilla regis prodeunt,* verse 1, though the opening figure of the hymn verse is conceived and developed in a more imitative fashion. Yet the textures, particularly of the latter halves of the pieces, are remarkably similar; and the incorporation of repeated notes into the figuration is characteristic of Bull (Ex. 2-34). The fact that the following two verses are not characteristic does not necessarily argue against verse 1 being Bull's piece, for either composer or copyist could have prefaced two older settings with a newly composed one.

Complications outside the province of style are posed by several individual pieces in this group. The first is the fact that the two verses called

Ex. 2-34   Bull (?), *Vexilla regis prodeunt,* verse 1, b. 37-

Bull, In Nomine d, b. 51-

Jam lucis orto sidere are settings of different tunes. While the second of the two could have been mistitled in the source (see comments below on the so-called *Telluris ingens conditor* verses), it may also be an example of successive polyphonic verses setting different tunes for the same hymn. This is a practice that reflects the interchangeability of texts and melodies according to liturgical occasion, and one that was known in both vocal and organ settings. In *Cantiones Sacrae* (1575) two successive settings by Tallis of the verse *Procul recedant somnia*[73] set respectively the tune for Sundays (that of the *Ant* verse as *Te lucis ante terminum*) and the ferial tune. Two successive sets of verses on *Bina caelestis*[74] in Add. Ms 29996 set the tune for the day for matins, St. John the Apostle and the tune for the octave day and for the Sunday within the octave. Thus the two verses entitled *Jam lucis orto sidere* appear to be settings of the same hymn for use at different times; the second verse, however, is the only known organ setting associated with this text.

Te lucis ante terminum is another special case, about which John Caldwell had the following to say:

> A knotty little technical exercise such as Bull would have delighted in. The theme is stated in the top voice, twice, at different pitches, with some gaps and omissions. But the true *cantus firmus* is in the tenor, as an ornamented faburden. This is one of the few post-Reformation examples of composition "on the faburden," and the only one known to me amongst the keyboard music.[75]

As is the case with all faburden settings, a great deal of imagination and allowance for distortion is required to locate the actual notes of the melody. However, there are no faburden settings known to be by Bull, and the full melody does appear in the treble in this settings. In view of these facts, two interpretations appear reasonable: 1) the piece is a treble setting for some incidental purpose made by Bull—the unusual ending out of the mode would seem to exclude it from alternatim use—or, 2) it is a setting, perhaps conceived in faburden, by an earlier composer. This author prefers the latter interpretation, but in any case cannot see that the piece is a faburden setting by Bull himself, as Caldwell interprets it. The treatment of the plainsong in *Salvator mundi* 3 is also anomalous with respect to Bull's usual procedures. In none of his settings is the plainsong so thoroughly broken as it is here. Again, this is an earlier practice which is strange to find applied to a tune that was currently serving as the basis for larger, nonliturgical compositions for both keyboard and consort.

The seven verses called *Telluris ingens conditor* are apparently a copyist's aggregate. If, as it appears, the copyist was not familiar with English plainsong practice, then he may have simply grouped together settings which shared the first four notes of one on *Telluris ingens conditor*, assuming subsequent variance to be the result of the idiosycracies of broken style. Since they are all canonic, Caldwell suggested that the verses on *Aeterne rerum* in this group of seven were written for a "technical [didactic?] rather than a liturgical purpose."[76] Though the fact that they are canonic certainly does not exclude them from liturgical use (the second of the anonymous hymn verses from Add. MS 29996 copied into *Bu* is canonic), such an interpretation may help explain why the normal upward limit of a'' is disregarded in two of the verses: the cantus of one extends to c''', another to b''-flat.[77] While this is not an unusual situation, pieces in which such an extended range is found were intended to be played an octave lower, without the diapason rank.[78] In those pieces, the bass never decends below tenor c. Such is not the case here, however, for in both verses the bass goes frequently below tenor c, making the standard octave transposition impossible. At least one organ in the cathedral at Antwerp had an extended compass, to c'''; and Bull's advice to the cathedral at s'Hertogenbosch stated that the compass of their proposed organ should likewise be extended from a'' to c'''.[79] Yet the proposition that Bull was taking advantage of the new compass available to him runs up against three obstacles: no authenticated plainsong settings of Bull employ this compass, there are no known settings of the hymn by Continental composers which would corroborate its use, and the style of the verses is uncharacteristic of Bull. That the pieces could have had a technical or didactic, rather than practical, intent may help to explain their unprecedented range, but the questions of who in fact may have written them and why the copyist of *Ant* chose to include them in his collection still remain.

The two Alleluias present no stylistic problems not already encountered in the hymn verses, yet they appear to represent opposing liturgical practices. *Alleluia: Per te* sets only the soloist's portion of the chant, leaving the *jubilus* to be sung. Preston's *Alleluia* from his Easter Mass[80] and an *Alleluia: Per te* by Tallis hitherto known as "Fantasy" also set the precented portion of the Alleluis, but include, in addition, a section which sets the *versus*. Judging from Preston's and Tallis's pieces, and the alternation between choir and organ they imply, the *versus* of the *Alleluia: Per te* in *Ant* must be missing. *Alleluia: Post partum*, on the other hand, sets the complete Alleluia with its jubilus continuously, and leaves the versus to be sung by the choir. Two kinds of alternation therefore appear to have been possible: 1) *Alleluia* (organ – *jubilus* (choir) – *versus* (organ) – *jubilus* (choir), and 2) *Alleluia* + *jubilus* (organ) – verses (choir) – *Alleluia* + *jubilus* (organ).

The hymn verses and Alleluias of *Ant* should be considered anonymous, with the exception of *Vexilla regis prodeunt*, verse 1, which is a good deal like Bull's work. If Bull did write all these pieces, he would have to have done so at a point when he was under the influence of some mid-century organ music, including Tallis's more sober style (not that of his two *Felix namque*) and, to a certain extent, Blitheman's style. But the question of why he might have written such pieces in the first place still looms. It is easier to imagine Bull taking copies of older liturgical settings with him to the Continent, where he expected to find use for them, than it is to see why he would have chosen to compose for an extinct rite and in so uncharacteristic a style.

Any overview of Bull's work in plainsong setting must obviously exclude these spurious pieces from consideration. Rather, the composer's progress has to be traced from his earliest attempts, written in imitation of his forebears, to the highly individual achievement of the *Salve Regina* verses. Particularly strong are the stamps of Blitheman and Tallis on the earlier music, in which the primacy of prosaic phrase and metrical structure is established as a corollary of cantus firmus setting. As in mid-sixteenth century organ music, Bull structured his compositions through a series of articulations effected by cadences and changes of rhythmic speed, usually allied with changes in texture and figuration. Well-worn though these principles were, Bull established an identity for himself with the virtuosic bicinium, for which he seems to have been largely responsible on the English scene, and with the bubbling, rhythmically stratified textures of his larger settings. Bull stuck by cantus firmus setting throughout his career in England and always sought new ways to make it work. While his efforts may have superficially influenced Sweelinck and others, a triumph such as the 11/4 In Nomine was clearly not to be equalled by himself or by others. Bull chose instead to turn in earnest to meeting the requirements of a new patronage and new musical environment when he left England.

3

Preludes and Fantasies

A number of problems of attribution arise in the course of the present chapter. For the sake of simplicity and caution, therefore, all works which have a reasonable claim to authenticity are included in the list, which is not to be taken as canon. Two works in *MB* 14 are excluded. The first is a "Dorick Musique" (*MB* 14:59) found without ascription in Cosyn's hand in *Bu;* it bears few attributes of Bull's music, and its particular dorian transposition figures in no authenticated works. The second is the hexachord fantasy, *MB* 14:19, which identity has previously gone undetected. It is a keyboard transcription of Eustache du Caurroy's *Trenthuictiesme fantasie: A l'imitation des six monosyllables En laquelle sont contenues les six espèces de Diapason, divisée en la division Harmonique et Arithmétique,* the last five-part fantasy from his posthumous *Fantasies a iii. iiii. v. et vi. parties* (Paris, 1610), and published in *Les Oeuvres complètes de Eustache du Caurroy,* ed. Blaise Pidoux (Brooklyn, 1975), p. 104.

One piece not in *MB*, Prelude G7, is also included here. It is proffered as Bull's work with little reservation. Of the two canonic pieces, *MB* 14:50 and 51, the second seems much more likely to be by Tallis than by Bull (see especially the comments in Neighbour, p. 231n.), while internal evidence in the first piece gives little clue to its authorship. Bevin's ascription may be allowed to stand, though it is worth noting that he is not always reliable in this matter. The works are:

Prelude d1	*MB* 14:30,1
Prelude d2	14:1,1
Prelude g	14:16
Prelude a1	19:84
Prelude a2	19:83
Prelude a3	19:82
Prelude a4	14:57
"doric"	

Prelude a5	14:58
"doric"	
Prelude C	14:61
Prelude F	14:60
Prelude G1	19:121
Prelude G2	19:118
Prelude G3	14:2,1 and 14:2a
Prelude G4	19:117
Prelude G5	19:119
Prelude G6	19:120
Prelude G7	*FVB*, no. 117
Fantasy d1	*MB* 14:10
Fantasy d2	14:11
Fantasy d3	14:12
Fantasy d4	14:1,2
Fantasy g	14:15
Fantasy a1	14:4
Fantasy a2	14:5
Fantasy C	14:6
Fantasy F	14:13
Fantasy G1	14:2,2
"sol, ut, ♮, mi, fa, sol, la"	
Fantasy G2	14:14
"re, re, re, sol, ut, mi, fa, sol"	
Hexachord Fantasy 1	14:17
Hexachord Fantasy 2	14:18
God Save the King	14:32 (*LyA 1* text in *SK* 1:33)
Fantasy on *La Guamina*	14:3
Fantasy 1 on *Vestiva i colli*	14:8
Fantasy 2 on *Vestiva i colli*	14:9
Fantasy on *A Leona*	14:7

The Preludes

Although the keyboard prelude in the sixteenth century was, in general, too miniature a genre to reveal much about a composer's attitude, it appears that Bull did take seriously the composition of such pieces. More preludes survive from him than from Byrd, Gibbons, or Farnaby, and several of them are well-developed works. Bull may have been required to produce a large number of teaching preludes, for four survive: Preludes a1, G1, which appears as late as 1663 in *Musicks Hand-Maide,* G2, and

G3.[1] In its source, *Ant,* the last of these precedes and is paired with a piece in the same key, Fantasy G1. The pairing is satisfactory, yet quite possibly an arbitrary choice of the scribe, for the prelude and the fantasy are not otherwise related.

With the exception of three in contrasting keys that are grouped together, the preludes in *Tr* are scattered about the collection. *Bu,* on the other hand, gives its selections at the end of the group to which they belong by final, thereby suggesting that a given prelude can be used in combination with any of the preceding pieces. Such is the case with Prelude d1, whose presence in *Bu* was overlooked by the editors of *MB* 14. (*Bu* gives f sharp as the penultimate note in the left hand, b. 14, and an improved reading of b. 18; see Ex. 3-1.) The prelude might be used as a companion, for instance, to Pavan d1, with its rising third suggestive of the prelude, or to either of the variations on *Why Ask You?* or *Bonny Sweet Robin.* Prelude G4 could likewise be paired with one of the many G pieces which it follows in *Bu;*[2] yet another possibility is offered by the *Pa* version of this prelude, which precedes the Pavan "St. Thomas Wake." Here Bull chose an existing piece, revised it in details of figuration and ornamentation of the final cadence, and used it to open his contribution to the publication.

The two remaining preludial pieces in *Bu,* a4 and a5, are both called "dorick musique," an appellation that refers more generally to the mood of the piece rather than specifically to the final. Charles Butler described the Dorian mode as consisting of "sober slow-timed Notes, generally in Counter-point, set to a Psalm or other pious Canticle, in Meeter or Rhythmical vers: the notes answering the number of the Syllables"; such elements were supposed to move to "sobrieti, prudence, modesti, and godlines."[3] Dowland's translation of Ornithoparcus's *Micrologus* characterizes it as the "bestower of wisedome, and causer of chastity."[4] The style of Prelude a4 and its relationship to the fantasy which follows it in *MB* 14, as well as to Prelude a5, calls its authorship into question. Prelude a4 appears to be an arrangement or transcription of a consort work in three parts by a somewhat older composer or by a composer who was

Ex. 3-1   Bull, Prelude d1, b. 18 (*Bu*)

more harmonically and contrapuntally conservative, such as Gibbons.
Cosyn preserves a shorter and apparently later version (*MB* 14:57a) of
the same piece, slightly dressed up for keyboard by elimination of the
long dominant pedal and addition of a fourth voice near the end. His
ascription to Gibbons is convincing, yet Cosyn failed to list the *Bu* version
of the piece as Gibbons's when he indexed that collection.[5] Prelude a5 is
surely authentic, although its opening gesture seems to acknowledge some
inspiration from the former piece. It is a harmonically rich work, rather
loosely constructed from a motivic point of view, with a characteristically
ruminating quality. Either Prelude a4 or a5 would, in any case, be a good
preface to one of the In Nomines which it follows in *Bu* (see Table 4).
Tregian's two "dorick" preludes, in C and F, are more reserved than
Prelude a5, exceptionally expansive in texture and sure of movement.

The association of preludes with pieces which precede, rather than
with the piece which follows, can also be seen in the single example from
D2. There, Prelude G6 follows the later version of the Quadran Pavan,
to which it is clearly connected by the otherwise perplexing pavanlike
structure of the first 14 measures and a use of the second half of the
passamezzo moderno bass.[6] A single prelude, a3, is also given by *We*,
and without apparent association to other pieces. Yet the figuration of b.
7–9 suggests it would be a fine piece to play before the "Chromatic"
Pavan. Prelude g, given by *Vi* as "Fantasia," may be a reworking of the
one of Gibbons in *Pa*, for both pieces are woven throughout from the
same "running" motive. (Ex. 3-2).

Finally, *Tr* ascribes two more preludes to Bull, the brief G5 and the
stately a2 which precedes the "dorick" prelude in F. A third prelude then
follows, anonymously, in G. The piece (*FVB*, no. 117) begins like a2, but

Ex. 3-2   Gibbons, Prelude in G (*MB* 20:2)

Bull, Prelude g

includes a longer and more fully developed imitative section before dissolving into the very typical figuration at b. 10. With all caution in reattributing on the basis of style, this author takes this to be Bull's piece and certainly one of the handsomest of the preludes.

More than in any other genre of Bull's keyboard music, the mind behind the fantasies appears to be one that was at once diverse and indecisive. A wide variety of approaches to free composition without cantus firmus or fixed forms may be observed; yet no one emerges as Bull's preferred manner, that which he chose to explore and develop over a longer period of time. The lack of a well-defined fantasy style (such as Byrd had) must reflect in part the fact that Bull underwent changes as a result of his movement from one musical culture to another that affected not only what kinds of pieces he wrote, but how he wrote them. Such changes are so great, in fact, as to raise serious and sometimes unanswerable questions about attribution, consequently rendering stylistic criticism a tricky and dangerous task. The situation is exacerbated by the blanket ascription of the entire contents of *Ant* (save six pieces) and *Vi,* the two most important Continental sources for the fantasies. The available edition offers little help in this matter, for the sequence there follows neither a hypothetical chronology, preference for certain sources over others, nor the order of the keyboard modes. In the present discussion, therefore, the fantasies are divided by English and Continental period, then by type within those periods.

Fantasies d1, d2, d4, g, and God Save the King

The very earliest English pieces that are today broadly termed fantasy—fancies, voluntaries, points, verses—are either transcriptions of vocal or instrumental works, or are modeled on the textures and procedures of plainsong settings. Newman's *Fansye* in Mulliner is an arrangement of a piece found in the Dallis Lute Book,[7] and the texture of Shepherd's three *versus* in the same collection suggests a vocal inspiration. Other pieces such as the voluntaries of Alwood and Farrant (Mulliner, nos. 17 and 20) and Blitheman's "3 pts." (*Be,* f. 9) reveal by a more deliberate movement of the bass line with respect to the upper texture an affinity with plainsong settings in which the bass carries the tune. As noted, one such piece, Tallis's *Alleluia: Per te,* has been hitherto called "Fantasy." Another untitled piece in ChCh 1034, ascribed to John Ambrose, attains a similar texture in four parts and, like Tallis's *Alleluia,* ends with figuration. It, as well as some of the pieces in Mulliner, could also prove to be a plainsong setting.

That plainsong settings fall within the genealogy of the fantasy is suggested by the use of the term *verse* or *versus* for pieces that were either modeled on the two-, three-, and four-part textures of plainsong settings or were in fact actual settings, the tunes of which scribes failed to recognize or identify. As late as the middle of the seventeenth century Tomkins gave the title "Verse" to a fantasy by Byrd in the two-part Redfordian style.[8] Such evidence substantiates an association between the style of setting verses of plainsong and the style of free composition without a plainsong, an association that continued well beyond the time when composers were called upon to provide organ verses for liturgical use. It is with this relatively early stage in the development of the English keyboard fantasy—the emulation of old-fashioned plainsong settings—that the first fantasies of Bull connect. Fantasies d1 and d2 belong to the two-voice and Fantasy g to the three-voice style. Both reflect traditional ways of elaborating plainsong.

The roots of Fantasies d1 and d2 go back at least as far as Redford, whose plainsong compositions in two parts place the tune in the bass, heavily disguised, against a free treble part of faster motion. Blitheman's use of this texture can be seen in his *Te Deum* in Mulliner, a decidedly archaic work by comparison to his *Gloria tibi Trinitas* set. Tallis (and others) chose this technique for his In Nomine and Byrd used it for settings of the *Miserere, Clarifica me, Pater,* and *Gloria tibi Trinitas*.[9] No plainsong settings of this type survive from Bull, though one of the hymn verses from Add. MS 29996 copied into *Bu* and the two fantasies in this style may indicate some interest in it. The real successor of the Redfordian two-voice style, however, is not to be found among plainsong settings, which leaned toward extensive use of the bicinium technique in the last quarter of the century as a replacement for the older two-voice style. Rather, it is found in works such as the two of Bull, Byrd's "Verse," and a fantasy by T. Holmes in *El* (no. 96), in which the old technique is put into the service of free, plainsongless composition.

In earlier two-voice plainsong settings occasional points of imitation occurred, bringing with them an increase in the motion of the normally slower left hand or, conversely, a decrease in the motion of the right (Ex. 3-3). With the requirement of depicting a *cantus prius factus* removed, the motion of the two voices could be closer and imitation could become more central than incidental. This is in fact the case with all of the pieces in question. Imitation is Byrd's point of departure in his "Verse," and runs sometimes occur in both hands at once. Yet elsewhere in the piece Byrd betrays the early origins of the style with passages in which either left or right hand moves more slowly than the other. Bull's references to the older rhythmic stratification in Fantasies d1 and d2 are allied, like

Byrd's, with bravura, both with the significant addition of ostinati. Later imitations of this style such as Farnaby's *Duo* and Sweelinck's two-voice fantasy[10] never admit such passages of stratified motion. They reveal a closer acquaintance on the part of their authors with the works of Byrd and Bull than with earlier models.

Fantasia d1 begins as a quasi-canonic composition based on a theme which is derived from scalar motion. An essential upward fourth (a'–d'') is elaborated by a descending and ascending gesture, then transferred to a downward fifth in a two-bar codetta which compresses the preceding motion. This opening, which is imitated at the octave by the left hand, sets the melodic tone of the piece, one of distinct yet unpredictable contours. Unlike Byrd's "Verse," in which melodic invention has been somewhat updated, Bull's piece insists upon a style taut with old-fashioned syncopations and modal ambiguity (Ex. 3-4). After the close of the first section, at b. 23, Bull steps up the motion with motives designed, as in the three-part plainsong settings, to provide interest by imitation at short intervals. Indeed, the texture here often resembles that of a three-part

Ex. 3-3   Redford, *Deus Creator omnium*, v. 1 (*EECM* 6:42I)

Ex. 3-4   Bull, Fantasy d1, b. 48-

setting with tenor cantus firmus from which the tenor has been removed. Without the skeleton of the inner-voice plainsong, however, Bull feels compelled to depart from his norm and introduce a certain amount of periodization, as does Byrd. The four-plus-six segment from b. 24 to 34 is paralleled, and amplified, by a four-plus-seven segment from b. 34, and is then followed by two eight-bar segments. Such syntax can never last long with Bull; here it is succeeded by the fragmentary one-bar dialogues that lead up to the descent into the ostinato section. The onset of the ostinato very nearly marks the Golden Section of the piece.[11] That is, the length of this first section, ending in the middle of b. 82, bears the same relationship to the total length of the piece as the second and third shorter sections (ostinato and closing) do to the first:[12] The precise mathematical moment occurs at the repetition of the bass motive (b. 83, fourth eighth-value), the point at which the figure first becomes ostinato.

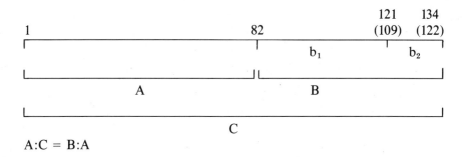

$$A:C = B:A$$

The ostinato into which the left hand devolves at the major structural point is a chromatic alteration of the first five notes of the opening theme (Ex. 3-5). Above this figure the right hand rhapsodizes with increasing speed and with no reference to the lower voice, rhythmically or melodically. The utter disembodiment of the previous texture and temporary suspension of forward movement attained in this passage is prevented from destroying all sense of the piece's cogency by a certain psychological role that it takes within the larger form. The angular, nervous right hand against the obsessive, off-beat left hand creates a polarity of consuming intensity. After the appropriate amount of suspense has been built, imitative dialogue is wrested back and a sense of return obtains. The principal is the same as in *Christe Redemptor omnium,* a piece that also dates from early in Bull's career. The eventfulness of the final section depends not only upon the anticipated return to a texture of regular imitation and dialogue, but also upon the revival of a scalar motive which in this rhythmic formulation served as a codetta to the opening theme (Ex. 3-6). Finally, the clear, determined harmonies and expanded four-voice texture bring the piece to a close on firm ground.

The three sources of this piece differ considerably in matters of accidentals and ornamentation. As noted, *Bu* gives the finer choices. Meanwhile *MB* conflates the sources, disregarding in this case the lavish ornamentation of *Be,* but occasionally admitting idiosyncracies from that late source. In performance, particular attention should be given to *Bu* variants of b. 8, 58, 66, 82, 83, 103, 105, 109, 110, 121, and 122 noted in the textual commentary. In addition, b. 7 should read as in Ex. 3-6; b. 18, left hand, is printed a tone too high; b. 65, right hand, should read a'–c''-natural, etc., conforming with the minor-mode reading of b. 65.

While Byrd's debt to Redford in his "Verse" is evident in his use of the two-voice texture common in the older composer's work, Bull has gone a step further in Fantasy d1 by incorporating the ostinato technique common in earlier organ music, such as that of Redford and Cabezón. The technique is carried still closer to its origins in Fantasia d2, where ostinati appear in both treble and bass and are treated with a generous measure of melodic and rhythmic freedom. The treble ostinato seems to

Ex. 3-5   Bull, Fantasy d1, cantus, opening point

Ibid., bass, ostinato

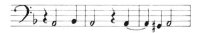

Ex. 3-6   Bull, Fantasy, d1, b. 7-

Ibid., b. 121-

have its roots in fifteenth-century Netherlandish music[13] and was well ingrained in English music by the time of Taverner and Redford. Antonio de Cabezón, who visited England in 1554–55, employed numerous ostinato passages in his tientos.[14] Cabezón's use of ostinato, schematic and cantus firmus-like, is later echoed in works which treat the ostinato as a kind of descant, essential to the piece yet independent of its texture. The second ricercar from the third mass of Frescobaldi's *Fiori musicali* is such a piece, unusual for its rubric "con obligo di cantare la quinta parte senza toccarla."[15] Monteverdi might have given the same performance directions for his *Sonata sopra Sancta Maria* from the *Vespro della Beata Vergine* (1610).[16] At a time when a plethora of pieces based on popular bass ostinati (like the chaconne and passacaglia) are appearing, Monteverdi's remarkable work reaffirms the viability of treble ostinato as a structural device. Bull, too, had not forgotten how effective this kind of treble ostinato could be when he wrote his *Salve Regina* verses, a much later work than Fantasies d1 and d2. However, the freedom with which Bull uses ostinato in Fantasy d2 bespeaks an origin not in this more rigid, Continental type of treatment, but in the more fluid one of his English predecessors.

In England during the sixteenth century the ostinato came to be used either for structural continuity, as in the opening of the *Santus* from Taverner's Mass *The Western Wynde*,[17] or as a means of melodic development. In Bull's works of his English period he used the former approach in *God Save the King*, the latter in Fantasy d2. Here, the freedom of Redford in works such as *Eterne rex altissime*, *Externe rerum*, and *Iam lucis* is recalled (*Mulliner Book*, nos. 26, 74, 75). In these pieces the ostinato may be defined as a cell, containing a rhythmic pattern and a set of pitches, from which a melodic line emerges. This peculiar motivic process may also be seen in Alwood's "In nomine," in Mulliner. There the theme is lengthened, interrupted by rests, or truncated to serve the needs of the lower voices. Byrd's use of the same theme in a section of his string Fantasy 6/F is more Redfordian than is Alwood's, for he varies the motive with a characteristic fluidity that lends a freshness to each statement, the final one of which appears at transposed pitch.[18] Bull's approach in Fantasy d2, beginning with the right hand of b. 55, takes the final step backward, recalling Redford's freedom in *Eterne rex altissime*. After a two-fold repetition of the motive, the pitch content changes and only the rhythm remains, itself occasionally varied by the addition of a dot. When the ostinato passes to the left hand the process is a similar one: melodic variation yields cadences on A, F, and D while the rhythmic patterning keeps a feeling of periodicity in the section. Finally, the whole section is balanced by a return of the ostinato to the right hand before the brief coda (b. 75ff).

While Bull's attention to melodic detail in the long ostinato section of Fantasy d2 is remarkable, the preceding section lacks the sense of purpose of the analogous part of Fantasy d1. Having set out to do an extraordinary thing in the ostinato section of the latter piece, he prepares for it well by introducing dialogue in increasingly shorter periods that foreshadow the unit of the ostinato figure. In Fantasy d2 he loosens the reigns and allows figuration to take over about b. 45; attention wanders until the treble melody emerges in b. 54ff. If improvement can be laid with any certainty at the door of practice, then Fantasy d2 must be the earlier of the two. In any event, both pieces must date from before the major plainsong settings, particularly the In Nomines. Plainsong setting would have been a natural place for Bull to experiment with the older two-voice melodic style; yet the evidence is that he chose not to, having earlier tried his hand at the style.

The *MB* transcription of the piece omits the substantial ornamentation of its source, *Tu*. Though this appears to be a later addition, it is not excessive and can serve as a guide to what may be done in performance. The following details from the source should also be noted: b. 12, treble, second note, the b'-flat is not cancelled but the seventh note is; b. 69, treble, thirteenth note is c''-sharp, fourteenth note is b'-natural, and twenty-third and twenty-ninth notes are f'-sharps; last bar, the left-hand rhythm is ♩ ♩ , not 𝅝 .

Slow, even motion, consistently imitative texture, and the lack of a title in its only source, *E1*, have invited speculation that Fantasy g may be a setting of a broken plainsong.[19] The three-voice plainsong style of Redford and of the anonymous hymns in Add. MS 29996, in which the decorated plainsong allows of a similar rate of motion among voices in a freely imitative texture, is surely the background of Bull's piece. Pieces of this type were often designated by the term "meane" (e.g., Redford's *O Lux with a meane* in Mulliner). Blitheman used this approach as did Byrd in his Fantasia C3.[20] Two features of the "meane" style in which a plainsong is present or implied, however, weigh against a theory that Fantasy g contains an unidentified plainsong. The first is the relative rates of movement among the voices. Although the decoration of the plainsong in the Redfordian style permits its voice a slightly faster movement, approaching that of the free voices, there yet remains some distinction among them, particularly when the plainsong-carrying voice is the bass. The bass lines of Tallis's *Alleluia,* Blitheman's "3 pts.," and Alwood's *Voluntary* in Mulliner (which, though it may not be a plainsong setting, is surely a product of this tradition), all move at a slower rate than the upper voices. The second feature, also observable in these pieces, is that the bass line retains a more stepwise character of movement than the upper voices, often in spite of the introduction of imitative points involving wider intervals. Neither of these features is present in Fantasy g. Both the rate of movement and type of movement are very nearly the same in all voices, the bass line occasionally becoming more, not less, angular in its assuming of a harmonically supportive role (b. 19–21, 54–55).

Striking, even suspicious, is the total absence of figuration. Stark writing and emphasis on treble melody recall the style of several of the hymns in *Ant*. Yet the sensitivity of melodic line and thematic process of the fantasy are significantly different. The theme, conceived in two halves of four and five notes respectively, generates the entire linear content of the piece and lends it a strongly conservative character through the omnipresent flat 6–5 melodic inflection. The opening imitation between middle and bass voices is pointedly altered, both rhythmically and by diatonic displacement of the second half of the theme to bring the two voices to a simultaneous close on III. This is the first of a series of cadences on the mediant, counterbalanced only by half-cadences on the dominant, never by a full cadence in the tonic. All points derive from one or both of the halves of the theme (Ex. 3-7), a procedure much like that of Byrd in his string Fantasy 4/G and in many of his motets.[21] This motive-to-motive process, one of smooth derivation rather than high contrast, has been seen in Bull's plainsong style and in the thematic process of Byrd's fantasies. In pieces such as Bull's In Nomines, however, figuration, not melody, is at the heart of thematic transformations. Here, the quality is clearly more vocal; long rests in the treble voice and wide registral displacements enhance the poignant quality implicit in the germinal E-flat–D. The addition of a fourth voice and stretto which it allows (b. 52–54) are catalysts for the conclusion, which occurs finally on G, refreshingly distant from the B-flat area emphasized throughout.

Such intensely melodic thinking, careful balance between imitation and homophony, absence of figuration, and emphasis on a nontonic degree are uncharacteristic of Bull's fantasies and plainsong settings as we know them. (Ending out of the key is another matter, and not unknown to Bull. See the discussion of *God Save the King,* below.) Ellis's ascription has never been challenged, yet neither is it supported by external evidence. If we are to take this as Bull's composition, it will be useful to think of

Ex. 3-7 Bull (?), Fantasy g, b. 5-, cantus

it as an early creation, one in which he tried his hand, as Byrd did in his Fantasy C3, at an earlier style.

Fantasy d3 raises a similar problem involving a different style. There is a type of fantasy, represented in its early stages by Strogers's single piece in *Tr*, which maintains an imitative texture through a series of points for the majority of the piece, then gives way to accompanied figuration. The polarities of imitation and figuration as demonstrated by Strogers's piece are manifested in varying mixtures throughout the English fantasy tradition. Farnaby's fantasies follow Strogers's format, while Byrd introduces homophonic tripla in several of his works as a substitute for sheer figuration. Gibbons's fantasies stick to the imitative throughout, with one exception (*MB* 20:10). Fantasy d3 belongs to the tradition of Strogers and his successors and is the only piece of its kind ascribed to Bull. Like Fantasy g, we have neither pieces by Bull with which to compare it nor corroboration of the attribution from other sources. Furthermore, this piece again exhibits stylistic anomalies that call its authorship into question.

Only a brief section at the opening of Fantasy d3 is concerned with imitation. The point is quickly abandoned in favor of brief transitional dialogues (b. 21–22) which connect with the following section. Based on an ascending sequence, this section eventually gives way to the simple harmonic progressions, entertained by accompanying figuration, that occupy the center of the piece (b. 44–103). During this section imitation is occasionally introduced as an alternative to figuration (b. 58ff., 76ff.) though it remains subsidiary to the harmonic progressions. Toward the end of the section harmonic rhythm is stepped up and a quasi-imitative figuration in two voices, derived from the previous point, is displaced in order to effect the chain of syncopations which are resolved at the arrival in b. 105. Here begins the first of two triple-meter sections; the first subsumes eight divisions to the semibreve, the second six. The pacing of motion from imitation to figuration, from convulsive rhythms to gliding triplets, and the secure handling of harmony in so free a style are difficult to accept as the work of Bull, though they are certainly the work of a skillful composer—one, like Byrd, who was comfortable with an incidental use of imitation. Yet, for all its qualities, Fantasy d3 lacks the purpose and efficiency of Byrd who, at least in his fantasies, never combined triple meter with figuration to such an extent.

The suggestion at the head of the piece in *MB* 14 that it might be the work of its scribe would be a welcome one if there were pieces of Cosyn that matched this one in quality. Neither those of his anthology from which this piece comes, with their overworked figuration, nor the fantasies in *El*, short and severe with a minimum of figuration, bear the slightest resemblance to Fantasy d3. Moreover, the notion that a copyist would attribute his own piece to a well-known composer seems far-fetched.

In addition to Cosyn and Bull, *Co* also contains works of Gibbons. Might Cosyn have misattributed a fantasy of Gibbons to Bull? There is in the same source a short fantasy ascribed to Gibbons (*MB* 20:6) on the theme of Fantasy d3. The similar treatment of the opening point (Ex. 3-8) suggests some relationship between the two pieces. Other features of the larger work are also comparable to those in pieces of Gibbons. Of special note are the handling of sequence and the texture of the passage preceding the first triple-meter section. Sequence used as a means of development is a well-worn technique in the works of Gibbons. The stepwise sequence, spanning from a to f' (b. 23–26, reworked in the succeeding bars) echoes a similar passage in another d-minor fantasy of Gibbons (*MB* 20:8, b. 23–25). There, too, the sequence is reworked in the subsequent passage. Later in the same piece a texture obtains through the displacement of a voice in imitation to create an offbeat, chasing effect (b. 44–45). This texture is no handprint of Gibbons, but is frequently found in Bull's music as well. Despite similarities, basic differences persist. Gibbons only once allows a fantasy to be given over entirely to figuration after an initial period of imitation; and in that piece (*MB* 20:10) the imitative period occupies fully one-third of the total length, not one-seventh as in Fantasy d3. Furthermore, in no fantasy of Gibbons are triple-meter sections to be found.

For all the problems posed by an attribution of Fantasy d3 to Bull, an equal number are posed by an attempt to attribute the work to Gibbons, the only other likely candidate. Thus, in the absence of conclusive

Ex. 3-8   Gibbons, Fantasy in d (*MB* 20:6)

Bull (?), Fantasy d3

proof to the contrary, Cosyn's ascription must be accepted with reservations. Cosyn either copied the piece from *Bu* before it disappeared from that source and assumed that the piece was Bull's, or he copied it from somewhere else. In any case, this excellent work should not be overlooked merely because its authorship is uncertain. Performers will want to note: b. 17, alto, first note is a f'-sharp; b. 44, alto minim g', is missing; b. 137, left hand should read as in Ex. 3-9. The indication of change in transcription to reduced values at b. 104 is dangerously buried in the critical notes. The original meter signature at this point is ⌀ with white notation, the left hand notated Ⅱ ⌀ and the right hand ⌀ ⌀ ⌀. This signature indicates a division of the semibreve into three minims,[22] which only takes place at b. 122, where the notation is blackened (left hand notated ♩. ♩ . ♩). If the correct signature of C3 is assumed to have been intended at b. 104, tripla proportion (with respect to the original notation) can be applied successfully to the passage, and sesquialtera (notated here and often elsewhere as *61*) at the ensuing transition, b. 121–22. Choosing a broad tempo for the first section of the piece, about ♩ = mm. 48, the minim in the *MB* transcription at b. 104ff. would be played at mm. 72 with the same tempo maintained for the dotted quarter at b. 122ff.

The use of ostinato as a means of structural and melodic development in Fantasy d1 and d2 may be contrasted with the skeletal applications of the technique in a number of other fantasies. In consort pieces of Fayrfax and Lloyd, tetrachord-based tenors provide ostinati against which the outer voices move.[23] Such pieces belong to the same tradition as that of the anonymous "upon la mi re" in Add. MS 29996 and hexachord fantasies, the earliest keyboard example of which is probably that of White in ChCh 317.[24] As late as Tomkins's *Offertory* (dated 1637), ostinato can be seen as a means of building a large-scale keyboard work.[25] In all these examples, it is a repeating *cantus prius factus,* sometimes subjected to rhythmic alteration, that provides the framework for free composition. This is a genre that elicited a definite scheme from Bull, as can be seen in a comparison of *God Save the King,* Hexachord Fantasy 2, Fantasy G2, and *Salvator mundi* 1.

In each case Bull begins with bicinium, proceeds with a middle section involving either the rhythmic stratification characteristic of plainsong

Ex. 3-9   Bull (?), Fantasy d3, b. 137, left hand

settings or still more adventuresome figuration as an extension of the opening, and concludes with toccatalike or imitative textures. The two approaches to making a conclusion are seen in the hexachord fantasy, which continues to invent excited figurations up to the end, and in Fantasy G2, which indulges in a display of contrapuntal artifice. *God Save the King* exalts the imitative rather than the virtuosic. Its penultimate section is outfitted with running sextuplets that advance the motion to its peak; then follows a resolute three-fold repetition of the ostinato in a more sober texture of quarter-values, ending the piece on an A-major chord after thirty-four repetitions of a ground outlining the C-major triad. Though the composer has made some attempt to prepare for this event through the a-minor tonality of b. 120–21, the effect is nevertheless an astonishing one. Morley would have found the situation abhorrent, for to him closing "out of the key" was "one of the grossest faults which may be committed." Called upon to explain further, he continued, "for every key hath a peculiar air proper unto itself, so that if you go into another than that wherein you begun you change the air of the song, which is as much as to wrest a thing out of his nature, making the ass leap upon his master and the spaniel bear the load."[26] Such admonishment would have impressed Bull little, for he was familiar with the process by which the final note of a plainsong required that its setting end in a key different from that in which it began. By virtue of this requirement, *Veni Redemptor gentium* 1 admits the same tonal asperity as does *God Save the King,* C-major to A-major. Thus it was the familiar, not the unfamiliar, that the composer was exploiting when he chose to harmonize the last note of the ground with A rather than with C. The power of the choice lies not with simply ending "out of the key," as if by accident or happenstance, but with the willfull overturning of the piece's predominant tonality.

God Save the King exists in two versions, nearly identical up through b. 110. *MB* 14 prints the version given by William Kitchiner in *The Loyal and National Songs of England* (London, 1823), transcribed there by Edward Jones from *Pe 18,1.* (The title of the piece, given in the manuscript owned by Pepusch, leaves little doubt that Bull composed the work before he left England.) In the new Sweelinck edition and in the older one of Seiffert are printed the version from *Ly A1.*[27] Another piece, based on the same theme and having the same ending (final eight bars) as the Lynar version of *God Save the King* is found in Lüneburg, Stadtsbibliothek MS KN 208 (f. 34': "Fuga") and is also printed by Seiffert (no. 13). The relationship between these three works has been convincingly discussed by Alan Curtis and is summarized here.

Sweelinck at some point obtained a copy of Bull's original piece and decided to change the ending, substituting brilliant figuration for stately, quasi-imitative homophony, and bringing the piece to a close in the key. This is the version that was later copied by the Lynar scribe. The other piece on the same theme is probably a work from the school of Sweelinck; it is too weak to be from the Dutch composer himself. The fact of the identical ending to Sweelinck's version of Bull's piece may be accounted for by the likelihood that its composer was emulating the original piece of Bull/Sweelinck and copied its ending right into his own piece.[28]

Curtis's interpretation of the facts is indeed plausible, but the matter of a satisfactory text for the Bull version remains. That printed by *MB* 14 is based primarily on Kitchiner's print, with many of its mistakes and omissions corrected. A few details from *Ly Al,* however, may actually restore a better text or at least provide alternatives. In b. 73 *Ly* gives e for the tenth note of the left hand, more consistent with the preceding figuration than c, and in b. 106 gives b' in the alto on the first beat rather than g', lending the harmony an appropriately colorful turn at the point before the sextuplets break out. In the entire preceding passage *Ly* avoids doubling the g'' at the lower octave when it occurs in the theme; three times by replacing it with rests, once by substituting a c''. Whether this is an improvement, and whether it was intended by Bull, is arguable. Other variants of *Ly* preceding the changed ending are more drastic and appear to be actual rewritings.

The Hexachord Fantasies

The hexachord was a popular subject for imitative ensemble and keyboard music during the sixteenth and seventeenth centuries. In keyboard examples from around the time of Bull the theme served either as cantus firmus ground against figurations, as in Byrd's *Ut re mi fa sol la* (*MB* 28:58) or, more commonly, as the basis of imitative points with or without cantus firmus. An example of the latter type, a second hexachord fantasy of Byrd (*MB* 28:64), reserves one voice for the monorhythmic cantus firmus, but in specimens from Sweelinck, Cornet, and Frescobaldi that technique is abandoned in favor of a freer use of the theme.[29] Bull left two works based on the hexachord, one related to each of the above two types.[30] Hexachord Fantasy 1 is a chromatic, imitative composition employing the hexachord cantus firmus in a unique modulating scheme. Hexachord Fantasy 2, by contrast, is an essay in figuration against a ground.

The fundamental process of Hexachord Fantasy 1 is the same as that of Byrd's second setting, for the theme serves as a cantus firmus against a series of points. Both pieces include a section in tripla and place the theme on degrees other than the tonic. The peculiarities of Bull's scheme, however, are as follows: The hexachord is stated six times ascending and descending in the cantus/alto, occupying 12 semibreves. Each successive statement begins a whole tone higher, starting with a statement on g and ending with one on f'. At this point (b. 39), where the next starting note in the series would again be a G, the theme passes to the bass (and eventually the tenor) where the process is repeated, starting on A-flat and ending with f-sharp. One statement on g, balancing the first and rounding off the section, precedes the final four on g', evenly divided between triple and duple meter. Both Byrd's second hexachord fantasy, which uses six of the 12 possible transpositions, and Frescobaldi's *Recercar con obligo del basso*,[31] which uses eight transpositions of its *ut mi fa re* obligato, stop short of Bull's comprehensive plan.

In Hexachord Fantasy 1, the imitative points whose texture accompanies, or harmonizes, the notes of the cantus firmus, are freely invented and derive neither from the hexachord nor from one another. In the resulting concord of counterpoint and modulating cantus firmus, triads on all 12 degrees obtain, demanding that certain notes function in a manner not envisioned by the temperaments of the day. Pythagorean tunings, by their preference for pure fifths, left too few good thirds for even fleeting excursions into remote keys to be tolerated. Mean tone temperament provided more good thirds by sacrificing the purity of the fifths, yet not in all 12 keys. In b. 14, for example, an A-sharp in the tenor is required as the third of a chord of F-sharp major. In normal mean tone there would be no A-sharp, B-flat being conceived as the third below D. With F sharp serving as the third above D, a diminished fourth would result between F-sharp and B-flat, far too large an interval to be treated enharmonically as a major third. The problem posed by the performance of this piece in contemporary temperaments is not the presence of chords distant from the tonic, as adjustments in the tuning (at least of stringed keyboard instruments) could be made to accommodate the unusual. Bull's "Chromatic" Galliard uses the chord of F-sharp major repeatedly and the chord of C-sharp major once in the third strain. Since there is no B-flat in the piece, a third to F-sharp could be provided by retuning that pitch, and with minor adjustment of C-sharp (or of F), the brief occurrences of chords on that degree could be tolerated. Yet the hexachord fantasy requires distant chords on both sharp and flat sides, resulting in the need for either an equalized, enharmonic temperament or an expanded scale (split keys) providing both sharps and flats.

The lack of evidence for either of these provisions in England during this period, along with textural features of Hexachord Fantasy 1, have raised doubts as to whether the piece was in fact conceived for a keyboard instrument. Tradition has it that viols and lutes played in equal temperament, thus enabling the performance of passages which were impossible on the keyboard.[32] On the basis of this, J. Murray Barbour provided the following explanation: "It seems almost as if Bull had written a Fancy for four viols, and then led by some mad whim, had transcribed it for virginals and tuned his instrument to suit."[33] Steele, pointing to awkward and ineffective voice crossings as well as the problem of a temperament, also concluded that the piece was for viol consort.[34] The sustained, consistently imitative texture and the absence of figuration are further suggestive; and the very use of a modulating ground which necessarily cuts through the tessituras of other voices seems better suited to a medium in which individual lines are delineated by timbre. The fact of the transcription ascribed to Bull of du Caurroy's hexachord fantasy lends some support to the theory that the chromatic one, as Barbour suggests, may have originally been a viol piece. At least one other musician prior to the present century recognized the potential of this work as an ensemble piece. Alessandro Poglietti, who copied—and hopelessly garbled—the text of Bull's piece, also arranged it in score for a quartet of strings. The strongest piece of evidence in support of the transcription theory, however, is offered by a pair of hexachord fantasies ascribed in English sources to Alfonso Ferrabosco II, but argued by Edward Lowinsky to be the work of Alfonso della Viola.[35] The fantasies, which may be thought of as two halves of one work, exist in two versions for four and five parts, respectively, and in keyboard arrangements.[36] In the first half the hexachord cantus firmus is heard eight times, each repetition one half-step higher than the previous, beginning with a statement ascending from c' to a' and ending with one ascending from g' to e''. The second half of the piece reverses the process by using an eight-fold repetition of the hexachord inverted and in descent from e''–g' to a'–c'. The requirement of an enharmonic temperament and the presence of frequent crossings between the upper voices are found in Alfonso's piece, as in Bull's, and contrast sharply with Byrd's second fantasy. Byrd avoids transpositions of the hexachord that would run into enharmonic difficulties (with two tolerable exceptions), and the alto never crosses the cantus when the upper voice is carrying the cantus firmus.

What, then, is to be made of the keyboard piece of Bull? It is doubtful that Tregian included it simply as a novelty if it could not in fact be played: bald transcriptions of consort or vocal works whose performance on the keyboard would serve no purpose are uncharacteristic of the anthology. That Bull's fantasy was somehow workable as a keyboard piece seems the more likely in view of keyboard versions of the Alfonso fantasies. Such arrangements, which have been overlooked in previous discussions of this problem, provide evidence that some system existed which permitted pieces with enharmonic notation to be played at the keyboard. In an attempt to justify the harmonic audacities of Bull's fantasy, Apel pointed to the existence of instruments with split keys, enabling the performance of enharmonic music.[37] Nicola Vicentino described such an instrument of his invention in 1555 (*L'Antica musica ridotta alla moderna*) and in 1561 (*Descrizione dell'arciorgano*), and the "Universal-Clavicymbel" of Charles Luyton was lauded by Praetorius in 1619 (*Syntagma musicum*) as "instrumentum perfectum si non perfectissimum." In a letter of 1622 Titelouze mentions "une certain espinete faite exprez" for playing music of the enharmonic genre; Mersenne several times cites such an instrument in his treatises, giving in the *Harmonie universelle* (1636) some of the possible configurations of split-key keyboards.[38] Apel believes that the chromatic hexachord fantasy was intended for just such an instrument. Curtis, however, maintains that these instruments were not widely known in the North.[39] We lack, indeed, a single example or reference from England. Yet Frank Hubbard has shown that Italian harpsichords were not only known, but were emulated in England in the sixteenth and seventeenth centuries. It should, therefore, not be excluded that instruments with split keys reached England and were known there, at least within a narrow circle. That we have no example from England of a harpsichord with split keys[40] may be as much a symptom of the general lack of surviving instruments from that country as it is a proof that such instruments were never known there.[41]

As noted, Hexachord Fantasy 1 exists in several sources as the work of Alessandro Poglietti. Dart explains this by the fact that *Vi* was once in the private collection of Emperor Leopold I (reigned 1658–1705); Poglietti could then have had access to it during his tenure as organist of the court chapel (1661 until his death in 1683).[42] Poglietti's version of the piece is of little use as a textual source since it is so debased. However, in one place in the first twenty-one and a half measures (now missing from the *Vi* copy) what appears to be a linear *non sequitur* in *Tr* is corrected: the cantus should resolve to a c' (semibreve) on the third beat of b. 6, not drop out. Subsequent variants are less helpful, and should not be taken seriously. They represent substantially different readings, not corrections. *MB* contains one obvious wrong note: b. 76, alto, third note should be f'-sharp. The critical note fails to mention an interesting variant of *Tr* found in b. 100: the bass line, third beat, reads c–A, two eighth-notes, which is more rhythmically motivic.

Hexachord Fantasy 2 is Bull's longest fantasy. It shares with *God Save the King* and *Salvator mundi* 1 certain aspects of overall form and peculiarities of Bull's mature bicinium style. Twenty-three complete statements of the hexachord, ascending and descending, plus one *Vorimitation* in ascent only, are divided into a number of sections of greater or lesser length by changes of figuration, rhythmic rate, number of voices, and cadences. Such techniques are those of Bull's plainsong settings, yet here the problem of variety within form is a greater one. In a plainsong setting for nonliturgical use, structural articulations could be placed without regard to the intrinsic organization of the tune (cf. the variety in Bull's placement of the final section in the In Nomines). Where a melodic ground is present, however, some choices have to be made which will mitigate the regularity of the melodic unit. Thus the twelve-bar unit is broken in the middle (b. 181, 283) or the hexachord itself in midcourse (b. 105, 142) creating relief in both length of period and cadential degree. The rhythmic rate accelerates and decelerates twice in the piece, yielding four waves of motion:

b. 1–89 / 90–141 / 142–210 / 211–92
    I   II   III   IV

In wave I, the bicinium, four, eight, then sixteen divisions per semibreve occur, advancing the motion to its point of highest activity. Bull then proceeds directly to the first of a series of textures in which two voices, then three, are joined in figuration, bypassing the familiar rhythmically stratified textures which follow the bicinia in *God Save the King* and *Salvator mundi* 1. Wave II, initiated by a tonic cadence and the addition of a third voice, obtains divisions of six, then twelve, against the cantus firmus. Wave III repeats the process by reworking the two textures of the previous section in four (from b. 150) rather than three voices, and by tonally mirroring its predecessor. Thus cadences on G, G, a, and G (b. 90, 105, 121, 129) are answered by cadences on a, a, G, and a (b. 142, 157, 172, 181). Standing apart from these is the cadence on C in b. 163, calculated to support, as mediant, the a minor tonality of the section. Relief from the density of the texture in b. 165–80 is granted at b. 181ff., where the opening is recalled and the level of highest rhythmic activity resumed in a kind of harmonized bicinium. At an analogous spot later in the piece (b. 246ff.) the texture of b. 130ff. is recalled, slightly enriched again by the addition of a harmonizing voice, in order to relieve the density of the foregoing passage. These sharp textural contrasts occur at the points of highest activity in the middle of the piece and lowest activity in the conclusion, respectively. Bar 211 brings wave IV, with the first stage of the decreasing activity that defines the section. The rate drops as low as six values per semibreve before summoning back the motion of the opening with a return to duple meter, b. 278. Wave IV is mostly in triple meter, while wave I is in duple; it inverts the rhythmic increase which began the piece in order to reestablish the authority of the opening. Wave III, like

II, advances from six to twelve divisions against the semibreve, but complicates it by combining fours with sixes and sixes with nines (sesquialtera proportion cross-rhythms). It goes a step further than wave II by advancing to sixteen divisions in a return to duple meter that recalls the bicinium. The general form of the piece is thus a bilaterally symmetrical one: the last wave rhythmically mirrors the first while contrasting with it in texture and meter; the third tonally mirrors the second, but serves as a rhythmic development of it.

The axis of symmetry, b. 141, is the real center in terms of hexachord statements (23.5 [statements] × 12 [semibreves] = 282). A different calculation of total length, however, will take into account the doubling of the values of the cantus firmus in b. 271–82, still without including the four-bar extention at the end, for a total of 288. According to the Pythagorean monochord, the interval of the sixth is produced by the proportions 5:3, or a fourth (4:3) plus a third (5:4). Applying this harmonic proportion to the structure of the piece with 288 as the basis for its length, b. 180 emerges significant. That is, 288 divides evenly by 8, producing segments of 36. Five of these segments, or the temporal equivalent of the hexachord as represented by 5:3, add up to 180, the bar preceding the significant return of the highest point of rhythmic activity and recall of the texture at the opening. Thus there are two internal points of highest structural importance, each calculated on a different theoretical length and each serving a different end. Bar 142 is the axis of bilateral symmetry, the basis of the piece's formal logic; b. 181 forms an asymmetrical axis which, though in dissonance with the former division, yet partakes of the same structure by coinciding with the rhythmic climax before the conclusion.

The sequence of events in Hexachord Fantasy 2 invites a rhetorical interpretation. Gerd Zacher has undertaken such an analysis of two hexachord fantasies by Frescobaldi, a composer whose works have elsewhere been related to the traditions of classical rhetoric.[43] Zacher applies the eight divisions of the *chrie,* or traditional didactic *dispositio,* to both hexachord fantasies (capricci) from *Il primo libro di capricci, canzon francese e recercari* (Venice, 1626). This specialized approach to analysis would appear to be a promising one for a work such as Bull's Hexachord Fantasy 2 which, like Frescobaldi's hexachord fantasies, is highly sectionalized and invites extramusical interpretation.

What might Bull's rhetorical paradigm have been? Though many works on rhetoric in English and Latin were published in England during the sixteenth century, one—at least for present purposes—stands out. Thomas Wilson's *The Arte of Rhetorique* (London, 1553)[44] is the most complete treatment in English and the most original. Its sources are chiefly the anonymous *Rhetoricorum ad C. Herennium libri quator,* Quintilian's *Institutio,* Erasmus's *Ecclesiastae,* and works of Cicero.[45] The book went through seven editions before the close of the century and was popular in both literary and ecclesiastical circles, for its copious examples are drawn from both Classical and Christian literature.

Wilson's *Rhetorique* treats all five of the classical categories of the subject: *inventio, dispositio, elocutio, memoria,* and *pronunciatio.* His divisions of the *dispositio,* or oration proper, are compiled from Cicero, Quintilian, and *Ad Herennium.*They are as follows:

    i. The Enterance or beginning.
    ii. The Narratio.
    iii. The Proposition.
    iiii. The Deuision or seuerall parting of things.
    v. The confirmation.
    vi. The confutation.
    vii. The Conclusion.

After enumerating the seven steps, the author gives a brief definition of each:

> The Entraunce or beginning is the former parte of the Oration, whereby the will of the standers by, or of the Iudge is sought for, and required to hear the matter.
> The Narration is a plaine and manifest pointing of the matter, and an euident setting forth of all things that belong vnto the same, with a breefe rehersall grounded vpon some reason.
> The proposition is a pithie sentence comprehended in a small roome, the somme of the whole matter.
> The Deuision is an opening of things, wherein we agree and rest upon, and wherein we sticke and stande in trauers, shewing what we haue to say on our owne behalfe.
> The Confirmation is a declaration of our owne reasons, with assured and constant proofes.
> The Confutation is a dissoluing, or wyping away of all such reasons as make against vs.
> The Conclusion is a clarkly gathering of the matter spoken before, and a lapping vp of it altogether.[46]

Later, Wilson expands upon these definitions, gives many examples, and informs the reader that the third step, the proposition, is optional.

The opening of a bicinium with imitation in two voices has been cited as a peculiarity of Bull's style. It is this "priuie twining, or close creeping in" of voices rather than the "plaine beginning" in two voices simultaneously, characteristic of the older bicinium, that Wilson would have called insinuation, designed "to win fauour with much circumstance."[47]

But in a bicinium the surreptitious entry of voices is limited to two; thus Bull chooses to introduce progressive degrees of animation through steadily decreasing note values, as if to stir up his audience. Vicentino's counsel for word setting shows how close the association was between rhythmic rate and the orator's speed of delivery:

> The movement of the measure should be changed to slower or faster according to the words. . . . The experience of the orator teaches us to do this, for in his oration he speaks now loudly, now softly, now slowly, now quickly, and thus greatly moves the listeners; and this manner of changing measure has great effect on the soul.[48]

The entrance, or *exordium*, is followed by the two rhythmic levels of wave II, both expressions of triple subdivisions of the minim. This is the narration, the opening of the matter "that the hearers may fully perceive what we goe about."[49] Francis Bacon, recognizing the correspondence between rhetorical and musical devices, saw that it was not only the rate of motion but also the kind of motion that was important in musical rhetoric: "The *Tripla's*, and *Changing of Times*, haue an Agreement with the *Changes of Motions;* As when *Galliard Time*, and *Measure Time*, are in the *Medley* of one Dance."[50] The rhythmic rates of waves I and II with their corresponding figurations and textures having thus established the terms of the argument, wave III divides the argument into two sides, those things "wherein the aduersarie and wee can not agree, and what it is, wherein wee doe agree." Here, in the division, it becomes clear that the dispute involves duple versus triple metrical divisions. Bars 142–62 state the conflict between fours and sixes, then between sixes and nines, by combining the triple subdivisions of the narration with the established duple ones of the entrance. Agreement is accorded in b. 165–80 in the groups of twelves, reworked from the narration, where they were set forth. Confirmation of the duple is made at b. 181ff, the point of harmonic proportion, by quoting the opening bicinium at its highest rhythmic level, "making the strongest reasons that we can," and expanded to four voices so that the argument "may seeme strong and of great weight." The same texture, contrarily stated, begins the confutation: "In confuting of causes the like may be had, as we vsed to proue: if we take the contrary of the same."[51] The biciniumlike texture, therefore, is given a counter-statement in triple meter, resulting in twelve rather than sixteen subdivisions, and the thick texture of b. 165–80, in which agreement has also been found, is restated with nine rather than twelve subdivisions. The lighter texture and deliberate movement at b. 246ff. signals the beginning of the conclusion, a "gathering of the matter spoken before," or the material of b. 130–40. The decreasing motion of wave IV, which counter-balances the increasing motion of wave I, can here be seen as a part of the deliberate nature of the conclusion. Invoking Cicero, musician and rhetorician Charles Butler observed in his *Principles of Musik* (London, 1636) the necessity of controlling the rates of movement within a piece: "Haere note that slow-timed Musik, nou and then interposed, dooeth grace the qik: and that the most artificial runing Discent, if it bee continued too long, will at the last wax tedious, even to the vulgar: as *Tulli* did wel observ:"[52] The "gathering of the matter spoken before," or the first part of the conclusion, is followed by the second part, called "amplification," or "augmenting and vehemently enlarging that, which before was in fewe woordes spoken to set the Iudge or hearers in a heate." Hence, the augmentation of the values of the cantus firmus in b. 271–82, followed by an amplification of the second kind, "not ascending by degrees, but speaking that thing onely, then the which no greater thing can be spoken."[53] The final authority then rests with duple meter, a resolute four-voice texture, and the *descending* hexachord which bring the piece from a (the rival tonality emphasized in wave III) to a final close on G.

Although neither the application of a rhetorical model nor the results obtained can be proffered unequivocally, the natural logic of Bull's fantasy is well-described by Wilson's directions for the oration:

I	II	III	IV
entrance	narration division	confirmation confutation	conclusion

However challenging to credibility rhetorical analysis may be, there is abundant evidence for its applicability, at least to vocal music, in the sixteenth century. Claude Palisca and Willem Elders, among others, have recently cited the influence of rhetoric in music of the humanist age;[54] and George Puttenham's *The arte of English poesie* (London, 1589)[55] is a mine of information on the subject of music and poetry (a separate branch of rhetoric from logic, in the English scheme). Instrumental music is another matter. While considerable documentation exists to support the theory that Continental composers in the sixteenth, seventeenth, and eighteenth centuries were thinking along rhetorical lines in instrumental composition, little exists from England from the period we are presently considering.[56] Yet composers had the same education, which included Classical rhetoric, as other professionals and must have been looking for ways of building larger musical structures without words or, finally, without cantus firmus. Rhetoric, a common ground of statesmen, poets, preachers, and lawyers, would have been a natural place to go in search of models.

Whether or not the application of harmonic proportions of the monochord to temporal dimensions is a valid technique at this point in history is difficult to say. The proportion cited in Bull's Hexachord Fantasy 2, at any rate, has an important correspondence in the structure of the piece as it is perceived through other methods of analysis. Likewise, the Golden Section in Fantasy d1 confirms and is confirmed by a structural event, the ostinato. Correspondence between harmonic as well as other numerological proportions is, as Marcus van Crevel has emphasized in his valuable analyses of Obrecht masses, a phenomenon rooted in the dominant neo-Platonic philosophy of the late fifteenth and sixteenth centuries.[57] This philosophy, generously infused with Cabalist and Hermetic influences, was strong in Elizabethan and Jacobean England. It figures, as Frances Yates has shown, prominently in the works of John Dee, Philip Sydney, Spenser, Shakespeare, Robert Fludd, and others.[58] Connections between this philosophy and the music of the age have probably been hampered by the fact that composers tend to leave behind few words,[59] yet further investigation may show such connections to be valid and useful. Certainly, too little work has been done in relating music of this era to classical rhetoric[60] and to cosmology for a systematic critical approach to emerge from either. The usefulness of such applied philosophy should be viewed less as a way to the development of new analytic techniques than as a means of increasing our understanding of the minds behind the music. If both mathematical and rhetorical systems are at work behind Bull's Hexachord Fantasy 2, then music's position music within the seven liberal sciences is not confined to the quadrivium, where it is usually found, but rather joins it with the trivium. Our rhetorician, Thomas Wilson, had placed it there in "A brief declaration in Metre, of the seuen liberal Artes, wherein Logique is comprehended as one of theim," published in *The rule of reason,* 1551:

> Grammar dooeth teach to vttre woordes
>   To speake both apte and plain.
> Logique by Arte, settes foorth the trueth,
>   An dooeth tel what is vain.
> Rethorique at large paintes wel the cause,
>   An makes that seme right gaie,
> Whiche Logique spake but at a woorde,
>   And taught as by the waie.
> Musike with tunes, delites the eare,
>   And make vs thinke it heauen:
> Arthmetique by numbre can make
>   Rekeninges to be euen.
> Geometrie thinges thicke and broade,
>   Measures by line and square:
> Astronomie by Sterres dooeth tel:
>   Of foule and eke of Faire.[61]

Fantasies G1, C; Fantasies on *La Guamina*, *A Leona*, and *Vestiva i colli*

All of these pieces bear some measure of the influence of Italian or Northern styles and appear only in Continental sources. Both Italian keyboard
music and Italian vocal music, which gained great popularity in the last
decade of the sixteenth century, had made their marks in England by the
time Tregian began compiling his anthology. Pieces by Morley (*FVB*, no.
[124]) and Farnaby (*FVB*, no. [233]) emulate features of the Italian keyboard style or directly adopt one of its traditions, intabulation of vocal
works. Philips, whose intabulations from as early as 1593 in *Tr* are apparently of Continental origin, is also represented by the only piece; (except for Sweelinck's own) that shows any significant confluence with
Northern style: his fantasy, *FVB*, no. 84. The genres and styles of Italian
vocal intabulation, the Venetian toccata (see Galeazzo's Prelude, *FVB*,
no. [99]), and the Sweelinckian fantasy had no lasting effect in England.
The later fantasies of Byrd, Gibbons, Cosyn, Lugge, and Weelkes (who
elsewhere embraced Italian manners) continue along the established lines
of the English fantasy tradition. The fact of Italian fashions in England
before Bull's departure may cast doubt on an assumption that pieces
showing this influence and surviving only in Continental sources were
written after 1613. Two cases in point are Fantasies G1 and C, yet in both
pieces distinctly non-English elements argue for a later dating.

In Fantasy G1 figuration is only once forestalled long enough to allow
imitation in four voices for more than one bar's duration. Its treatment of
the three points is sparse by English standards, yet by Continental standards the imitative sections are themselves too short and the handling of
the subject uncharacteristic. The opening point is dismembered after b. 11
by the loss of the two weighty semibreves which announce it. What remains of the subject then becomes the basis of the second and third
points. After a few transitional bars of winding figuration (b. 42–47) typical of Cornet, the right hand and left hand assume distinct roles, taking
either block chords or figuration.[62] Though the fast rate of harmonic
change is unlike the Venetian toccata, the idiom is rooted there and is
distinguished from normal virginalistic harmonic elaboration or melodic
decoration by a more motivic conception of figuration, frequent trading-
off between hands, and registral interpenetration of the scales. Bull seems
less sure here of how the passage should proceed than does Morley in
his fantasy (*FVB*, p. 59), Philips (his "Fantasie de Petro Philippi")[63] or
Sweelinck (Ex. 3-10). Dialogue treatment of the theme announced in b. 55
is shunned for more filler figuration before it is answered and further
pursued (b. 60ff.). The following texture, so like a basso continuo realization, and the keyboard recitative which ends the piece have few par-

allels in English music. These two techniques, which go hand in hand in
Italian music of the period, had found little acceptance in England before
Bull's flight (and would not, for some time). The discovery of keyboard
monody as an alternative to established types of figuration is already
evident in the works of Merulo, but becomes a feature of major contrast
with Frescobaldi (Ex. 3-11).

Fantasy C (not ascribed in *Ant*) is laid out on the pattern of the
Venetian toccata as best represented by Merulo: rhapsodic–imitative–
rhapsodic. The solid, chordal opening gives way to an extended harmonic
elaboration which entails a good deal more motivic repetition and sequence than an Italian would have deemed appropriate. The middle section develops with some seriousness of intent a point built around a fourth,
the interval which encloses the figurations of the opening section. Sustained chords and scalar figuration announce the return to the toccata
style. The subsequent texture (b. 65–83) is related to, but less interesting
than, that in b. 60–66 of Fantasy G1. An effective flourish at the end of
the piece unfortunately does not compensate for the inertia of the
foregoing.

Although there is some evidence of Italian influence on English keyboard music around the turn of the century, the incidence of keyboard
recitative in Fantasy G1 and the remarkable resemblance of Fantasy C to
the Venetian toccata have no parallels in England. Examples of the latter
from composers in Northern Europe are numerous, including the "Fantasie de Petro Philippi" and one toccata in particular of Sweelinck (*SK*
1:15). In view of such features, the piece's unique Continental source,
and the strongly indicative altered fourth at the final cadence (see the
following paragraph), it may be assumed that the two works date from
the Brussels-Antwerp period.

The following should be noted in Fantasy G1: b. 41–42, alto, 2nd
note–1st note: c' ♩ , b ♪; b. 64, tenor, 1st note, f'-sharp; b. 72, cantus,
all c's should be c-sharps. And in Fantasy C: b. 26, cantus, 1st note, f'-
natural, 4th note, b'-flat; b. 89, all f's should be f'-sharps. The raised
fourth, altered by the editors with no mention in the critical notes, is rare
in English but common in Continental music of the period.[64]

Four fantasies in *Ant*, show the influence of the *canzona
d'intavolatura*, a keyboard arrangement of an instrumental or vocal composition. Fantasy *La Guamina* is an adaptation of an ensemble canzona
which itself exists in two versions. The more complete one was apparently
the basis for the fantasy, for it was published in Antwerp in 1612.[65] Furthermore, the triple-meter middle section of the fantasy corresponds in
some way to that of the larger canzona; the alternate version of the canzona has no triple meter.

Ex. 3-10 Sweelinck, Echo Fantasy, b. 132- (*SK* 1:14)

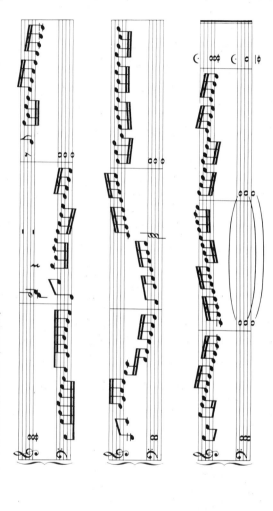

Ex. 3-11 Frescobaldi, Toccata terza (1615), b. 23- (*FK* 3, p. 11)

La Guamina falls into three sections, following the typical duple–triple–duple metrical plan of canzonas. The first section is divided into two paragraphs of 10 and 15 bars, respectively, the first characterized by the motive on which the fantasy is based, the second by two new themes. A fourth new theme opens the triple-meter section, which balances the opening, and eventually receives a syncopated treatment. The final section, a short recapitulation, compactly restates the opening. The fantasy, while based only on the initial point of the canzona, uses that point motivically as a means to unification. The composer has seen in the two halves of the theme independent motives which could be used to generate both imitative textures and registral dialogues, conveying the spirit of the ensemble composition. At one point, the descending and ascending halves are combined simultaneously (Ex. 3-12). Such a grouping of voices for registral contrast, implicit in ensemble style and found in the model mainly in the triple-meter section, was deemed serviceable in the keyboard arrangement. The note-against-note homophony of the triple-meter section itself was rejected. Thus the opening theme (first half) is resumed, in a triple-meter transformation characteristic of Frescobaldi's canzonas. Eventually it is overtaken by a version of the second half of the theme in diminution, unifying the triple-meter section with the opening one (Ex. 3-13). The urge to introduce syncopation as a means of variety in the midst of tightening the continuity may well have come from the abundant use of a similar figure in the second half of the canzona's triple-meter section (Ex. 3-14). Relief from this high level of rhythmic activity is offered by a brief excursion into figuration (b. 66–69), after which the syncopated motive returns for summary before the closing section. The proportions between outer sections in the fantasy and the canzona are the same; that is, the coda is just less than one-third the length of the opening section. Yet the effect in the fantasy is not simply to abridge the opening as a means of restoring balance, but to add further comment and sum up the foregoing. By lengthening selected notes of the theme (both halves)—not merely by augmentation—the recapitulation is stretched out, anticipating the final release of energy at b. 83. There both halves of the theme are heard together, for the first time and in diminution, bringing the piece energetically and concisely to a close.

The fantasy is a refreshing contrast to the plethora of schoolbook examples, so often given to an overuse of stereotyped figures and slavish imitation of the model. The considerable freedom with which the composer has dealt with his model permits both retention of the ensemble spirit and attainment of an idiomatic keyboard style. Nowhere are to be found either arid, stock diminutions or long passages of filler figuration. It is the work of a Northerner, one who like Philips (in his fantasy in *Tr*)

Ex. 3-12   Guami, *La Guamina,* theme

Bull, Fantasy *La Guamina,* b. 30-

Ex. 3-13   Bull, Fantasy *La Guamina,* b. 43-

Ibid., b. 53-

Ex. 3-14   Guami, *La Guamina,* b. 43-

had learned how the artifices of imitation as practiced by Sweelinck could free keyboard composition of its dependence upon the vocabulary of figuration it had developed in the course of emergence from the decoration of vocal and instrumental pieces.

By contrast, a fantasy on *A Leona* is of little intrinsic interest as a keyboard piece. Though its model cannot be located, the work bears none of the marks of stylish rewriting seen in the other arrangements, it is not thematically unified, and the figuration used to ornament the reprises of each of the two sections serves as little more than a weary reminder that material is being repeated.[66] Evidence provided by the character of the second strain (b. 46ff. in particular) suggests that the model for this piece was an ensemble canzona. Unlike the treatment of the triple-meter section of Fantasy *La Guamina*, however, no attempt was made here to render the material more suitable to the keyboard.

Like Fantasy *La Guamina,* two fantasies on Palestrina's madrigal *Vestiva i colli* paraphrase their model with freedom in the use of given materials and rigorous application of contrapuntal devices.[67] The opening point (a) of Fantasy 1 is the madrigal's setting of the words "Vestiva i

Ex. 3-15   Palestrina, *Vestiva i colli*, b. 1-, cantus

Ibid., b. 41-, cantus

Ibid., b. 62-, bass

Ibid., seconda parte, cantus and alto

Bull, Fantasy 1 on *Vestiva i colli*

colli" (Ex. 3-15). Its treatment, including cadential figuration, lasts 15 bars. The second point (b) derives from "e le campagne intorno" and is likewise given a section of 15 bars. Beginning with b. 30 the fantasy quotes the entire theme (madrigal, b. 41–44). Because the anacrustic rhythm has already been set up in (b), (c) sounds like a fusion of (a) and (b): the upward fourth of (a) has been set in the rhythm of (b), followed by its characteristic shape, the enclosed fifth. A 12-bar treatment of this motive is answered in a parallel passage which ornaments and slightly extends the material. The beginning of this section, b. 43–56, treats the upward fourth; the latter part, from b. 51, the enclosed fifth. A 15-bar closing section, calculated to balance the opening, makes explicit what is implicit in the madrigal. The closing theme (d) appears to be derived through augmentation and extension from (b), which has just been reiterated in the close of the previous section. In the madrigal, however, this theme belongs to the opening of the *seconda parte,* so widely separated from the beginning of the *prima parte* (and its derivative in b. 41) that the connection is only implied.

The second fantasy opens with lower voices rather than upper and, instead of pairing voices for imitation, skillfully elides the cantus and alto to avoid a parallelism. At b. 15 a thematic transformation (b) provides a link to the following section by preserving the rhythm of (a) on one pitch (Ex. 3-16). This is the characteristic of theme (c). Here the new theme is combined with a kind of countersubject closely related to (b) of Fantasy 1 and reflecting the contour of the opening of the madrigal's *seconda parte.* Bar 35 brings an episode based on an upward third (madrigal,

Ex. 3-16   Bull, Fantasy 2 on *Vestiva i colli*

b. 62ff.) which was briefly touched, in inversion, in Fantasy 1 (b. 25–26). These eighteen bars provide significant textural relief prior to the final stretto, which is based on a hybird of the repeated-note and fourth-motives, all in diminution. Broadly speaking, the piece, like Fantasy 1, falls into five sections; the first and second, and third and fourth, belong together (see below). The proportions between the third and fourth sections are necessarily different, since Fantasy 2 devotes more attention to the third-motive. The two fantasies are not really a pair corresponding to parts one and two of the madrigal. Fantasy 1 may be considered an arrangement of both parts, while Fantasy 2 treats only material from the first part and cadences on the final of the *prima parte*.

Fantasy 1:	bar	1–15	16–29	30–42	43–56	57–71
	cadences		D	D	D	a A
	section length	15	14	13	14	15

Fantasy 2:	bar	1–14	15–25	26–34	35–52	53–63
	cadences		a	D	D	D D
	section length	14	11	9	18	11

The techniques displayed in making these arrangements are, as in Fantasy *La Guamina*, so different from those of the fantasies of Bull's English period and so different from arrangements by other English composers as to raise doubts of his authorship. Yet there is no external evidence against the ascription other than the general untrustworthiness of *Ant* in this matter. The seemingly anomalous style is probably attributable to a wide separation in dates of composition between these works and authentic English works such as Fantasies d1 and d2. More mature and secure in their use of techniques foreign to the English fantasy, the former pieces probably postdate Fantasy a1, dated 1621, and a2, its companion. If the same composer had anything to do with the Fantasy *A Leona*, it was either as an early attempt at Italian-style intabulation or a copy he made as an example of a technique he would further refine with an English eye for thematic process, generously disciplined with Northern contrapuntal artifice.

A discrepancy between source and transcription occurs in three of these pieces; each time the situation is the same. In Fantasy *La Guamina*, b. 79, tenor, third note is an a, not an f-sharp; in Fantasy *A Leona*, b. 98, cantus, third note is a c', not an a; the analogous situation in Fantasy 1 on *Vestiva i colli*, b. 54 is noted in the critical report. In this type of ornamented suspension cadence, it may well appear more idiomatic for the melodic voice to drop a third below the note of resolution before the ornament; yet the threefold appearance in this source of the same formula speaks strongly in favor of accepting it in this context.

Fantasies d4, a1, a2, F, and G2

The influence of Northern European, rather than Italian, keyboard music is encountered in five pieces from *Ant* and *Vi*. Fantasies a1, a2, and G2 exhibit features of a style that is identified with Sweelinck. Fantasies d4 and F may be connected with the more general tradition of soloistic writing which sprang up in the early seventeenth century on the Continent, and with the works of Cornet, respectively.

Fantasy d4 is preceded in *Vi* by an incomplete piece, also called there "Fantasia," which is printed in *MB* 14 as a prelude to the fantasy. It may have originally been complete, continued on another page of the manuscript, or the scribe may have decided not to finish copying it. It is, after all, not very interesting, though the melodic outline A to D drawn by the cantus at the outset may imply some connection between the two pieces. The fantasy is a substantial work built on a series of short, well-defined melodic ideas. Two lower voices introduce (by Vorimitation) and then accompany the long-breathed phrases of the solo line. The dramatic spacing of the entrances of the cantus, the careful registral separation between solo line and accompanying voices, and the abundant coloratura suggest that the treble line (except for b. 34–40) is conceived for a solo organ registration.

It is difficult to define the precedents of this piece. Solo-voice writing of this type can be found in many of the "echo" pieces of Liège 888 and in some of the short versets in ChCh 89 (see the discussion of the *Salve Regina* verses in chapter 2). Yet the dialogue character of the former pieces and the brevity of the latter differ from the lengthy, soloistic Fantasy d4. The suggestion of a *cantus prius factus* is a particularly noteworthy feature, present in the sharp definition of phrases and in the deliberate statement of each melodic segment in Vorimitation, then in long values in the cantus before the onset of coloratura. This technique, however, is identified with later generations, especially with Scheidemann, and has no equal in the first quarter of the seventeenth century. Viewed as a fantasy on freely invented materials, the piece again appears anachronistic. Such pieces appear in the work of A. van den Kerckhoven at the middle of the century (see especially the one in d minor),[68] but are not known in music of the first quarter. A work which may be a predecessor of this genre, and possibly of Fantasy d4 as well, is the *Fantasia per sonar Le Cornetto* in Liège 888.[69] The piece (or pieces) consists of four short and independent segments of rudimentary Vorimitation in the lower voices between righthand passages of florid melody. No longer values, such as in Fantasy d4, precede the coloratura, and the phrases themselves are short, about the same length as those of the "echo" pieces in the same source.

While no parallel for this piece can be found from around Bull's time and no choral or psalm tune can be located that fits its phrases, a further problem is posed by the style of the figuration.[70] Aside from repeated notes, which could as easily be Sweelinck's as Bull's, there are none of Bull's characteristic figurations in the solo voice such as are found in the two *Salve Regina* (especially the first setting, verse 5, b. 10–11, and the second setting, verse 1, b. 20). The unusual Vorimitation by diminution (b. 32–40) also does not figure in either *Salve Regina,* works which are otherwise much concerned with the general technique.

The player is faced here with the problem of finding a tempo suitable for the wide range of values. Not only does the ratio of 1:32 in the cantus voice make establishing a uniform tempo virtually impossible, but at any tempo the sudden slowing down produced by a return to sixteenth notes in b. 43, 76, 111, and 122 defies any musical rendering. Although the editors' suggestion that the bars containing thirty-seconds may have been halved in value by the scribe seems at first implausible, one might nevertheless consider the possibility in performance. (Bar 31 can be treated freely, as a cadence should be, and could therefore be excluded from such alteration.) Two errors in the *MB* transcription should be noted: b. 7, cantus, sixth note is g'; b. 29, cantus, first note is e'', tied from the previous note.

Fantasy F is a canzonalike work, based on three themes (b. 1, 92, and 160) and devotes equal attention to imitative development and appropriate figuration. In John Steele's discussion of the work he points to several features of the late works in general by way of praising the quality of the fantasy. Sequences are kept in hand and are seldom repeated more than three times; "bravura" remains subordinate and never pushes the subject out of the picture; and cadences are frequent, especially deceptive ones.[71] Nowhere does Steele admit the possibility that the piece may not be Bull's, yet it appears in *MB* 14 as dubious, and in the Appendix of *MB* 19 Dart gives the following note: "Compare the second part of de Macque's Canzon chiamate le due sorelle, and Cornet's working in *Cp,* f. 65." On closer examination, Cornet's piece (Ex. 3-17) turns out not to be a working of Macque's canzona at all, but simply a fantasy based on a theme of the same shape, as is another of his fantasies. Nor are Cornet's the only pieces based on such a theme. One each by Byrd and Philips show a remarkable affinity with this type (Ex. 3-18), a rising second and falling fourth followed by another upward movement.[72]

More to the point than thematic similarities in a comparison of Fantasy F with works of Cornet is the style of the work, which has a great deal in common with Cornet's fantasies. Cornet's style falls directly between the extremes of figuration and imitation. The one is never allowed to wear out before the other takes over: his style reaches neither the severity of Sweelinck nor the flamboyance of Bull. Such is the case in Fantasy F. Although the work is quite long, as are many of Cornet's, each of its three sections are balanced internally by reference to, and deviation from, the subject on which it is based. Imitation avoids the artifices that Bull seems to have adopted in his later compositions, and figuration is restricted mostly to parallel thirds, scales, and triadic elaborations (b. 68). Both of these features are found throughout Cornet's music. Smaller details, such as the occasional interjection of thirty-seconds without fundamentally changing the rate of motion (b. 35, 37, 91, etc.) and the off-beat displacement of a voice (b. 112–13) are also widely found in Cornet's works, though the latter is of course known in English music as well. In general, however, the sense of continuity in Fantasy F

Ex. 3-17   Macque, *Canzon chiamate le due sorelle,* seconda parte (*MMB* 4, p. 58)

Cornet, Fantasy in G (*CK:* 5)

Cornet, Fantasy in G (*CK:* 6)

Ex. 3-18   Byrd, Fantasy G2 (*MB* 28:62)

Philips, Fantasy (*FVB* no. 84)

is greater than it is with Cornet. Transition from imitation to passagework is smoother, and a greater equilibrium between faster and slower motion is established. Contrasts are handled with an ear for texture and register not usually encountered in Cornet and phrases are thought out in shapes, rather than lengths (see especially b. 120–25).

The problem posed by Fantasy F is the same as that of Fantasy d4 and d3: they are isolated examples of styles that depart drastically from the known works of Bull and in some cases closely resemble the works of another composer. With Fantasies d4 and F the problem is intensified by the fact that the ascriptions in the sources are frequently wrong.

Fantasies a1, a2, and G2 employ bicinium techniques in ways which relate to Sweelinck's use of the two-voice texture. About one-third of the total length of Fantasy G2 is occupied with bicinium, based on a ground which is the theme for the entire piece. Unlike *Salvator mundi* 1, *God Save the King,* and Hexachord Fantasy 1, however, the ostinato does not remain in the right hand but passes to the left hand for the second half of the section. Such trading off can be found in a fantasy of Sweelinck containing an even longer section in bicinium (*SW* 1:9) and in another fantasy attributed to him (*SW* 1:32). Charles Raquet's fantasy, published by Mersenne as a musical example in the *Harmonie universelle,* also contains an extended middle section of bicinium in which the theme is heard first in the right, then the left hand.[73] Another feature of Fantasy G2, the ostinato, looks not to Sweelinck, but to Bull's earlier work. Sweelinck uses an ostinatolike technique in the pieces mentioned above, but the theme is never confined to the role of a ground. In both, the theme stated at the outset subsequently appears on different pitch levels and is occasionally extended through sequence as a means of development. The rigid ground of Fantasy G2 has no parallel in Sweelinck's music, but is based in a skeletal use of ostinato such as that of *God Save the King.*

Upon conclusion of the bicinium, the composer once allows the theme to be transposed tonally down a fifth, giving relief and forming a bridge to the three-voice section which begins there. The theme then returns to the cantus at its original pitch. The techniques of this section, especially the rhythmically stratified texture, are mostly familiar ones of Bull. However, there is a measure of imitative treatment (b. 64–76, 98–105) not encountered in analogous passages of other works which begin with bicinium. The last third of the piece, b. 113ff., abandons the ground for a more fully imitative working of the theme, appropriate to the four-voice texture. A wide variety of transpositions—tonal and real—which bring the theme to close on E, A, and F, and a passage in double diminution and augmentation before the concluding toccata flourish (b. 159–69), speak of the composer's knowledge of Continental contrapuntal techniques (as does Philips's fantasy in *Tr*). These features are perhaps among those referred to as "stylistic considerations" by the editors of Sweelinck's keyboard works in casting doubt on the authorship of the work.[74] In reference to the authorship of Fantasy G2, Dart further notes that "Its use of ostinato with diminution and augmentation is typical of him [Sweelinck], whereas it is unknown in Bull."[75] Such rigorous use of ostinato as found here is *not* typical of Sweelinck; and techniques of diminution and augmentation are to be found not only in this piece but also in Fantasies a1, a2, *La Guamina,* and the first fantasy on *Vestiva i colli.* In any event the light cast of b. 159–68 has none of the tightening effect usual for Sweelinck's passages in diminution. Two wrong notes appear in the *MB* text. Bar 108, cantus, last note is e'', and b. 146, cantus, first note is b'.

Sweelinck sometimes introduces two-part writing in the middle, rather than using it at the beginning of a work. This was his choice in the chromatic fantasy and two other fantasies (*SK* 1:1, 3, 4). In these instances the texture is reduced to allow free reign to the motoric figuration which serves as a means of development. This technique, as well as that of augmenting the theme so that it serves as a cantus firmus, is a way of providing monothematic works the variety which might otherwise have been furnished by successively contrasting points of imitation. Fantasies a1 and a2 show this approach, each time framing a rhythmically active mid-section with opening imitation in slower motion and a closing section involving more imitation and/or solemn chordal textures.

Fantasies a1 and a2 are companions to one another, not so much by the similarity of their themes (and not at all by their location in the sources, for each is from a different one), but by their simultaneous use of both original values and diminution. Fantasy a1, "on a theme of Sweelinck," states its palindromic subject first in the bass, then in the tenor in diminution, and finally in the cantus again in original values. Having established these two levels for the subject, the piece is then free to use them separately (cantus, b. 22–30) or, as at the opening, together (b. 42–46). Two sections in which running sixteenths accompany a single voice and then a pair of voices frame a brief return to the texture of the opening—expanded finally to four voices. This delay in the completion of the texture is a touch that we can imagine having occured only to an English composer. When the motion again settles, however, the texture returns to three voices and remains so for nearly half of the closing section. The earlier segment in three voices fails by this thinness to rekindle the excitement inherent in a return to imitation after a period of figuration. The tonic extension (b. 78–91) begs, as before, for urgency such as that which so effectively charges an analogous passage in *La Guamina* (b. 75–86).

The work collapses where it might have pulled together through the application of further diminution and/or stretto.

Fantasy a2 may also be some kind of tribute to Sweelinck, for its theme is that of the Dutch composer's chromatic fantasy. However, as Alan Curtis has shown, the sources of the chromatic fourth (Curtis's term) are many—vocal, lute, and keyboard music—and date from the middle of the previous century.[76] Curtis could point to close connections between Sweelinck's piece and works of Dowland but, due to the lack of precise datings for the sources involved, found it impossible to say for sure whether it was Dowland's work that influenced Sweelinck's. Bull, as an Englishman, would certainly have known works such as Dowland's though no evidence of the chromatic fourth is to be found in the works of his earlier period. The presence of Fantasy a2 in *Vi,* along with a text of Sweelinck's chromatic fantasy attributed to Bull and dated 1621, surely suggests that Bull at least knew Sweelinck's piece.

Bull goes a step further in Fantasy a2 than in the previous piece by presenting the subject rising slowly from the bass to the tenor, then leaping out in the treble in double diminution. This rather upsetting effect is followed by the bicinium on the chromatic fourth at its intermediate level of diminution, in the quarter-values absent from the exposition, and stated in its descending as well as ascending forms. A second section, biciniumlike, brings the theme in two voices in a manner analogous to the previous piece and finally ends the effort by weak stretti of the theme in double diminution. There is the sense here that too much has been attempted in too short a space. Neither Fantasy a1 nor a2 succeeds on Sweelinck's terrain so well as the hybrid English-Dutch Fantasy G2, or the Italian-Dutch Fantasies *La Guamina* and *Vestiva i colli.*

Both pieces contain errors in transcription or misinterpretations of *Ant*'s muddled texts. In Fantasy a1, b. 8 should have only three voices; the inner one might well read ♮–a–b–c'-sharp; b. 34, bass, fourth note is c. Fantasy a2, b. 26, cantus, third beat read e' f' e' d'; b. 28, tenor, fifth note if f-sharp; bass, second and third notes, two quarters. Players may also wish to consider a revision of the *MB* reconstruction of b. 33–36 which gives a stronger articulation on the dominant in the second bar and a more idiomatic descent in the last bar (Ex. 3-19).

In summary, it may be reiterated that the changes which Bull seems to have undergone as a result of his migration from England to the Continent and the many incorrect ascriptions in the sources of his music both work against confident attributions and, hence, a full stylistic appraisal of the fantasies. Close examination unearths doubts about the authorship of Fantasies d3, d4, g, F, and *A Leona.* The early Fantasy g and stylish d3 are hard to put aside; they are both good pieces and, though as dif-

Ex. 3-19   Bull, Fantasy, a1, b. 33-36, suggested reconstruction

ferent from one another as they are from Bull's authenticated works, are nevertheless from the hand of a composer of his own background. Fantasies F and *A Leona* are another matter. Further consideration of either piece as Bull's should be reserved, and an eventual rearrangement of the fantasies should relegate them to an appendix.

An overview of the apparently authentic works still raises the inevitable issue of the place of Bull's fantasies within the English tradition. In this connection Bull's consort fantasies should be acknowledged. Two are extant, one each in three and four voices, the latter of which has also been attributed to Coperario.[77] The ease with which these pieces fit the style of late Elizabethan and Jacobean consort music attests to a willingness on the part of the composer to write in a current style, at least under some conditions. Why, then, are the keyboard fantasies so unlike those of his English contemporaries? The phenomenon could, of course, be a function of the particular pieces which have survived. Yet Tregian gives a good sampling of the work of the major composers he includes (Gibbons excepted), and the fantasies of Bull which he transmits have little in common with those of Byrd, Farnaby, Gibbons, or other composers. The two other English fantasies in *El* and *Co* (g and d3) only raise further question. Unless there is a substantial missing link in the sources for his English fantasies, Bull must have been little interested during the year of his mature production in pursuing the keyboard fantasy.

It does appear that Bull was attracted by certain archaic features of the English tradition—especially the two-part style—and certain other more progressive features of the Continental style. The crux of this dichotomous attitude is figuration, for it is this aspect of the music that takes over and rules the work in the absence of features that might better align his music with one tradition or the other. What Bull largely abjures in both is a thorough-going use of imitation, whether of the kind practiced by his younger English contemporary Gibbons, or of the kind found already in Italian keyboard music of the sixteenth century. Bull's music has often been regarded as an enigma, a bridge between old and new in which certain links are missing. Yet there is also a continuity, crossing boundaries of time and genre, which stems from the primacy of figuration in the composer's mind.

4

Pavans and Galliards

The following list of works discussed in this chapter consists of pieces which we take with reasonable certainty to be Bull's and is ordered by the authority of the sources. The arrangement within each group (defined by final) proceeds from pavan and galliard pairs to single pavans, then single galliards, with preference given to those printed in *Parthenia,* then to those found in *Bu, Tr, Ant,* and other sources, in that order. The list includes most of the pieces in *MB* 19, but several exceptions are mentioned below.

Pavan and Galliard d1	*MB* 19:66a and b
Pavan and Galliard d2:	19:67a and b
Melancholy	
Pavan and Galliard d3:	19:68a and b
Symphony	
Pavan d4 (incomplete)	19:69
Galliard d4	19:70
Galliard d5	19:71
Galliard d6:	19:72
Lady Lucy	
Galliard d7	19:73
Pavan and Galliard g1	Appendix III and
	MB 19:78
Pavan g2:	19:76
The Spanish Pavan	
(Discussed in Chapter 6)	
Pavan g3	19:77
Pavan and Galliard a1:	19:86a and b
Fantastic	
Pavan and Galliard a2:	19:87a and b
Queen Elizabeth's Chromatic	
Pavan and Galliard a3	19:88a and b

Galliard a4:	19:90
Vaulting	
Galliard a5:	19:92
Italian	
Galliard a6:	19:89a and b
Piper	
Galliard C	19:103
Galliard D:	19:113
The Prince	
Pavan and Galliard G1:	19:126a and b
"St. Thomas Wake"	
Pavan and Galliard G2	19:131a and b
Pavan G3:	19:127a
Quadran (Discussed in Chapter 6)	
Pavan and Galliard G4:	19:127b and c,
Quadran (Discussed in Chapter 6)	19:127d, e, and f
Pavan and Galliard 5:	19:128a and b
Trumpet	
Pavan and Galliard G6:	19:129a and b
Lord Lumley	
Pavan and Galliard G7	19:130a and b
Galliard G8:	19:133
Lord Hunsdon	
Galliard G9:	19132b and c
Regina	
Galliard G10:	19:132a
Regina	

The terrain of Bull's pavans and galliards is a rich but untidy one. Pavan and Galliard G1, which are actually variations, were included along with another pavan and galliard pair and two separate pavans in Parthenia. A galliard setting (*MB* 19:126c) from *We* of the same tune was attributed to Bull by Dart. There is, however, little in this unimaginative piece to support an ascription to Bull. Dart himself withdrew the claim in the second edition.

Tregian indicated that no. 48 in his book, a galliard he ascribed to Bull, was to go with no. 34, Bull's "Fantastic" Pavan (al). Yet the pavan had already been provided with a galliard, no. 35, and the second galliard fails to live up to it. Particularly disappointing are the opening of the first strain, which is at a loss to establish the galliard rhythm, and the repetitive, long-winded third strain (12 bars here versus four in Galliard al). The futility of reworking the 16 bar third strain of the pavan into a 12-bar strain for the galliard is proved in the feeble decorated repeat. (Galliard al chooses different material for strain III.) Strains I', II, and II' are competent.* However, the piece as a whole is no match for the terse and eventful Galliard al, nor is it a worthy partner to the pavan. In his 1620 collection, Cosyn claims this piece as his, an ascription that seems far more likely than that of Tregian. Cosyn also appears to be right in his ascription of the "Pavin in Gamut flatt" (Pavan gl) to Bull. In spite of its omission from *MB* 19, the work bears numerous attributes of Bull's work and is here considered authentic.

Bu, which provides the greatest number of pavans and galliards of any source, also poses the most problems of attribution. Since there are no ascriptions in hand I, the matter of authorship rests in most cases either with concordances or with Cosyn's index. Several pieces remain— one pavan, three galliards, and two pairs—which can only be dealt with on stylistic grounds. No particular anomalies threaten the credibility of the incomplete Pavan d4, Galliards a5 and C, or the G7 pair. However, the authorship of the F-major pair (*MB* 19:109a and b) is less secure; for present purposes the pieces are considered anonymous. Likewise, the other galliard in question (*Bu,* p. 275) also remains anonymous. Three features of the piece would seem to exclude an attribution to Bull. It ends out of the key in which it began (Galliard G8 begins in a different key from that in which it ends, but the tonic is firmly established by the third bar); the plain style of strain II is one Bull avoided; and the treatment of its decorated repeat as a *petite reprise* is nowhere encountered in Bull's music. Weelkes's ascription of another galliard in *Bu* (p. 212; *We,* f. 148; pr; See *MB* 19, p. 223) to Richardson seems correct. (The latter two galliards from *Bu* are transcribed in full in Cunningham, Appendix I.)

Finally, an "Air" (*MB* 19:91) found in W. H. Cummings's *God Save the King* (London, 1902), transcribed there by Sir George Smart from *Pe 18, 1,* is evidently the first strain of an incomplete galliard. Nothing in the six extant bars is particularly at odds with Bull's style, but the matter— like the fragment itself—is of little importance.

Pavans and Galliards from *Tr* Not Included in *Bu*

Bu, Tr, and *Pa* together contain all of the pavans and galliards save six that are dealt with in the present discussion.[1] The overlap between *Tr* and *Bu* is considerable, yet both sources give some unique texts. Those

---

*In pavans a bar is considered a semibreve, in galliards a dotted semibreve (without regard for how the piece is barred in *MB*). Strains are referenced by Roman numerals, and a superscript stroke indicates its repeat.

in *Tr*, Pavans g2 and G3 and Galliard a6, appear to be among the earliest, as does Galliard d7, which is also found in two Continental sources. *Bu* invariably gives the finer texts of pieces it has in common with *Tr*, but in two instances, Pavan and Galliard G6 and Pavan G4, the improvements assume the form of substantial rewritings. Likewise, *Pa* provides a revised text of its two pieces found in *Tr*, Galliards d5 and G1. Thus *Tr* gives in general the earliest pieces and earliest texts, although the other major manuscript was certainly compiled earlier, and the print was at least issued before Tregian completed his anthology.

A few preliminary observations on some earlier works in *Tr* will be helpful in beginning an examination of Bull's pavans and galliards. The first, Galliard a6, raises the issue of appropriate rate of movement. Its striking feature is an unprecedented exploitation of thirty-second-note passages, the sort of youthful experiment that Bull, preoccupied with virtuosic means, would have undertaken. He must have soon realized that it was not a viable step to take: while admitting a profusion of divisions 16 to the minim in two later pavans, d2 and G6, he abjures it in galliards except where—as in Galliard D—short motives of thirty-seconds are used to momentary, ornamental effect. A number of features of Bull's setting of the Spanish Pavan also point toward an early date of composition. Noteworthy are the motive in the first variation, which fails to break out of its semibreve's space, and the schematic procedure in the three succeeding variations. Eighths appear in the right hand, then left, then in both. The texture in this fourth variation recalls that of Byrd's early *Hugh Aston's Ground* (before 1591) and Philips's Passamezzo Pavan (dated 1592 by Tregian), which Bull's piece otherwise resembles in several respects. The strumming left-hand filler that crops up here and there looks back at least to *My Lady Careys Dompe*. Such passive left hand writing was expunged from two bars in the considerable revision for *Bu* of the Quadran Pavan and was replaced with more engaging imitation. Finally, the triple-meter fifth variation belongs to an older tradition, as again found in Philips's Passamezzo Pavan. Bull pointedly rejected this practice when he removed the final tripla variation found in the *Tr* version of Galliard G1 in preparing the piece for publication in *Parthenia*.

While these three works are each based on preexisting materials, a fourth, Galliard d7, was independently conceived. Dart's suggestion that its appearance in two Continental sources, *Cp* and *Du,* identifies it with the lost "Galliard, Madamoyselle Charlotte de la Haye"[2] is pure conjecture. There is at least one other galliard in that source, Pepusch's no. 18, vol. 1, and another in Pepusch's no. 26 (also lost, see Appendix II), which could equally well be identified with this one. The unusual situation here in which the Continental sources give better texts than the English one indicates that the piece was transmitted by reliable means, perhaps by Bull himself. Dart's recognition of the style as early accords with the possibility that Bull may have taken the piece with him on his first Continental journey, but internal evidence suggests that the work may date from some time before his leave in 1601–2. Whatever its precise date may be, the galliard is a fine effort, combining an appropriately limited number of thematic ideas with restrained figuration and good textural variety. In it he also demonstrates two important principles, irregular strain lengths and the cantus firmus strain. The former figures in a significant number of Bull's pavans and galliards from both earlier and later periods; the latter is a special feature that attracted composers from Philips through Scheidemann.

Bull built Galliard d7 on strains of eight, nine, and 14 bars. Strains of odd and uneven lengths are a notable feature of another apparently early galliard, d6, Pavan G6 (before 1609) and Pavan g3, a late work. Bull's lifelong emphasis on variety in strain-lengths—noticeably suppressed in the *Parthenia* pieces—directly contradicts Morley's prescription. In pavans, says Morley, "you must cast your music by four, so that if you keep the rule it is no matter how many fours you put in your strain for it will fall out well enough in the end." The galliard, Morley continues, "is a lighter and more stirring kind of dancing than the Pavan, consisting of the same number of strains; and look how many fours of semibreves you put in the strain of your Pavan so many times six minims you put in the strain of your Galliard."[3] These stipulations represent more accurately the practice of Morley's teacher, Byrd, than they do that of the sixteenth century in general. A consort galliard by Bassano in Tregian's anthology Egerton 3665 is built out of strains of 11 bars each;[4] two keyboard pavans, one in the *Dublin Viginal Book* (no. 5) and one in *So* (no. 33),[5] contain strains of five and 13 semibreves, respectively; and Philips's widely disseminated pavan in *Tr* (no. 85) is laid out in strains of 13, 11, and 15. While Bull's considerable flexibility in choice of strain lengths may be seen as following in the tracks of the exceptional and as such constituting an antithesis to the Byrd-Morley tradition, it may also be interpreted as an outgrowth of Bull's experience in cantus firmus-style plainsong setting. Plainsongs rarely provided the opportunity for regular periodization without making arbitrary choices in the harmonization of the cantus firmus; cadences on degrees related to the mode simply had to fall where they fit, creating phrases of irregular length. While Bull sometimes tried to exert control over this situation and once tried to use the requirements of the cantus firmus to advantage in a scheme of progressive phrase lengths (his *Christe Redemptor omnium*), he normally made no attempt to harness the plainsong with a preconceived periodicity.

Given such a background, the proclivity for uneven and unequal strain lengths in Bull's pavans and galliards is no less to be expected than is the regularity in those of Byrd, who in his plainsong settings usually sought to impose some periodic organization, and who throughout his life was interested in regular, strophic forms.

Bull approached the task of putting together strains of uneven length through one of two means. He either coupled a phrase of even length with an uneven one, an additive process indigenous to both song and dance music, or he elided the end of one phrase with the beginning of another, eclipsing the cadence of the former. This latter process effectively contracts shorter even segments into a longer odd one and has obvious roots in cantus firmus technique, where the continuity of figuration takes precedence—at least in Bull's style—over melodic logic. In Galliard d7 it is the process of addition, rather than contraction, that accounts for strain II. Thus after an initial strain of four–plus–four bars, Bull continues in strain II with an internally symmetrical phrase of four bars, then upsets the balance with a consequent phrase of five bars resulting from an extension of the cadence. Similar ways of working can be seen behind Galliard d6/III, a strain of three–plus–four bars, and in the second strain of Alman D2, which is built in units of three, four, and four bars. In each case a longer segment follows a shorter one, effectively stretching the material and creating a certain amount of tension by delaying the cadence. The five-bar phrase in Galliard d7/II begins by heralding an extension of the previous material, the interval of the treble motive heard at the outset of the first phrase widened from a fourth to a fifth, and ends by returning to the dominant, rounding the whole.

Strain III is based on a procedure found in final strains of several pavans, but one which composers in general tended to abandon after trying it once. Cantus firmus-like strains close pavans in *Tr* by Philips (no. 85) and by Morley (no. [169]), a version of which was elaborated by Farnaby (no. [285]). Byrd's Pavan F2 (*Tr*, no. 93), a parody of Morley's passes judgment on the idea by dissolving Morley's cantus firmus into motives of melodic and imitative value.[6] Gibbons just once explored the procedure in an a-minor pavan (*MB* 20:17), but makes reference to it in the second strain of a d-minor galliard (*MB* 20:23). Bull alone more than once built the final strain of a dance movement on the cantus firmus idea, realizing in doing so that the skeletal voice, as in a real cantus firmus setting, could lie in one of a number of voices. Thus Galliard d7/III states its theme in the alto, and Pavan a2/III poses its poetically ascending line in the cantus. The latter placement is used, if in a perfunctory way, in the final strain of the Coranto C2 "Battle" (identical with no. 183 in Praetorius's *Terpsichore*), ascribed to Bull in *Ant*. The cantus firmus procedure is exceptional, even in the case of Bull, who gives us three examples. Such popularity as it retained, however, must have been connected with Philips's pavan, dated 1580 by Tregian. Philips's piece was popularized in England through settings for mixed consort, lute, and cittern, and on the Continent in lute arrangements as well as in Sweelinck's keyboard setting.[7] Stiff and sometimes clumsy keyboard writing, the retrospective nature of cantus firmus technique and a probable *terminus ad quem* of 1603 for Pavan a2 support a dating of Galliard d7 from no later than around 1600, and possibly somewhat earlier.

A comparison of Galliard d7 with the one of Scheidemann in the same key which adjoins it in *Du* reveals two striking similarities. Scheidemann, like Bull, elected an irregular plan, composing strains of 11, 12, and 12 bars. Furthermore, the German quotes the Englishman in his own language by basing his third strain on the same cantus firmus as that of Galliard d7. The tribute is important evidence of a direct musical connection between the two men, and attests to a continued intrigue with the cantus firmus idea as it was so boldly pursued by Bull. The aforementioned galliard of Gibbons may also have been inspired by Bull, for in addition to a middle strain in cantus firmus character, Gibbons's piece also uses uneven strains (8/9/8) and bears occasional melodic resemblance to Bull's d7.

The text of Galliard d7 given in *MB* relies largely upon the superior one supplied by *Du*. In one instance, however, a variant from *Tr* and *Cp* may represent the original reading. In the last bar of strain II, the top voice of the left hand, third beat, should read ♪ ♩ (-a), avoiding the doubled third and consistent with the final bars of I, I', and III'.

Bull's galliards may be viewed as falling into two categories defined by the note values that dominate the movement. Galliard d7 is an example of the first type, in which the outside tempo is determined only by the feasible speed of the eighths and the propriety of the dance itself. Two further galliards in *Tr*, d5 and G1, both included in *Parthenia*, exemplify the second type, a display piece which loses some of its lightness through the slower tempo required by an extensive use of sixteenths. Such an approach, while rare for Byrd, figures in a good half of Bull's galliards.[8] Neighbour asserts that the greater brilliance created by a preponderance of sixteenth-notes and the resultant slowing down of the dance is a later development in the galliard, as evidenced by the examples in *Parthenia* from the younger composers Bull and Gibbons.[9] This theory would seem to be supported by a number of other galliards by Gibbons of this type, galliards in *Tr* by Bull's and Gibbons's contemporaries Richardson and Tisdale,[10] and by Tomkins's galliards, which push the dance to its utmost limits. However, the evidence in *Parthenia* may equally attest to a balanced attitude on Bull's part, for both galliards in that source dominated by sixteenths, d5 and G1, appear to have been written earlier, and the two ruled by eighths, d4 and G4, were probably composed anew for the publication. By writing two new galliards in the older style Bull may have been wanting to demonstrate that he was not addicted to the virtuosic type, his most extreme example of which was the early Galliard a6. The older composer Byrd, on the other hand, seems to be saying in his Galliard C4 (*Pa,* no. 5) that he was also capable of writing in the newer style; in doing so, he had some comments on its capabilities and limitations (see the discussion of this piece in connection with Bull's Galliard D, below).

As in two other two-strain galliards, d3 and a5, Bull lays out in Galliard d5 strains of six and eight bars. The piece also shares several other features with a5, the most notable of which is an emphasis on the mediant in the middle of the first strain and on the dominant in the second. The tonal balance between strains that this sets out to achieve is unfortunately undercut by a redundant dual cadence on the second and fourth bars of the first strain. A slow tempo, required by the high level of activity in II', makes this defect particularly obvious. In the second strain consecutive repetitions of the intermediate harmony on the second through fifth bars weaken the strain, though the effect is somewhat mitigated by a modal change at the midpoint. The several variants given by *Pa* represent an improvement in the text over that in *Tr.* Though some of the weaknesses of *Tr,* such as b. 4 and 16, may be passed off as corruptions, smaller differences, such as those in the left hand of b. 18 and 21, can best be accounted for by the fact that the composer refined the text for publication.

Galliard G1 and its pavan, treated below with works written specifically for *Parthenia,* are not conventional dances, but variations on a two-strain theme known only through these settings and the one in *We.* Again, the *Pa* text gives a more refined reading than does *Tr,* but also includes a major variant not found in the case of Galliard d5: the entire last variation is omitted. This triple-meter variation and the second and third variations with their bicinia both display techniques associated with plainsong setting and, as such, imply an early origin. Bull's second thoughts in var. 3 provide variety by substituting a harmonization of the third quarter of the melody in parallel thirds for the more faburdenlike one which he had previously used here (and repeated in the following variation). There can be little doubt that the galliard was written before the pavan, which only appears in *Pa.* Yet a feature in the pavan raises the question of priority with respect to the original version of the melody. Each strain of the pavan begins with an anacrusis, completely foreign to the rhythmic syntax of pavans. It is hard to imagine why Bull would have chosen to set the melody in this way had the anacrusis not been a part of the original conception of the tune. The melody as given in the galliard would, after all, have adapted well into normal pavan rhythm by simply doubling the value of the first note and proceeding from there. Furthermore, the one variant in melodic design between the two dances, an arch through e'' in the second phrase of the galliard's version, would surely have been retained in the pavan if it were original, for it greatly improves the topography of the tune. The situation seems to be that the galliard, though earlier, was written on a variant of the tune devised by Bull for his purposes at the time; the later pavan then set the original tune.

Pavans and Galliards in Both *Tr* and *Bu*

In addition to the original Quadran Pavan, three pavan and galliard pairs—dl, al, and G6, a single pavan, G5, and two single galliards, a4 and G9, all in *Bu*—would be included by Tregian in his keyboard anthology. Of these, G6, like the Quadran, shows evidence of having been considerably refined for *Bu* while surviving in an earlier version in *Tr*.

A proliferation of thirty-second notes in the pavan of the G6 pair and the reference to plainsong-setting style in the second and third strains of the galliard argue for an earlier date than the death of the dedicatee, 1609, as would the fact of the piece's revision for *Bu*. Byrd quoted from the pavan in his Pavan C3 (*MB* 27:33), and Bull reworked its material—perhaps by way of responding to Byrd's "comments"—in in his own Pavan and Galliard G2 for *Parthenia*.[11]

Bull puts his material together in all three strains of the pavan through the familiar additive process, yielding lengths of 11, 11, and eight bars. The four-bar segment that opens strain I could have been answered by another of four bars (as Byrd did in his Pavan C3/III), or by one of six bars, for a total of 10 in the strain. Conversely, the dominant cadence on the seventh bar requires a later rather than earlier answer and suggests that the strain could also have been 14 bars. As it stands, however, the dual cadence of b. 10–11 seems wrong and places a static drag on the end of the strain that is scarcely overcome by the right hand's brilliant excursion. The problem of where the main cadence should occur is encountered elsewhere in Bull's work, particularly in Pavan d1, yet in the present piece the composer seeks straight away to overcome the difficulty he has made for himself. In the ninth bar of the repeat he introduces a rocking figure which carries the motion through to the eleventh bar, somewhat masking the flaw. By shifting the intermediate harmonic emphasis by one bar in II, Bull succeeds in setting his proportions right. Here the main cadence in the tenth bar now answers a dominant articulation in the sixth bar so that the repetition of the dominant at the end of the strain fulfills the usual expectation of cadential extension. In both strains it is a seamless effect that Bull is striving for, rather than one of clearly delineated units. Having found a wrong way and a right way to deal with cadential placement in uneven lengths, Bull completes the composition with a third strain of even length yet, almost perversely, runs into the same problem as before. The beautiful two-bar theme which the opening of strain III shares with Pavan G5/III and which Bull retained in his considerably later Pavan G2 (see Ex. 4-1) is worked into a four-bar phrase by sequencing it at a fourth above. The second half of the strain, however, collapses through a lack of melodic incentive and harmonic movement: the cadence seems to arrive prematurely, as it did in I, in spite of its normal placement here in the seventh of eight bars. The otherwise lovely rocking figuration recovered from the end of I' then gives the air of an unconscious attempt to dispell the sinking feeling. Again as in I', Bull shows how much the overlaying of figuration can downplay structural shortcomings when he opens up a texture of consistent and ingratiating imitation. The cadence still arrives too soon, but by this time the music needs an extra passive bar to unravel the momentum of the continuous sixteenths. Significantly, it is the decorated repeats that speak the most eloquently in the pavan. Strain I' moves smoothly and convincingly from the broken homophony of the first phrase to a short-lived, off-beat imitative figure (adopted by Byrd as the point of his C3/III), then through low-lying parallel thirds reminiscent of the early Pavan G3, and on to the rocking figure. In I', then, are contained the elements of figuration and imitation that dominate the repeats of II and III, which are themselves designed to be less and more imitative, respectively.

Bull made no attempt to adapt the material of the pavan for the galliard, as he later did in Galliard G2. Instead, he chose two simple and sharply contrasting ideas, the first to serve as the basis for strain I and the second for the remaining strains. The 8/8/10 plan, reversing the pavan's order of two longer strains of identical length followed by a shorter one, ensures that the strains treating the same material will be of different lengths. The bilaterally symmetrical strain I attains straight away in its second half the g'' not heard in melodic context until strain II in the pavan, thereby setting a relatively higher pitch of energy for the faster dance. Likewise, the a'' that serves only a decorative function in the pavan has already been reached in strain II of the galliard, and is to be insistently sounded twice more in the final strain. Texture as well as melodic structure contributes to the unusual intensity of this galliard, which Bull must have thought of as commensurate to, rather than a foil for, the intensity

Ex. 4-1   Bull, Pavan G6/III

Bull, Pavan G5/III

Bull, Pavan G2/I, b. 9-

of the pavan. A brief smattering of syncopated imitation suggestive of Bull's plainsong settings are used passingly in strain I' of the pavan; Bull then turns with a full sense of purpose in the last two strains of the galliard to developing a relatively mechanical motive (pointedly referenced by Byrd in the unusual third strain of his Galliard C3) as a counter-statement to the melodic riches of the pavan.

The identity of strain II with the style of plainsong setting is sensed in the motive's shape and rhythmic character as well as the stretto imitation to which it is subjected, reinforced through the characteristically blunt sequence by a tone. Bull achieves a balanced and symmetrical strain by not pushing beyond the one sequence, felicitously referring back to strain II of the pavan with the deceptive cadence and resultant cross relation in the fifth and sixth bars. The analogous style of strain III comes even closer, by motivic reference to that of Bull's plainsong settings. (Ex. 4-2). Here the two-bar segment built on a descending motive is sequenced first by a fifth, then by a tone, reaching the secondary dominant and finally returning to the dominant where it began. Thus a neat phrase structure, based on pairs of bars, is underlaid with a clear I–IV–V–I progression (expressed in terms of the dominant) before aiming back to the tonic, resulting in a succinctness that contrasts notably with the pavan. The decorated repeats again provide balance which here might have been lost through the weight of the second and third strains by comparison to the first. While I' achieves a thickening effect with its quick-moving parallel thirds and sixths, II' lightens the imitative main strains with the same figuration and with the introduction of an off-beat alto line, also found in other early galliards (d6 and d7). The similarity of II and III demanded that III receive a substantially different treatment in its repeat from that of II. Accordingly, Bull devised ways to further enliven the imitation in III' without increasing the rate of motion or introducing new figurations. As in the pavan, the densest textures occur toward the end of the piece, the lightest in the middle.

Most of the *Bu* variants in the pavan improve the integrity of the four-part texture or add motion where it was deemed lacking, though the ones in b. 13 and b. 50–51[12] (conveniently printed in *MB*) do give a better linear result. On the other hand, the improvements in the galliard substantially affect the internal balance of the piece, refining the counterpoint where needed and providing a greater variety of motion. Of the two endings for the galliard provided in *MB*, neither is quite right. The first, from *Bu*, gives a tidier first bar and a cleaner effect in the two subsequent bars

Ex. 4-2 Bull, Galliard G6/III

Bull, in Nomine a4, b. 41-

than the second, which adds Cosyn's cluttered chords to the rather hap-
hazard initial bar also in *Tr.* Something is wrong, however, in the final bar
of *Bu,* which has been corrected in *MB* to read as in Ex. 4-3a. A comparison of the last minim of this reading with that of *Tr* and *Co* shows
that the subdominant chord on the first half of the beat is almost certainly
incorrect. The bass lines and harmonies, at least, of all three sources
should be the same, requiring a tonic chord in first inversion followed by
the same in root position. Thus it is the left hand, not the right, that has
been incorrectly notated in *Bu;* it should conform to the tonic harmony,
as shown in Ex. 4-3b.

A comparison of the texts of the dl pair in *Tr* and *Bu* by no means
makes it clear whether the superiority of the latter is to be accounted for
by the composer's revisions or slackness in Tregian's transcription. Yet
the structure of the pavan's first strain suggests that it was written at a
time when Bull was still grappling with the same problem encountered in
Pavan G6, that of cadential placement and proportions. Bull set forth a
mirror scheme based on multiples of four for the pavan, consisting of
strains of sixteen, eight, and sixteen bars, and repeated the pattern on a
smaller scale in the galliard in strains of ten, six, and ten bars. The plan
must have been a conscious one, for Bull seems to have taken an abstract
interest in such correspondences. As noted, the 11/11/8 plan of Pavan G6
is scaled down and reversed in the accompanying galliard's strains of
8/8/10; the mirror scheme of Pavan a2, 16/18/16, is turned inside out in
strains of 12/8/12 in its galliard. The idea is applied with partial success
in the dl pair, for it allows one shorter strain in the middle of the piece

Ex. 4-3a Bull, Galliard G6, last bar *(Bu)*

Ex. 4-3b Bull, Galliard G6, last bar *(Tr* and *Co)*

where the least self-sufficient material naturally requires the completion provided by the third strain. The plan did not work, however, when Bull's failure to grasp the implications of the foursquare strain resulted in a miscalculated cadence. As Neighbour points out in his discussion of Byrd's pavans and galliards, the 16-bar strain was an outgrowth of the older eight-bar type.[13] In the earlier pavans, the cadence usually occurred on the seventh bar and was extended to the eighth. Thus, when Byrd began writing strains of 16 bars, it was logical to retain the seventh bar cadence and make a rhyme on the fifteenth bar. This structure, which Neighbour usefully terms "twin cadence," provided Byrd with a stable base into which a maximum of flexibility could be worked. Bull only occasionally wrote pavans with equal strains of 16 bars—d2, d3 (2 strains), gl, al, a3, and G2 (actually in imitation of Byrd) are the only examples—and even then he rarely employed the actual "twin cadence" scheme. Rather, he seems to have been more interested in alternate strain lengths, and alternate ways of dealing with the 16-bar strain when he did use it.

In Pavan d1/I Bull introduced asymmetry by placing the intermediate cadence at b. 6 and by extending the chord, in twin cadence fashion, on b. 7. This required the second cadence in b. 13, rather than b. 15, an exigency rendered more pressing by having enjambed the beginning of the second phrase, descending from a'', with the end of the first. In effect, two bars are left over at the end of the strain during which nothing new happens. As Bull had done in Pavan G6/I', he introduces a figure in the second half of the strain, at b. 10, which is intended to provide a new impetus for carrying the music beyond the premature cadence. It is yet insufficient to correct the imbalance caused by the miscalculation in b. 6–7. In the repeat, however, soaring decoration in the penultimate bar does much to downplay in retrospect the cadence two bars earlier and helps establish some priority of the latter point.

Strain II begins with a reference to the descending third heard at the peaks of I. A deceptive cadence at the midpoint energizes the strain while focusing attention on the harmonic rather than the melodic realm. The modal contrast at the juncture of II' and III, major to minor subdominant, echoes that heard between I' and II. Without accomplishing a full-fledged twin cadence in strain III, Bull does dispose his ideas symmetrically, bringing the intermediate cadence on the eighth bar and beginning the new phrase with the strain's melodic summit on the following bar, but without overlapping phrases as in strain I.

At the outset of Galliard d1, Bull chose to paraphrase the opening strain of the pavan. Recasting the 16 bars of Pavan d1/I into a strain of 10 bars would result not in stringing together two-bar units, as in Galliard G6/III, but rather in a more predictable four-bar unit followed by one of six bars. Though there is no particular magic in making such a strain work, the effect here is a subtly polished one owing to the ambiguity of the intermediate cadence. Clearly, b. 4 marks the end of the first phrase of strain I, but the chord of E major, approached in a phrygian cadence, becomes a secondary dominant when the chord of A major is soundly struck on b. 5. The double meaning of b. 4 captures the litheness of the movement, carried through consistently by a minimum of imitative devices and a steadfast avoidance of any heavy-handedness in the figuration. Bull here chooses what suits his purpose and refuses to force the rest to fit. Therefore, while strain I is faithful to that of the pavan—at least as far as the first phrase and subsequent melodic descent are concerned— strain II makes only initial reference to the corresponding point in the pavan, slipping quickly away to the dominant and avoiding the slackening effect of the pavan's subdominant at that point. In strain III Bull takes the same attitude toward the material in the pavan that he did in galliard a1: the 16-bar strain of the slower dance is too long-breathed and lyrical to offer much in the way of maneuverability, so it is avoided. Rather than devising entirely new material as he did in galliard a3, however, he begins by tying the movement together with a quotation from the opening of strain I, then proceeds with a light-hearted (if aimless) idea which lends itself well to snappy decoration. The potential of this simple descending-third motive to drive the music forward rescues the strain from arriving at its final cadence too soon, a danger forewarned by the early placement of the intermediate cadence and one which Bull had not escaped in the first strain of the pavan.

Two corrections in the *MB* text should be noted: in the pavan the second note of the tenor, b. 9, should have a double stroke ornament (*Bu*), and in the galliard the sixth note of the tenor, b. 5, should evidently be a c'-sharp, as *Tr* has it, conforming with b. 15.

The "Regina" Galliards (G9 and G10) are two versions of the same piece. The former, which is followed by a variation, is an example of the virtuosic type, while the latter is mostly confined to eighth notes. The main strains of Galliard G10 are identical to those of G9 as regard melody, harmony, and many details in the articulation of the homophony, yet G9 is more elaborate and more adapted to the keyboard. Galliard G10 could therefore be an earlier version, possibly a keyboard reworking of a consort piece actually associated with Queen Elizabeth, to which repeats have been added that could be managed in the proper tempo of the dance. The strumming fillers in the left hand which end several phrases may be designed to substitute for the sustaining power of wind and bowed instruments. These and the unusually playful and soloistic treble divisions of strain II' could be interpreted as looking back to a consort original. A second possibility is that Galliard G10 is actually a later work, a simplification of Bull's G9. Its appearance in *D2* along with the fuller and more elaborate version found also in *Tr* and *Bu* may imply that another composer (or even the scribe) lifted and somewhat simplified the main strains of Bull's galliard, replacing his decorated repeats with ones that could be more easily played without slowing the piece down to accommodate a plethora of sixteenths. Such a reductive reworking as implied by this sequence would surely exclude Bull's hand. Galliard G10, then, appears to be either an earlier version by Bull of G9, or a later version of it by someone else. Whichever hypothesis one accepts, Galliard G9 remains the definitive piece.

The three strains of Galliard G9 are exceptionally regular in construction, each consisting of two phrases of equal length. Strain I introduces right away the sixteenth-note motion that will determine the movement of the piece. In its decorated reprise is heard for the first time the long-short-short motive which, along with its inversion, characterizes much of the variation. A bland second strain does little more than establish a structural D'', though strain III restores the tunefulness of the opening with two parallel phrases, the first cadencing, as do many contemporary popular tunes, on the supertonic.[14] Its repeat animates the texture by inserting rests and eighth notes for the quarters in the main strain, effectively shifting the accent to the second half of each beat. A refreshing absence of sixteenths allows room for their free play in the ensuing variation. The same restraint can be seen in the initial section of the Quadran Galliard: the material is subjected to a largely scale-wise and easygoing treatment in preparation for the virtuosic variations which follow.

In the variation of G9, Bull begins by announcing that the motive from I' is to do important duty. Continuous sixteenths in the repeat and the addition of passing eighths to the second strain make it clear that this is a display piece, not merely a royal amusement. The third strain returns to the motive of the first, supplemented by its rhythmic inversion. In a schematic response to earlier material, Bull develops the repeat out of mostly right-hand rather than left-hand decoration. The initial motive is recalled to close the piece. In spite of several attractive passages, there is not in Galliard G9 the inventiveness in figuration, the freedom of rhythmic treatment, the kaleidoscopic textures, or the adventuresome phraseology of Bull's most successful galliards. There is not even the simple liveliness of Galliard G10. It is as if the composer had been required to work with given materials that did not inspire him.

The number of strains in Bull's pavans and galliards has no chronological significance and no bearing on his conception of the dance, except for what the choice of length may require of the tonal plan. Bull most likely wrote the two-strain Pavan G1 expressly for *Parthenia,* while including the older two-strain Galliard d5. On the other hand, three-strain Galliards d6 and d7 appear to number among his earliest. Galliard a4 is a two-strain dance from Bull's maturity which, though it admits sixteenth-note motion, does not become encumbered by it. Its various appellations in the sources, "dancing," "vau[l]ting," and "thumping," must all refer to the spirit of the piece which is engendered by the leaping octaves in the left hand set in dotted rhythm. The two ideas contained in this motive, the one intervallic and the other rhythmic, govern the development of the piece. The decorated repeat of strain I carries on the left-hand octaves, stripped of their characteristic rhythm in order not to detract from the more active right-hand figuration. In the second phrase, a halt on the second half of each beat in the right hand allows the dotted rhythm to be restored. In strain II the rhythm alone remains of the motive, stretched in the second bar to predicate the hemiola that brings with it the melodic climax of the piece. A certain regularity has been established up to this point, stemming from strains of eight bars and their division into phrases of four. The regularity is subverted in strain II', however, when decoration in the manner of strain I' interrupts one bar before the mid-point the sixteenths that began the strain—a simple but effective structural stroke.

An unusual degree of emphasis is accorded the bass line of the texture in Galliard a4 by virtue of the prominent dotted motive of the left hand, though it is adequately counterbalanced by occasionally omitting the rhythmic aspect in favor of right-hand activity, or by transferring the rhythmic aspect to the melody, as in strain II. The long-short-short motive in Galliard G9 also frequently appears in the bass of that piece, drawing attention to the lower register when treble decoration is absent. The same balance between treble and bass emphasis, and variants of the same motives, are to be found in Galliard D, one of Bull's most original and engaging works. The fact of the work's first appearance in *Vi* points neither to a Continental origin nor to a particularly late date of composition, for its dedication, which is presumably to Bull's patron Prince Henry, places the work within Bull's English period, and the piece is closely connected with Byrd's Galliard C4, "Mistress Mary Brownlow" (*MB* 27:34).

The dotted rhythm indispensable to Galliard a4 first assumes importance in Galliard D in the second half of strain I, where it serves in its two characteristic forms,   and   , to articulate the melody. The latter takes a role in the figuration of strain II, then III (Ex. 4-4), where its function is strongly reminiscent of that in Galliard a4. The original, slower form (Ex. 4-5) plays a part in melodic development when it reappears in the second half of strain II. This motive, in its decorated form, undergoes a further transformation to become the foundation of the

6/4 bars of strain III (Ex. 4-6). The motive   which works hard at breathing life into Galliard G9 is mainly confined in Galliard D to the first strain and its repeat, but returns briefly to get the repeat of the second strain going. An unusually proliferous surface in this galliard, comparable to some of Bull's plainsong settings, is underpinned with foundations of equally unusual solidity. Each of the three strains consists of eight bars divided into two phrases of the same length, a structure which Bull makes no attempt to confound in the decorated repeats as he had in Galliard a4/II'. The mirror construction of the tonal plan, in which outer strains in the tonic frame an inner one in the dominant, is further stabilized by intermediate cadences on the dominant of each strain. Foursquare phraseology also lies beneath the exceptionally active surface of Byrd's Galliard C4, though the older composer aims, typically, for a greater tonal variety in the second strain, ending there on a secondary dominant whose resolution will begin the final strain.

Byrd's Galliard C4 begins with a pointed reference to Bull's piece in its thumping left-hand rhythm, found nowhere else in Byrd's galliards. In the firmly parallel second phrase, the rhythm is extended to the melodic realm in a passage closely akin to the second phrase of Bull's first strain (Ex. 4-5). Unlike Bull, Byrd reserves diminution of the motive for the next strain, which he begins with two bars that are virtually identical to the two Bull uses to close his third strain (Ex. 4-4). The ensuing three or so bars utilize the smoothly contoured motive that begins strain I' by way of contrast to the angular announcement at the beginning of strain II. A return to dotted rhythms in the final bars of the strain brings the motive in diminution into a play with the melody, as it does in the sixth bar of the repeat, without actually involving it in the melodic process. Byrd, in fact, appears to want to avoid having the rhythmic motive generate the melodic, as Bull does in the second half of his strain II (Ex. 4-6). As if the make another point by reference to Bull, Byrd shows that the tempo of the dance can be determined by factors intrinsic to the material and not only by the requirements of figuration. Thus a rather broad pace in the first half of the piece, necessitated by an uncharacteristically fast rate of harmonic change, suits well the exigencies of the sixteenth-and thirty second-note figuration of the second half of the piece. Bull, by contrast, sets up the requirement in both realms at once, introducing a fast harmonic rhythm (see b. 6 in Ex. 4-5) as well as the ♩ ♪♪ motive right away in the first strain. The older composer indeed seems to be demonstrating to the younger that he has in his own music a substitute for such an ornamental figure when in I' Byrd decorates his line with the tracing thirds found in abundance in Bull's music, but not in Byrd's (Ex. 4-7).

From the decorated repeat of strain II to the end of Byrd's galliard

Ex. 4-4 Bull, Galliard D/III, b. 7-

Byrd, Galliard C4/II

Ex. 4-5 Bull, Galliard D/I, b. 5-

Byrd, Galliard C4/I, b. 5-

Ex. 4-6 Bull, Galliard D/II, b. 5   II', b. 5   III, b. 1

one-half of the bars are concerned with sixteenth-note motion. To this
unusual circumstance the composer adds the unique feature of a six-note
thirty-second figure (perhaps partially by way of connecting the galliard
to the prelude which precedes it in *Parthenia*) and in doing so outstrips
Bull on his own ground. The thirty-seconds in Bull's galliard have little
motivic significance, yet Byrd develops in II' the complex motive
♩♪♪♫♫♫, and a slightly simplified variant of it in strain III, with

Ex. 4-7   Byrd, Galliard C4/I', b. 4-

Ex. 4-7   Bull, Quadran Pavan 2 (G4), var. 3, b. 24-

considerable fervor. Byrd's point of view again comes through clearly: fast note values, even where they are ornamental, as they are in II', should have deeper meaning; they are never gratuitous embroidery. Furthermore, once introduced they ought to be followed up, as they are when they are given a place in III, and not be abandoned as they are after the brilliant melodic descent at the end of Bull's strain I'.

The same applies to less distinctive features, so that the off-beat open fifth sonority in the bass, first heard in the last two bars of I', gains prominence in strain II as a tenor then bass punctuation. The same notion returns in the decorated repeat of strain II, where it provides a rhythmic precedent for the stretto imitation at the interval of an eighth in the sixth bar. The syncopation finally emerges melodic in a big way in strain III, b. 4–7. Such off-beat punctuation never waxes linear in Bull's galliards but serves only to animate a texture by way of a kind of written-out arpeggiation (see Galliard d6/III and III', and Galliard d7/III and III') or simply treble bass exchange (Galliards G6/III' and G8/III'). Byrd, in effect, has taken a passive and subservient idea, distinguished only by its weak rhythmic placement, and brought it gradually out of the shadows of accompaniment, giving it a focus.

Bull's approach, by contrast, was to boldly state at the outset the full meaning of his off-beat idea in the second phrase of strain II, decorate it in the repeat, and go on to something else. His subsequent idea forms the basis of a passage in 6/4 of unprecedented length for Bull, and is an organic derivative—as shown in Ex. 4–6—of the motive imitated in off-beat fashion but without retaining its original quality. If Bull introduces this metrical alternative in a galliard, it is almost always in the third strain. Byrd, on the other hand, is often interested throughout in the interplay of 6/4 and 3/1 (hemiola) with the basic 3/2, and evidently calculated that the regularity of the structure he used allowed him considerable latitude in the matter. In much of Bull's music the opposite is the case: both uneven and irregular strainlengths as well as the tempo requirement of highly charged figurations worked against freedom on the metrical level. In Galliard D, however, he simplified the tonal and larger metrical structure to a sufficient degree that more variety on the smaller metrical scale was possible. He therefore permits himself a four-bar excursion in the third strain into the alternative meter, but also ends his *first* strain and its repeat with a single bar of 6/4. Closing a strain thus is common in Byrd's galliards; and if Bull was trying his elder's language at this point, then Byrd surely did not let the attempt go unnoticed: the last bar of Byrd's C4/I' is like Bull's in details of texture, motive, and metrical ambiguity (Ex. 4-8). Yet, since Byrd has allowed considerable metrical variety throughout his piece, there is no need in strain III to provide a great, new contrast. Instead, he does just the opposite, beginning the strain ambiguously and projecting into simultaneity that which Bull found necessary to define in succession. He then proceeds, after one bar of 3/2, with the remainder of the strain in 6/4, ending it with one more ambiguous bar in 3/2. Things are fully and finally squared around in the decorated repeat, where Byrd removes the ambiguity from the last bar and adds a final chord.

The relationship between these two works naturally raises the question of chronology. Neighbour finds that Byrd's galliard "need not have been composed till shortly before its publication."[15] Since it seems as though it is Byrd who is parodying—and to a certain extent criticizing— Bull's work, and since in any event Bull left England shortly after the publication of *Parthenia,* the younger composer's piece must have pre-

Ex. 4-8   Bull, Galliard D/I, b. 8

Byrd, Galliard C4/I', b. 8

ceded the older's. Indeed, we might expect Bull's galliard to have been a fairly recent work exhibiting a certain involvement with Byrd's principles without wholly embracing them.

Although a policy of conflation has resulted in many instances of confusion in the *MB* edition, particularly in the earlier volume, it was used to advantage in deriving the text of Galliard D; the generally superior text of *Vi* has been supplemented with minor improvements from *D2*. Ex. 4–8, comparing b. 8 with the final bar of Byrd's Galliard C4/I', proves that the rhythm of the left hand as given by *Vi* in that bar and in b. 16 is the correct one. The temptation to opt for the reading in *D2* of b. 28 should be resisted, for as Bull showed in suppressing the dotted rhythm of the thumping figure in Galliard a4/I', there is a sense of balance which governs the level of activity permitted in one extreme of the texture versus the other.

Pavan a1 is one of Bull's most finely wrought works. Its three 16–bar strains are asymmetrically structured, yet the cadences are never misjudged. A wealth of luxuriant figuration in the decorated repeats remains faithful to the expressive intent of the main strains and achieves a rare degree of coherence: no decorative figure becomes an isolated event. Bull also integrates here melodic and tonal elements so that a structural soundness underlies this long and complex work. In the first strain Bull is at his most elusive, achieving the continuous, almost seamless effect toward which he seems so often to be striving. Accordingly, changes of rhythmic rate and submediant harmonies in b. 5 and 13 are more important in organizing the strain than are any clearly delineated melodic units. Yet the emphasis on F does more than clarify local topography, for it prefigures the tonal region which opens strain II—this pavan and its galliard are the only ones in which the middle strain begins in the submediant— and provides melodic precedent for the 6–5 motion above the bass that takes on motivic importance in strain III. At the close of strain I Bull suspends any definitive melodic arrival by casting, at the end of b. 14, a second treble line above the main one. This move has a dual function. Since the uppermost voice comes to rest on an E rather than on an A, the initial note of the repeat provides, in the right register, the satisfaction of completing the foregoing (i.e., resolving the g'-sharp from b. 14) as it begins something new. Secondly, the sweep of the new voice down two octaves from e'' to e gives impetus where harmonic stasis might engender slackness. Byrd would have appreciated the consistency and relevance in Bull's application of the four thirty-seconds motive in I'. The same motive that was used to such bristling effect in Galliard D/I' functions here in quite the opposite way, generating the melodic decoration itself. It is quitted for an easy flow of sixteenths in the midsection of the strain, but returns to round off the whole.

The slower movement and melodic passivity of the second strain achieve a restful effect after the abrupt change. Such sudden changes in the rate of movement never bothered Bull (cf. In Nomines a1 and a7) however much they may seem to threaten the coherence of the composition and however awkward they may be in performance. Bull again here evades periodicity. The first five-eighths of the strain gently wanders, and cadences on the tenth and twelfth bars subvert any notion of a definitive intermediate caesura; a VI^6 chord following the high A at the end of the twelfth bar is the single prominent event in a strain where one might have expected more tunefulness. The lack of profile, however, is largely hidden beneath the changeable yet tasteful surface of the decorated repeat. Approximately five ideas succeed in creating new interest, yet without milking the material. A steady stream of sixteenths arch through the texture in the first five bars before being fragmented into an exchange motive. This naturally leads to a brief excursion of imitation in the seventh and eighth bars based on the motive. Two bars of broken figuration bridge the two cadential posts before a fleeting recall of the thirty-second-note motive from I' highlights the melodic peak of the strain.

Elusive melody and equivocal phraseology, found in varying mixtures in the previous strains and counterbalanced there by repeats with supple decoration of unusually fine linear design, are replaced in strain III and its repeat with clear, motivically organized phrases and simple decoration. The first four bars of III reestablish the tonic as a means of providing the framework for the three sequences that generate the following six-bar segment. Here the melodic significance of the sixth above the bass resolving to a fifth finally emerges, providing the central material of the strain. The high F that begins the last phrase connects with similar points of emphasis in both earlier strains. Only a slight increase in motion is then permitted to decorate III, for its material is already well developed and self-sufficent.

In Galliard a1, as in Galliard d1, Bull avoided any rigid adherence to the pavan's material. Rather, he adapted and considerably abridged the first two strains and substituted new material in the third (unlike the spurious galliard which Tregian gives as an alternate). The two strains which are based on the pavan retain the melodic parameters of the slower dance, a'–a' and c''–d'– (d'' in the pavan), and the different material of III furnishes the opportunity to bring the structural line back to a' from c''-sharp, where the pavan had left it. However, Bull wisely forbids retracing the pavan's melodic structure to dictate the same melodic peaks; instead, he lowers the ceiling in each strain by a third to compensate for a higher temperature in the faster dance that would result from thick textures, a fast rate of harmonic change in the second and third strains, and a dominant sixteenth-note movement in the repeats. The first two factors account for the slow tempo required in this galliard as much as does the third, the same situation found in Byrd's Galliard C4 as well as in Bull's own Galliard a3.

The proportions created by strain lengths of eight, four, and six bars, and the balance resulting from their relative weights are nearly ideal in Galliard a1. The first strain appropriately paraphrases that of the pavan in half the number of bars, and its decoration draws from the vocabulary of the pavan's corresponding section. Strain II compresses the slackest material of the pavan into the densest but shortest strain of the galliard; its contrapuntal density dissipates in the repeat. The length of strain III splits the difference between I and II, obtaining a textural midrange as well between the two. Its four-part writing alternately moves toward contrapuntal independence and coalesces into note-against-note homophony. Here Bull follows Byrd's pattern of intermixing 6/4 with 3/2. The first four bars, forming two parallel subphrases which alternate between the two metrical interpretations, appear to eschew the cautious attitude toward such practice as manifested in Bull's Galliard D/III.

MB provides a good text for this pair, which has many variants among the sources. In b. 68 of the pavan, however, the third note of the cantus should be b', not d'', a reading which is suggested by concordance with b. 70, 72, and 74. The two sixteenths preceding the written-out trill are missing in *Bu,* and the notes in *Tr,* on which *MB* is based at this point, are different in each of these bars from those in *Bu.* In addition, the rhythm of the bass in b. 62 as given by *Bu,* ⊢♪ ♩ ♪♩ ♩ , might be considered decorative and therefore correct.

The unpretentious Pavan and Galliard G5 are found as a pair in *Bu,* while only the pavan occurs in *Tr.* The pavan opens with a harmonic progression, I–I–V–vi, that is identical to the opening of *Il ballo del granduca.* The resemblance ends after b. 3, however, and appears to be of no significance.[16] A comparison from the two sources (Ex. 4-9) may indicate some concern on the part of the composer for bluntness in the ensuing plagal caesura of the first strain. The progression occurs suddenly, in connection with an unexpected drop to the tonal region of the natural seventh, and is melodically highlighted in the decorated repeat by the lowered seventh in the treble answered by a lowered sixth above the bass in the following bar. Bull seems to be intent here upon a direct melodic course in each strain, for the descents in the outer strains and the ascent in the middle strain are unaided by intermediate peaks. This extremely unusual conception works satisfactorily in the first and third strains, but fails in the second. There the impetus of over-stepping is needed to establish the structural d''. The plagal progression in the fourth bar, replaying the downbeat harmonies of the second and third bars, weakens the melodic design and causes the passage to waver. Strain III contrasts markedly with the others by its predominant eighth-note motion, touches of (albeit heterophonic) imitation, prominent melody, and authentic close on the fourth bar. The decoration in the repeat, which presumably accounts for the designation "trumpet," is also of stronger character than that in I' or II'. This last third of the piece is musically effective in itself; yet in spite of the melodic connection between the opening of I and III, the final strain and its repeat threaten the rather passive nature of the first two-thirds of the piece. Whereas the same melody and its treatment in Pavan G6/III (Ex. 4-1) seemed organic and appropriate, the material jars slightly here, as if Bull were patching in an old, ill-fitting idea in the absence of a new one.

Pavans and Galliards from *Bu* Not in *Tr*

The strains of Galliard G5 are not based on those of the pavan which precedes it in *Bu*, though Bull plots a similar melodic course in the faster dance. He does so, however, in a more conventional way, arching through a pitch higher than either the initial or final melodic points in each strain. No departure from clear two-bar units is ever made, and the repeats strive for brilliance rather than variety. Because Bull so often related outer strains, the shapes which open I and II invite comparison. The latter may have been based on the former (Ex. 4-10), its elements reordered through a familiar process in plainsong-setting figuration. Whether or not the galliard dates from later than the pavan, as might be implied by its absence from *Tr*, it appears likely that it was conceived independently of the preceding dance. It uses none of the same material and makes only one apparent reference to it (the dissonant f' and b flat in the first bar of III', which echo the e''-flat and b'-flat in the fourth and fifth bars of the pavan/I'). The piece could have been chosen as a suitable companion for the pavan when it was included in *Bu*, whence the pair found their way into *Co*.

Ex. 4-9   Bull, Pavan G5/I, b. 3- (*Tr*); Ibid., (*Bu*)

Ex. 4-10   Bull, Galliard G5/I; Ibid., III

Processes of addition and contraction have been cited as responsible for uneven strain lengths in Bull's dance movements. The first strain of Galliard d6 furnishes an example of the latter. By moving the second phrase of the strain back one bar so that it overlaps and eclipses the cadential bar of the first phrase, the composer has produced a seven-bar strain where one of eight might have resulted. An analogous situation is found in the Coranto C2 "Battle," in which the second strain, initially eight bars, is extended by a 12-bar cantus firmus-like section. The eighth bar of the first phrase, however, becomes the first bar of the second, and the whole segment comes out as 19 rather than 20 bars. Unlike segments built up in even and uneven blocks, the conception in these works is foursquare, though the result is not, and the impression of a tactus having been left out always obtains. As if this effect alone were not sufficiently disorienting, Bull adds to the confusion in Galliard d6 by introducing a hemiola in b. 2–3 before any metrical norm has been established, begins the second phrase with a bar of 6/4, and continues with two bars that mix 6/4, 3/2, and syncopations of both. A strong tonic cadence in the fifth bar, however, helps establish some equilibrium, effectively providing a delayed cadence to the first phrase that counters the premature onset of the second. The strain is somewhat clarified by the decorated repeat, if only as a result of the thinning away of counterpoint, leaving bare the rhythms of treble and bass. The density of the first strain is matched in the second by a harmonic rhythm of six to the bar and persistent imitation between cantus and tenor. A seven-bar third strain was to have balanced the first, yet the material here is a weak successor to the tightly packed earlier strains, and is hard pressed to accomplish its goal. The simple scale pattern accompanied by a tinkering, off-beat figuration lacks enough muscle to bring the melodic line up to rest on d''. This assignment is the last stage of the galliard's unusually ambitious melodic plan in which the structural line of the piece is intended to ascend (violating both gravity and an arch doctrine of Schenkerian philosophy). Such an attempt might be viewed, along with the oddness of the first strain, as a manifestation of youthful adventure. Indeed, uneven strains and off-beat figuration, the latter of which Byrd used only when he could make something further of it, connect Galliard d6 with Galliard d7 and place it among the oldest of the pavans and galliards in *Bu*.[17]

The other piece with an ascending melodic structure, Galliard gl, approaches the job with more forethought on the part of the composer as to what the consequences of such an ambition are for the design of individual strains. It was deemed necessary to establish the ascent in microcosm in the first strain and to follow through in successive ones with a melodic structure of similar incline. In addition, each strain arches widely into the upper stratum of the treble register, exerting a strong magnetism on the line. Here Bull, unlike in Galliard d6, did not confound his structural goal with tricky strain lengths and an array of figuration. Instead, each strain is eight bars long, thus allowing for maximum metrical flexibility, and decoration is kept straightforward yet brilliant.

The eight-bar standard is used to advantage in Galliard gl, and metrical variety is accomplished through conflict rather than the more usual ambiguity. Strain I falls into units of two, three, and three bars, the central unit defined by boundaries of a quarter rest and the sounding of the highest note on the keyboard. The first downbeat in the midsection of the strain occurs with, and in part as a result of, the E-flats in the left hand; the use of the lowered sixth degree in two contexts—here as subdominant in the relative major area and in the second strain as phrygian approach to the half cadence—gives the first two-thirds of the piece a distinctly aeolian flavor like that of Pavan al. What happens in the middle of strain I can be seen in Ex. 4-11 as a breaking down of the meter, made possible by doubling the harmonic rhythm and sequencing a syncopated and anacrustic motive of four quarters' length. The metrical asperity remains

Ex. 4-11 Bull, Galliard g1/I

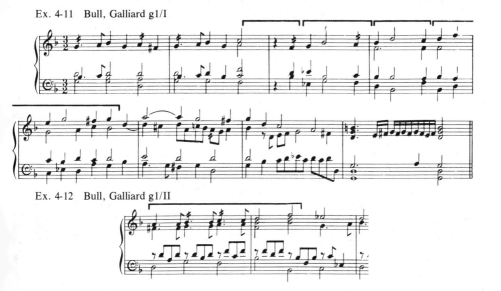

Ex. 4-12 Bull, Galliard g1/II

unresolved until three groups of four quarters have been answered by a group of 2 × 4 quarters and the top A has been reached.

Strain II produces a unit of four at the outset (Ex. 4-12) rather than in the middle, and on the level of the minim. The conclusion of the second subphrase in the fourth bar brings with it an ubiquitous filler figure in the left hand that sets off a thematic response in the treble; its consequent, the melodic peak in the fifth bar harmonized with the minor dominant rather than the mediant, resolves any doubt about the strain's symmetry which may have been raised by the enjambment in the previous bar. Early attainment of the mediant in the second strain and its definitive establishment at the end of the strain responds to the opening of I, whose harmonic progression asks for—but never affirms—the B-flat region. This organic relationship, reinforced by a melodic correspondence between the openings of the two strains, is carried further in III. Strain III begins with the dominant of the previous chord, as strain II had done in relation to the final chord of I. Both the weight of the mediant and the anacrustic nature of the fourth (cf. the second half of II) having been established, the strain begins by reversing the normal strong-weak sequence of the first two beats (Ex. 4-13). That the fourth-motive with which the strain begins is ultimately derived from the midsection of strain I is made clear when the later strain nearly quotes from the first (cf. b. 4–5 of Ex. 4-11 and b. 6-7 of Ex. 4-13). The chain of fourths throws an accent on every second beat, beginning with the second of the first bar, bringing a" in conjunction with the resolution of the metrical contradiction two bars earlier than in strain I (and in both instances with a phrygian cadence). This early arrival of the high point allows room for a second peak at the end of the strain, necessary to establish the g"; an unobstructed return to the tonic is then facilitated by abjuring the previously important E-flat, effectively expunging any mediant emphasis.

The unusually complicated yet finely balanced strains of Galliard gl

Ex. 4-13   Bull, Galliard gl/II

Ex. 4-14 Bull, Galliard g1/II, b. 3

Bull, Galliard g1/III', b. 1

did not lend themselves well to fanciful decoration. Hence Bull sticks with scales against which the harmonies and rhythms of the main strains, in a reduced form, are clearly sounded. As a part of his well-integrated conception, Bull extends rhythmic asperity to the lowest possible level with a familiar three-in-two figure in strains II' and III' (Ex. 4-14). Also noteworthy is his reinterpretation of the sixth and seventh bars of the second strain in its decorated repeat. By changing the harmony on the downbeat of the second of the two, the crucial E-flat is sounded for the last time in the piece, creating a cadential hemiola that gives final emphasis to the B-flat region.

In *Co,* Galliard g1 is given as the companion to a "Pavin in Gamut flatt," ascribed to Bull by Cosyn. Dart rejected the pavan as Bull's, claiming that it "shows all the characteristics of Cosyn's style, and none of those encountered in Bull's own music." His conclusion that the piece is "undoubtedly by Cosyn" falters under the slightest scrutiny. Rather, the work is thoroughly typical of Bull, and internal evidence suggests that it was indeed conceived to pair with Galliard g1. Pavan g1, like its galliard, is constructed from strains of both even and equal length (16/16/16). Thus Bull is experimenting with that which for him was exceptional, allowing the standard to impose squareness in neither pavan nor galliard. Strains I and II of the pavan cadence on the sixth bar, then follow with a phrase of 10 bars, while strain II is woven seamless in Bull's finest manner, motivically conceived suspensions always eluding the cadence. As in similar pavan and galliard pairs in which the slower dance is melodically diffuse, Bull here fashions the galliard from new material. However, melodic and rhythmic resemblance between strains II and III of the pavan and strain III of the galliard suggests that some thematic relationship was being maintained (Ex. 4-15). Perhaps still more important as a link between the two works is the function of the E-flat. In the pavan, as in the galliard, the lowered sixth functions in the first strain to introduce the mediant area and in the second strain as antecedent to the dominant in the phrygian cadence. The latter is never actually explicit, being reserved in its full form for the galliard.

Pavan g1 opens as do two other pavans, d1 and a2, with a trilling motive that can be expressed either as sixteenths or six-groups. Its decoration introduces animation not through the usual flowing sixteenths, but through a new rhythmic motive that actually gives focus to the preceding material. A sudden interruption of the motion at the beginning of strain II comes as no surprise in the light of an identical situation in Pavan a2 and, to a lesser degree, in Pavans a1, a3, and d1. The 6–5 melodic inflection, which eventually leads to the arresting e''-flat in the seventh bar, is both in keeping with the aeolian color introduced into what appears to be a dorian (transposed) piece and is highly typical of Bull's harmonic palate. In only one other dance movement, Pavan a3, does Bull employ a passage of imitation as dense as that found in the third strain of this pavan. In the third strain of that piece close stretto imitations serve to bring in something new at the last moment but prove difficult to decorate without diluting their substance. Here, however, the imitation is actually confined to the upper voices—the accompanying voices participating to the extent

Ex. 4-15   Bull, Pavan g1/II

Ibid., g1/III

Bull, Galliard g1/III

that they engage in the rhythms of the upper pair—and allows a type of ornamentation that enhances and energizes. The rhythmic impetus provided by a motive based on the anacrustic two-sixteenths recalls similar decoration of the first strain and effectively rounds off the piece. The triplets in the second half of II need not imply an early date of composition, as in the Spanish Pavan and the earlier Quadran, for Pavan g2 is a mature work in every respect. It is, rather, a decorative idea used selectively by Bull—one to which he would return in a later work, Pavan g3.

Pavan and Galliard a2 probably date from around 1603, the year of the queen's death. If the pavan is indeed commemorative, as Dart supposes and as the pathotic and eloquent mood of the piece suggests, then it could also date from after her death, though probably not by many years.[18] The pair, in any case, is among Bull's most inspired works, the product of an imagination working freely yet with exceptional intensity. The many melodic, harmonic, and figural ideas of the pavan, however, are not so closely integrated as they are in Pavan and Galliard al or Galliard gl, perhaps suggesting that the a2 pair predate the others. The trilling figuration that decorates the pavan in I, I', and II' and an idiosyncratic variant of the twin-cadence scheme in I connect it with Pavan dl; likewise, the cantus firmus-like treatment of III signifies a kinship with Galliard d7. Quasi-canonic (c.f. Pavan g1/II and III) and chromatic elements in the second strain look beyond Bull's own corpus toward works such as Byrd's canonic Pavan G6 (*MB* 28:74) in Nevell, dated "no earlier than the 1580s" by Neighbour and the third strain of Philips's "Pauana Doloroso" (and its galliard, *Tr*, nos. 80 and 81), dated 1593 by Tregian.[19] All these features accord well with a dating of the work from around 1600.

In the first strain of Pavan a2 Bull succeeds in doing what he had tried and failed to do in Pavan dl/I. In the latter piece a premature intermediate cadence in the 16-bar strain upsets the balance at the final cadence, causing a static and overly long tonic extension. Here the error is remedied by placing the cadential bars in the middle of the strain, in "twin-cadence" fashion. Yet by overlapping the beginning of the second phrase, from a'', with the second of the cadential bars, an asymmetrical proportion between the two halves is retained. The early placement at b. 8 of the melodic high point that starts the phrase is in part prepared by the phrygian cadence on b. 4, which leaves g'-sharp unresolved.

The bald, note-against-note homophony at a minim's pace which begins the second strain calms the waters stirred by the decorated repeat of the first strain. However, no such abrupt effect obtains here as in the corresponding spot in Pavan al, for the figuration at the end of I' is planned so as to prepare the first bar of II as a down beat with only a modal change. Bull sets strain II in the manner of a canon, but without rigid adherence to the imitation. The harmonic rhythm predicated by the subject conforms with that of the preceding strain which, unlike Pavan aI/I, is seldom faster than two to a bar. Canonic writing tends naturally to preclude much periodic articulation, and Bull takes little exception to those conditions here. A mild caesura in the seventh bar is defined more by the change of melodic direction in the leading voice than by a strong harmonic or rhythmic articulation; and a second subdominant cadence is undercut through the simultaneous entrance of the bass's imitation. In the repeat, only the second of the two retains any strength.

Beginning the third strain with the chord of the dominant which closed the previous strain and following it in the second bar with its resolution gives a weak-strong effect over the bar. Subsequent tonic cadences on the fifth and eighth bars work with this opening to create a three-bar periodicity which comes to a halt when the high A is reached. Beginning with the following measure, Bull changes both metrical unit (from three bars to two) and figuration to heighten the intensity of the reascent from f''-sharp, rather than merely effecting a parallel descent in the second half of the strain. Thus the last three notes of the cantus firmus are beautifully reworked in a style suggestive of its plainsong-setting origins, and the melody descends finally in the last four bars to c''-sharp. The subdominant, which harmonizes F-sharp throughout the strain, echoes its strong position in the earlier strains; emphasis on this tonal region appears to be a part of Bull's conception of the mode in this piece and in the al pair. Decoration, while mostly confined in I' and II' to the terms established in the main strains themselves, becomes more independent in III'. Melodic and imitative requirements having been waived, the repeat has only to concern itself with retaining the integrity of the structural line and its attendant harmonies.

Galliard a2 is independently conceived rather than being built on the material of the pavan and employs more than the usual amount of sequence as a means of structuring the strains. The result is a tightly knit and well-motivated piece that contrasts effectively with the diffuse, ruminating pavan. Strain I is built out of three units of four bars, the second of which becomes the subject of strain II. Its harmonization creates a cross-relation between G and G-sharp that is then exploited in strain III. Chromaticism, confined to the second strain in the pavan, thus assumes a wider role in the galliard. The decoration of the first is treated schematically, yet without stodginess, calling upon the four-sixteenths figure that springs from a strong beat in the first half of the repeat to occur *on* strong beats in the second half. The development in II of a form of the central motive of I is carried out through a threefold repetition of the idea, each on a successively higher level. When the motive finally takes a cadential turn, the strain closes in the major subdominant. The modal contrast effected by the third strain's departure in the minor subdominant is by no means unusual at this point. However, the juxtaposition of major and minor—consciously or otherwise drawn from the cross-relation of the first strain—is repeated three times more as the two-bar unit is sequenced, thereby gaining motivic prominence. The sequence reaches from D, where the strain begins, through the circle of fifths up to F-sharp, where the harmonic rhythm is temporarily suspended; the circle is then retraced, backwards and in compression, to A. This long ascent, and relatively shorter descent, corresponds in the tonal realm to that in the melodic realm in the third strain of the pavan.

A major caution must be taken in reading the *MB* text of the pavan, for all the thirty-second-note trilling figurations in *Bu* have been revised as groups of six sixteenth-notes. Thus bar two should read as in Ex. 4-16. Likewise, b. 1, left hand, beats 3–4; b. 3, right hand, beats 2, 3–4; b. 4, left hand, beats 3–4; b. 7, right hand, beats 3–4; b. 8, left hand, beats 3–4; b. 23, right hand, beat 4; b. 26, left hand, beat 4; b. 27, left hand, beat 4; b. 28, right hand, beat 2 and left hand, beat 4; b. 30, right hand, beats 3–4. (The fourth beats of b. 1, 26 and 27 are notated ♪♪♪♪♪♪♪♪; apparently a beam has been mistakenly omitted.) A variant from *Bu* in b. 75, tenor, last beat, which some players may prefer, is noted in the critical report. In view of the importance of chromatic alteration in the third strain of the galliard, the sharp on d', right hand, b. 50 in *Bu* should be taken seriously even though it is missing in the corresponding bar of the repeat. On the second beat, a sharp appears to have been erased. A suggested improvement in the reading of b. 50 and 62 is given in Ex. 4-17.

In Pavan a3 Bull is again careful as he was in Pavan a1 to avoid "twin-cadence" symmetrical structuring of the three 16-bar strains. A dominant half-cadence on b. 5, extended in the following bar, followed

Ex. 4-16   Bull, Pavan a2, b. 2 (*Bu*)

Ex. 4-17   Bull, Galliard a2, b. 50 and 62, suggested correction

by a new motive treated sequentially (and recalling the second half of Pavan a2/I) apportions the opening strain into a shorter and longer segment. The same cadence that articulates the intermediate point of strain I occurs in strain II on the seventh bar, but rather than being extended is challenged in the following measure on melodic grounds, with the peak of the strain, and on the measure after that on cadential grounds, with a strong mediant arrival. The strength of the latter might have settled the matter, leaving the impression of an eight–plus–eight structure, had another dominant half-cadence on the thirteenth bar, rhyming with the one six bars earlier, not reopened the question of priority between the various points. Finally, in the third strain, the situation is somewhat clarified when the intermediate cadence—again on the mediant—ushers in the sharply contrasting closing material. Even so, the phrases are elided so that the end of the first becomes the beginning of the second.

The resemblance of this closing material to that of Byrd's Fantasy d1 (*MB* 28:46), particularly in its earlier version (before 1591), is unmis-

Ex. 4-18   Byrd, Fantasy d1, b. 64-

Bull, Pavan a3/III, b. 10-

takable (Ex. 4-18). Whether there is an issue of parody here is a question for which no final answer is to be found in internal or external factors, yet it can be wagered with little risk that Byrd's piece is the earlier. He did not go out of his way in the fantasy, as he did in Galliard C4, to write in an unaccustomed style. Rather, the material in b. 64–66 and its decoration in the following bars accords well with Byrd's sensitivity to linear design and rhythmic suppleness and betrays no stylistic anomalies. Byrd has built his phrase out of a canon at a minim's interval between cantus, bass, and tenor, to which the alto adds a related free voice offset by a quarter beat. The resultant continuous eighth-note motion becomes continuous sixteenth-note motion in Bull's passage. By simplifying the texture to two pairs of voices, then a trio of voices against the cantus, Bull concentrates the intrinsic rhythmic quality of the idea and dismisses the carefully paced stretto imitations. If, as Neighbour suggests[20], Byrd's passage is a more fully developed stage of part of the third strain from his Pavan g2 (*MB* 27:3), then Bull's reductive formulation can scarcely have been the origin of the idea. Be that as it may, there are few passages from the two composers that better show the difference between Byrd, the musician always thinking in concrete musical terms, and Bull, the composer conceiving his ideas *a priori* for the sound of the instrument.[21]

The passage in Bull's pavan proves difficult to decorate and loses some of its effectiveness in the repeat. Byrd's decoration of the corresponding material in his fantasy is based on the same principle of reducing a contrapuntal texture to its essential rhythmic and melodic elements, and introducing an accompanying flow of sixteenths (Ex. 4-19). When, however, Bull so distills the material that its character depends more upon sonic than linear device, then decoration becomes superfluous and tends to water down the initial statement. The decorations of the other strains share many configurations with Pavan a1; they integrate with one another, as well as with the main strains, by drawing upon the motive ♩ ♫ from the ends of I and II as a central idea for II', and by reusing the five-note figure of I' to close II'. Bull's usual unity of the outer strains depends here on a use in II of the three-note group of eighths from I.

Three clear-cut phrases of four bars each, light-weight melody, and relatively unencumbered textures in the first strain of the galliard and its repeat offer relief from the density of the pavan. The promise is revoked in the latter half of the piece, however, with two strains of unparalleled contrapuntal activity. Substituting weight for duration, Bull wisely chooses strains half the length of the first one and provides variety in their organization by splitting the second 3 + 3 and the third 2 + 2 + 2. He manages to decorate strain II in such a way that an impression of increased activity obtains and carries the contrapuntal texture with its fast harmonic rhythm into strain III. Further complications of metrical ambiguity and a rate of

Ex. 4-19   Byrd, Fantasy d1, b. 67-

Bull, Pavan a3/III', b. 10-

harmonic change that sometimes reaches down to the eighth-note push the texture to its limits. The repeat, as in II', can only add superficial motion, here in the form of a motive from the second strain of the pavan, turned round (♩♫ → ♫|♪) to give a rhythmic spring. Although the galliard retains only the tonal, not the melodic, plan of the pavan, the inclusion in the last strain of both this motive and texture of such density that it defies effective decoration helps to unify the two. Such unity is largely formal, however, for where the pavan takes on new life near its end, the galliard loses vigor by allowing the unusual, admitted in strain II, to overstay its welcome.

Among genres of instrumental music, the "next in gravity and goodness" to the fantasy was said by Morley to be the pavan, "a kind of staid music ordained for grave dancing. . . ."[22] This quality is present in large measure in Bull's pavans, reflecting an attitude akin to that expressed by Dowland in his *Lachrymae, or seven tears, figured in 7 passionate pavans* (1605).[23] In fact, two major-mode pavans with eight-bar strains, G5 and G7, find Bull not quite at ease, feeling some conflict between the limitations of the shorter strain coupled with the brighter mode and his conception of the dance. An extreme form of his more usual attitude is met in Pavan d2, indexed by Cosyn as "Melancholy." The mood of the piece goes beyond the pathos of Pavan a2 and the diffuse expressiveness of a1 into a contemplative realm undisturbed by any excess of faster values in the main strains. In contrast to this the decorated repeats provide activity, but on a descending scale: in I' thirty-seconds dominate, in II' there is no motion faster than the sixteenth, and in III' decoration is confined to passing eighths. Such a systematic disposition of rhythmic rate usually implies a plan, one which may be implicit in Cosyn's title.

The melancholy temperament, as opposed to the melancholy illness, was viewed in the dominant occult philosophy of the late Renaissance as complex: not merely dark, depressed, and earthbound but, when tempered with other influences, creative, inspired, even prophetic. The inspired melancholic as genius is defined by Agrippa, depicted by Dürer in his famous engraving *Melencholia I*, and manifested in England by, among others, Chapman's *The Shadow of Night* and the late plays of Shakespeare.[24] The tempering of Saturn's melancholy, advised in the pseudo-Aristotelian *Problemata*, had come by Bull's time to be associated to some extent with dancing, as it had in earlier times already been associated with certain kinds of music.[25] James Cleland, in his advice to a young nobleman on "How you should play at Tennis, and Daunce," heads his list of mythical uses of the dance, "I Wil not ascend vp amongst the Gods to shew you them Dancing to asswage *Saturn's* Melanchollie."[26] The temperament of Pavan d2/I is indeed Saturnian—a shady and slow-moving world, soberly closed with a plagal cadence. Fiery opposition to this mood is met in the animated movement of the strain's repeat; it stirs a response in the subsequent strain where a more coherent language appears, based on a suspension motive. The contrast is less great in the repeat of the second strain: the mitigating influence of faster values having brought out more wakefulness in the main strain, the repeat is now content with a calmer motion. Finally, in the sanguine third strain both main material and decoration agree on an equaniminous eighth-note motion, with only appropriate differences between the two. Melancholy has been assuaged in the minor-major transformation from strain I to III, cholera appeased in the quieter values. Balance is also restored in the long dominant pedal of the strain, helping compensate for the scarcity of authentic cadences in the previous strains. Juxtaposing values as disparate as minims and thirty-seconds is a phenomenon encountered elsewhere in Bull's music. It can lead to a puzzling discontinuity and cause problems in establishing a workable tempo in performance. When, as in Pavan d2, a purpose for the initially unwieldy contrast can be envisioned, the music begins to explain itself.

The material of the pavan was hardly adaptable to a galliard, so new ideas were provided for the faster dance. Unambiguous intermediate cadences and a generous amount of sequence give clear articulation to the strains. The ascending melodic motive of the middle strain is framed by a descending one, providing like material in the sections whose rates of motion contrast most. The piece does tend to pick up speed with an increasing profusion of sixteenths, but it is balance here, rather than dialectic, that rules.

Both copies of Pavan d2 are in Cosyn's hand. Though there is no way of knowing exactly how detrimental this state of affairs has been in the transmission of the text, comparison of other pieces in *Bu* (hand I) and *Co* reveals inevitable corruptions. The most that can be done here is to expunge a good deal of the ornamentation, which is surely excessive by comparison to any other text of Bull's in *Bu*. Particular attention is drawn to the uncharacteristic ornamentation of successive notes in b. 8, 16, 32, 76, 78, 79, 94, and 95.

At the opposite extreme from the eccentric Pavan d2 is the unusually cool Pavan G7 and its galliard, both unique to *Bu* and lacking any ascription. A short opening strain with restricted melodic range and timid harmonic palate, complete absence of values smaller than the eighth in all main strains, and uninspired figuration in the repeats might speak against Bull's hand. Yet similar slackness is found in Pavan G1, undoubtedly by Bull, and certain details of the G7 pair favor the ascription: the crossing of cantus and tenor in b. 13, displacement of the bass on beat three of b. 14 by one sixteenth, repeated-note figuration in the galliard, and arpeggiation up to the last quarter or eighth at the ends of strains. The pavan's material is routinely accommodated in the galliard, a dance marked by neither virtuosity nor rhythmic variety.

The authorship of an F-major pavan and galliard in *Bu* (*MB* 19:109a and b) is less secure. Several features have led the present writer to exclude these pieces from the canon of works that may be considered with relative confidence to be authentic. The first is the 8/6 relationship between the lengths of the strains. In two-strain pavans and galliards Bull makes the two halves of the piece equal in length or precedes a longer with a shorter strain, but never the other way round. Only in three-strain movements does a shorter strain succeed a longer one. More importantly, Bull never follows a pavan with a galliard having the same strain lengths. Equally untypical is the unaccompanied scalar figuration in the first and fifth bars of I' and in the final two bars of the pavan. Bull is not content to let scalar decoration stand alone, unaided by rhythmically and harmonically defining chords in the other hand. A further detail, one pointed out by Dart, is the written-out trill in b. 21 of the galliard, an isolated instance of this ornament in a piece ascribed to Bull. Finally, the use of the same melodic material in a pavan and galliard of like strain lengths prompted a reorganization of the strains; thus strain I of the galliard comes out in segments of four plus four, rather than five plus three, and the final cadence of II is delayed to the last bar, rather than sounding in the penultimate one. Taken individually, any one of these features would not necessarily cast doubt on the authenticity of the work, for the pavans and galliards were always fertile ground for Bull's experiments. Collectively, however, they raise doubt.

Two separate galliards in *Bu*, a5 and C, also lack concordances. The first is a two-strain type having the same strain lengths and tonal plan as Galliard d5. Further affinities between the two pieces lie in their predominant trochaic rhythms and in placement and degree of intermediate cadences. The first strain of both pieces is articulated on the fourth bar by a cadence on the mediant, and the second strain at its midpoint by a cadence on the dominant. Though the pieces may have no direct relationship to one another, they do represent one type in two styles. The d5 piece is sonorous, richly decorated, and occasionally contrapuntal, while the a5 piece is simple, straightforward, devoid of sixteenth-note passages (save two written-out trills), befitting its designation "Italian." Galliard C is in a similar vein and, like a5, relies chiefly on the treble register. Hemiola groups in the second strain, bringing metrical reinterpretation and syncopation into play with the basic 3/2, give variety in a structure made regular by eight-bar strains divided symmetrically; eighth-note decoration characterized by repeated notes enhances the surface without challenging the fundamental movement of the dance.

In a final galliard in *Bu*, Galliard G8, Bull is found experimenting not with the internal proportions of strains, but with ways of counter-balancing internal regularity. He begins with a unique attempt at creating a kind of "twin-cadence" scheme within an eight-bar strain, resulting in cadences on b. 3–4 and 7–8. He may have chosen the unusual tonal plan of the first strain, which begins in the subdominant, in order to try to offset the periods of heavy tonic and dominant that this scheme affords. Bulges in the middle and at the end of the strain still are unavoidably obvious, especially since the dominant makes a premature appearance on the downbeat of b. 6. Decoration in the repeat takes the form of five-note figures (as in Pavan a1/I', a3/I' and II', and Galliard D/I') and trilling figures (as in Pavan G1/I' and Galliard G1/3d variation). The second strain, which avoids the two-bar cadence in the middle but retains it at the close, is largely a reworking of I to close on G, not D, and provides only textural contrast. Its decoration is entirely different from that in I' and breaks continuity with the foregoing. The two bars of closing tonic are set with a new idea (♩♪♪♩) followed by chopping chords such as those which close Galliard G5. The whole effect is a rather awkward one, lacking cohesiveness.[27]

Besides Galliard G8 only one dance, the incomplete Pavan d4, closes out of the tonic in its opening strain. This aspect of the tonal plan and the second strain's close in the tonic may signify that the pavan was originally just two strains and is therefore lacking only the decorated repeat of the second strain. The situation is unfortunate, for this is the only eight bar pavan in which Bull manages the expressiveness found in the longer dances, working into each strain a beautiful high point—the first a Lachrymae sixth—in anticipation of the melodic descent. Tasteful decoration in I' is followed with a folksonglike melody in II not unlike Byrd and underscored by a strong tonal contrast. This digression into simple tunefulness, which serves well to complement the restrained pathos of I, ends with a sudden leap of an octave in the melody, answering the sixth heard in I, and brings back the emotional climate of the opening strain.

Later Pavans and Galliards in *Parthenia*

It has been noted that Pavan G1 postdates the galliard based on the same tune and that the melody as it appears in the pavan likely represents the original version. Bull states the theme in unusually plain note-against-note style, sparing all imitation and decoration of the texture save what is needed to sustain the longer harmonies. For the variation he uses two figurations from the galliard, the trilling one which occupied the third variation and the passing eighths from the first variation. Whereas this figure has only a strain of sixteen dotted semibreves in which to do duty in the galliard, it is made soley responsible for the decoration of nearly all of the 16 bars of *breves* in the variation of the pavan. There is insufficient variety here to maintain interest in the section, already kept at a low temperature by the pallid theme, and the insistent ornament on the second of each group of eighths is wearing. Although none of Bull's contributions to *Parthenia* measure up to his finest pavans and galliards found elsewhere, the weakness of this particular piece raises the question of his motivation. All evidence points to the pavan's having been written, somewhat casually, as a companion to the earlier galliard, a piece which may have been a favored one of Princess Elizabeth.[28]

Galliard d4 must have been written to contrast with Galliard d5, which follows it in the print. The former employs three strains of eight bars each, all divided symmetrically into two phrases with an intermediate cadence on the dominant. The latter uses two strains of unequal length with ambiguity of caesura in both owing to repetition of the mediant in the first strain and dominant in the second strain. Galliard d4 sticks to eighth-notes throughout, versus the sixteenth-note movement which dominates d5, and preserves a uniformity by keeping the same level of activity in both main strains and repeats. The contrast is pointed, but does not prove Bull to be the master of the conservative style. Melodically, the piece is rather shapeless, the melody only passingly rising above the d" which frames it. The whole is planned along rather simplistic lines: strain I gives a partially ornamented treble which is answered in the repeat by an ornamented bass; strain III repeats the procedure. Meanwhile, strain II has its material laid out in a fully decorated treble, the repeat mixing treble and bass diminution. Encountered again here is the technique, found elsewhere in Galliards g1, G2, and Pavan g3, of altering the content of the main strain in its repeat. The ii⁶ chord in the fifth bar of the first strain is replaced in the repeat with a chord of the dominant, and the first three bars of the third strain are entirely rewritten. Here the alteration appears to be a result of Bull's plan of drawing attention alternately to bass and treble: when the harmony did not suit well, it was changed.

As noted earlier, Byrd quoted in his Pavan C3/III from the opening of Bull's Pavan G6. Oliver Neighbour has discussed at length the relationship between the two pairs, giving detailed attention to the ways in which the older composer's work criticized the younger's.[29] At least partly in response to Byrd's criticisms of Bull's thinking, Neighbour concludes, Bull wrote another pair—Pavan and Galliard G2—and published them in *Parthenia*. In the pavan Bull used strains of 16 bars and, in contrast to other pavans of like structure, employed Byrd's "twin-cadence" scheme each time, varying it only slightly in the third strain. The tonal plan of the second strain may also be a homage to Byrd, for the subdominant point of departure is found in the corresponding strain of no other pavan of Bull's, while it is by no means unusual for Byrd.[30] Again in Byrd's manner, Bull wrote a galliard on strains half the length of the pavan's and divided all but the first symmetrically into two phrases. Furthermore, he stuck to a fairly consistent and limited vocabulary of ornamentation in the repeats, abjuring the accretion of motives that typify his other large pavans, and attempted to instill in the decoration a linear quality which is often lacking elsewhere. He avoided the distinctive mechanical idea in Galliard G5/II and III, which Byrd had so effectively parodied (see Ex. 4-2 above), and of course excluded any substantial participation of sixteenth-notes in the motion of the faster dance.

The whole effort put Bull in a straitjacket, for the music nowhere

Ex. 4-20   Bull, Pavan G6/I

Bull, Pavan G2/I

rises to the level of inspired expression. After reducing the opening of
Pavan G6/I to a mere shadow of itself in a plain but effective eight-bar
phrase, (Ex. 4-20) the composer follows with a quote from the third strain
of his source, the same passage he had also used in the third strain of
Pavan G5 (see Ex. 4-1). Byrd had chosen not to quote this attractive bit
of melody, perhaps because it so explicitly requires sequence in any development. Bull obviously liked it, though, and substituted it here as the
consequent phrase for the rather dull use in Pavan G6/I. Unfortunately,
its memorable quality becomes lost in the worry of the close. In the
second strain Bull begins with a quietly tuneful and orderly half-strain
that shows more than a usual concern for lyric melody. The suspensions
on the ninth and tenth bars assert a strong motivic potential which is
never realized; rather than sounding like a consequent of the suspension
in I, it becomes a *non sequitur*, a pale match for the first half of its strain.
Bull finally lets down a bit in the third strain. Beginning with the inverted
tonic, as he had done in Pavan G6/III, he brings an early melodic peak
down to rest on an intermediate cadence of the major submediant. Then,
by not repeating the cadence as he had done in previous strains and as
was Byrd's custom, he invokes a twofold sequence as a means to internal
development. The passage finds Bull suddenly more at home, no longer
struggling with the lucid but unregimented melodic invention which Byrd
so easily mastered. The trade-off in the decorated repeat was inevitable,
however, for where Bull had previously been able to involve the figuration
somewhat with melody, he now found his idea too idiosyncratic for more
than a wandering bass line of sixteenths as decoration.

As if to prove a point, Bull reserved his most obvious quote from the
G6 pavan for the beginning of the galliard (Ex. 4-21). As Neighbour cor-
rectly observes, the phrase is recalcitrant to triple meter, having been

Ex. 4-21 Bull, Galliard G2/I

conceived for a duple context. Whereas metrical asperity introduced into a set pattern of strong and weak beats works to good effect in Galliard g1, the lack of an established metrical syntax at the outset of G2 creates confusion. The setting was perhaps designed to bring the strain's inter- mediate cadence a bar earlier than the midpoint, thus putting Bull's al- ternative to symmetrical strain division at the head of the galliard. (His variation of it in the pavan had been at the end.) However, articulation of the second phrase is a weak one, elided with a repetition of the dominant harmony in b. 4. Bull corrected the defect in the repeat, as he also did that of preempting the tonic resolution of b. 7. The robust and headstrong second and third strains of Galliard G6 bring nothing whatever to bear on Galliard G2. Here the final strains offer little in the way of character or melodic interest; the harmonic contrast between the phrases of III is the sole patch of color in the latter two-thirds of the piece. Assuming Neigh- bour's suggested chronology (Bull's G6, Byrd's C4, Bull's G5), Bull may have included this piece by means of defending his pride or paying tribute to Byrd, attempting in it to demonstrate that he could comprehend and utilize Byrd's principles as Byrd had used those of Bull in his Galliard C3. If, as they seem, the works in *Ant* discussed below are later than the G2 pair, they show the composer relieved of such concerns and function- ing with restored imagination, though perhaps with greater restraint than before he had tried to meet Byrd on his terms.

Two Pavans and a Galliard in *Ant*

Pavan and Galliard d3 and Pavan g3 appear to be authentic works of Bull, despite the fact that they show several departures from the composer's hitherto known style and that another pair ascribed to him in the same collection is evidently not authentic. In Pavan d3 Bull returns to the six- teen-bar plan in a unique two-strain example, but pays little allegiance to the "twin-cadence" scheme. Although enjambment makes it difficult to speak of clear phrases, the placement of intermediate cadences on the minor and major dominant tends to divide the strains into segments of seven plus nine and nine plus seven, respectively. Both strains attain their melodic high point during the first half, leaving free the second half of I for melodic development and the second half of II for rhythmic development. In the first strain emphasis on the melodic sphere brings with it a rich harmonic palate; attention to the rhythmic sphere in the second strain yields a harmonic stasis that in turn becomes the object of expressive decoration. The two strains relate not only through contrast, but also through similarity and with a rare degree of subtlety.

The inner-voice rhythm in the first bar is the core of the piece (Ex. 4-22). It becomes more prominent in its exposed position in the second bar, where the rhythm serves as the basis of imitation. In the second strain it is cast in a melodic mold of an upward third or second followed by a reciprocal downward turn (Ex. 4-23), while the original inner voice line is preserved at the outset of the strain as a further unification of the two halves of the piece. The idea is treated on two rhythmic levels—the original and its diminution—heard successively in the cantus at the outset (a & b), then separately in the alto (c) and cantus (d) in conjunction with the caesura, and finally reiterated by the cantus at its original rhythmic level (e) in a decorated form. This tightly knit (if simple) imitative scheme is preserved in the decorated repeat. Fine balance between imitation and figuration here is also to be noted in the first bar of I', where the harmonically static opening has been revitalized through an imitative point. The small matter yet demands no further treatment, for the point merges smoothly into the scalar figuration that decorates the rest of the strain. Techniques of "rhythmic imitation" and diminution, which give this work an unusual feeling of unity, look back to Bull's early encounters with Tudor vocal music and plainsong setting. At the same time, the unmechanical handling of his ideas and even strain lengths place the work well into his maturity.

The galliard is clearly based on the same melodic material, but with more aggressive aims. The melodic peak, e'', is again reached early in the first strain, but later repeated to further support the strain's goal, d''. In the second strain, its point an ornamentation of the pavan/II, the ceiling is pushed through by means of imitation to f'', and decorated by an a'' that in the pavan was reserved for much nearer the end. Bull replaces strains of equal length with unequal ones in the galliard and approaches their structure differently from other galliards of 6/8 design (d5 and a5) by making the second of the two ambiguous rather than clearly symmetrical. He was perhaps by now sufficiently confident of his art to risk both a continuous and bipartite strain within the same work. The latter is cast in a framework of tonal symmetry, the cadence in the fifth bar rhyming with that in the first to counterbalance the elided entry of the top voice in the fourth bar, which defines the onset of the second phrase. The opening bar of tonic, decorated with imitation in the pavan, is treated

Ex. 4-22 Bull, Pavan d3/I

Ex. 4-23 Bull, Pavan d3/II

lightly here with a familiar four-note scale figure that complements well the jagged bass line in the main strain. In strain II the repeated note figure derived from that in the pavan is unapologetically abandoned in the repeat amidst whirling sixteenths.

Attention to the direction and internal proportions of the strains in this pair as well as typical figuration mark it as Bull's. Uncharacteristic are the tight motivic organization of the pavan and close reworking of its material in the galliard, features which may be accounted for by Bull's having encountered the styles of composers such as Cornet and Sweelink. Steeped in counterpoint, Bull's own interest in artifice as a means of unity could have been rekindled on the Continent, forging the new style of Pavan and Galliard d3, as well as works such as the fantasies on *Vestiva i colli*. The other pavan and galliard in *Ant* bearing the same label, "Symphony" (and designated "de Chappelle" in the index), do not hold up well in comparison to the d3 pair. Both are in the same key, retain the same strain lengths (16/16 and 6/8), and in each case both pavan and galliard are built from the same material. Beyond this, the "de Chappelle" pieces mentioned in chapter 1 are graceless works that manifest a minimum of imagination and engagement with the material. Their composer cannot have been the same as that of the d3 pair, though he may have been trying to imitate Bull.

The editor has touched up the text of Pavan and Galliard d3 in a few

places where, typically, *Ant* leaves gaps. The suggested continuation of
the alto in b. 15 of the pavan should perhaps have been a' (semibreve),
for the c'' interferes with the cantus. In the galliard a suggestion is offered
for the tenor of b. 16 in place of that given in *MB* (see Ex. 4-24). This
alternative avoids stressing the second beat two bars in a row (it is weighted
in the previous bar by the suspension); it is also rhythmically consistent
with the tenor at the first entrance of the motive and provides the most
logical reduction of the line at the corresponding point in the repeat. The
small notes in the left hand, b. 7, should be ignored.

Bull's older proclivity for unequal and uneven strain lengths is combined with an attitude of restraint in Pavan g3. In it, as in Pavan d3, the
composer sticks to an unusually consistent four-part texture and achieves
a satisfying balance between pure melody and motivic unity, decorating
the strains in a manner that enhances their material without resorting to
radically contrasting figurations.[31] This is the only one of Bull's pavans
in which the second of three strains closes in the tonic. The feature in no
way suggest that the piece was originally two strains, for the third strain
is an integral response, melodically and harmonically, to the implications
of the opening one. Rather, Bull may have chosen the tonic close of strain
II as a means of maximizing tonal contrast at the point where the opening
was recapitulated, a structural element he wished to strengthen by setting
it in the dominant.

Strain I of the pavan opens over a descending minor tetrachord, the
treble moving in contrary motion and momentarily resting with the bass
on d''. Tonal direction is then reversed, and a series of ascending fourths
(G and C in the series are compressed into the fourth beat of b. 2) carry
the music sequentially to its peak, E-flat, with the melodic high point, g'',
in the treble. The mediant region implied by the long E-flat is diverted,
and the harmony turns back to the natural seventh degree, rhyming with
b. 5 and prefiguring the tonal area which opens strain II. In the opening
strain Bull attains perfectly what he so often seems to be striving for,
complete melodic cogency in one long phrase uninterrupted by caesura,
and sets about reworking the ideas to similar effect in the third strain.

Ex. 4-24   Bull, Galliard d3/II, b. 4, suggested reconstruction

There, the intentions of the strain are announced at the outset with an answer in the alto voice to the cantus at the opening of strain I. The bass line's ascent to F corresponds to a descent in the earlier strain and serves as the point of departure for a leisurely replay of the sequence, which was previously truncated. Here it rises through fifths rather than fourths and penetrates both melodic and harmonic realms. As a result, the g'' is strengthened by a harmonization with the tonic rather than with the submediant. The cadence on the ninth bar reaffirms the secondary importance of F and initiates a subphrase that is to account for the uneven length of the strain. A sequence of this phrase on the mediant, in delayed response to the implication of the E-flat in the first strain, closes the strain in four semibreves. The practice of adding extra bars of tonic extension to pavans and galliards was not uncommon for Byrd, but Bull seldom engaged in it. An extra bar at the end of Pavan G3 and three at the end of Galliard G4 served as codas after the music had been resolved. Here, however, Bull has keenly perceived an imbalance in the conclusion of strain III due to the three-bar subphrase. The addition of two bars to the end of the repeat does not merely extend the tonic, as it usually does in Byrd's pavans, but extends the final subphrase itself to balance the uneven antecedent, forestalling final arrival. The issue might never have arisen had Bull not seized the opportunity to extend two harmonies in decorating the second strain. The seventh and eighth minims of the strain were stretched by a value equal to their length to support a small digression upon the melody at that point. The 13-bar repeat of II, then, required a consequential one which, after having been created in strain III, required a final resolution.

Bull's interest in uneven strain lengths, stretching all the way back to his early plainsong settings and experiments in earlier pavans and galliards, pays off in this apparently late work, as does his preoccupation with asymmetrical and/or continuous structuring of strains. Yet he has not failed to set his unconventional thinking in relief with a middle strain of two six-bar phrases, the one ruminating, the other concise and motivic. The decoration of this strain, perhaps the most typical of the three by virtue of its collection of figurations, bridges that of the first and last strains. Strain I' is dominated by triplet movement, decorating the melody with a sensitivity to linear design that surely owes something to Byrd, and strain III' uses a combination of sixteenths in the bass and dotted figures in the treble. Rather than mixing elements throughout, as he often did, Bull here found a method for using a limited number of figurations in logical sequence; this involved casting the outer decorated strains as essentially duets for treble voices above a bass, a texture already implicit in the main strains. The texture is one Bull would have been far more likely to have known Continental music of the second and third decades of the seventeenth century than in English music of the first decade.

More than any other genre that Bull pursued, the pavans and galliards trace the composer's thinking at every stage of his career. His prolific production of these works throughout his life—the paucity of examples from his Continental period owing, one suspects, to the sources—attests to his vital interest in them as a testing ground for his ideas. Though few pieces stand out as masterworks, nearly every one is intrinsically rewarding to study and to play. From the relatively awkward early Galliard d7 or the experimental Galliard a6, Bull gradually emerged a master of daring and abundantly creative means, as evidenced in particular by the mature al and g1 pairs. Trying his seasoned hand on new ideas later in life, he produced the mysterious and complex "Melancholy" Pavan and Galliard in one vein, the dazzling "Prince's" Galliard in another. His interest in varied and uneven strain lengths and his use of the cantus firmus strain were not artifacts, but genuine part and parcel of the thinking of a composer steeped in plainsong-setting tradition. Where, as in *Parthenia*, he supressed them and tempered his conviction that keyboard figuration could solve structural problems, he all but failed. The few Continental works that survive, however, show the composer working in his later years with a renewed energy and remarkably restrained eloquence.

Almans and Corantos, Arrangements, and "Signature" Pieces

Some thirty pieces (all but two are in *Bu*, *El*, or *Ant*) consist of two or sometimes three strains and their reprises which, like the pavans and galliards, are usually decorated. The strains themselves are generally of four, six, or eight bars' length and have the character of almans or corantos, whether or not they are so called, or else are songlike in nature. There is the strong possibility that many of the works listed here are arrangements of popular or court tunes—some may even be masque music—yet concordances for only two have been located. Since these pieces are short, and stylistic evidence even more difficult to use here than elsewhere as a tool for testing authenticity, all the pieces included in the printed edition are given mention.

Coranto d:	*MB* 19:74
Brigante	
Coranto g1	19:79
Coranto g2:	19:80
Alarm	
Coranto g3:	19:81
Kingston	
Alman a1:	19:93
Duke of Brunswick	
Alman a2:	19:94
Germain	
Alman a3:	19:95
French	
English Toy	19:96
Duchess of Brunswick's Toy	19:97
"Most Sweet and Fair"	
Coranto a:	19:98
The Prince	

Dutch Dance	19:99
Alman C:	19:104
Dallying	
Coranto C1:	19:105
French	
Coranto C2:	19:106
Battle	
Welsh Dance	19:107 and Sabol, *Four Hundred Songs and Dances,* no. 395
Alman F:	19:110
Ionic	
Country Dance	19:111
Irish Toy	19:112
Alman D1	19:114
Alman D2	19:115
What Care You?	19:116
Alman G1:	19:134
Fantasia	
Alman G2	19:135
Coranto G1:	19:136
Joyeuse	
Coranto G2:	19:137
A Round	
My Self	19:138
(Discussed in chapter 6)	
My Grief	19:139
My Choice I Will Not Change	19:140
My Jewel 1	19:141
My Jewel 2	19:142
Bull's Goodnight	19:143
(Discussed in chapter 6)	

The absence of ascriptions in hand I of *Bu*, the blanket and sometimes erroneous ascriptions in *Ant*, and the fact that those in *El* appear to rest on Cosyn raise considerable doubt about the authenticity of many of these works. Serious though the doubts may be, they need not concern anyone who takes pleasure in these short pieces. Indeed, there is only one which seems certainly not to be by Bull and one whose concordance raises the question of authorship without answering it. These are Corantos C1 and C2 in *Bu* and *Ant*, respectively.

Coranto C1 could be French (as it is labelled by both hands in *Bu*), for keyboard arrangements of French tunes are known in England at the time.[1] More importantly, however, the piece exists in a fuller version in *Tr*, no. [228], ascribed to Edmund Hooper. There the piece has a usual 8 / 8 structure rather than the foreshortened and irregular one of 7 / 6 in *Bu*. In the second strain one of the two-bar segments has been removed with no appreciable damage in the pruning. In the first strain, however, the third bar in the second of two symmetrical four-bar halves has been lifted out, giving a bizarre *non sequitur*. The revision falls so wrongly on the music that one might take it for a scribe's omission—bars are occasionally left out elsewhere in the collection—yet the structure is retained in the decorated repeat. The priority of versions is less clear in the case of Coranto C2, found in Praetorius's *Terpsichore* (1612; no. 183). Praetorius gives the piece as "Incerti," and makes no mention of the designation "Battle" given in *Ant*. Several features of the music suggest that the composer was English, and even point to Bull. The first is the registral echo at the outset of II, an effect more native to the keyboard (cf. Corantos d and g2, and *Tr*, no. [19]) than to ensembles, where both dynamic and timbral changes can supply the needed contrast. The second half of the strain drifts into territory not found elsewhere in Praetorius's collection, that of the English cantus-firmus strain. Ten bars built on an ascending fifth, plus two cadential bars, are attached by elision to the seven preceding ones for a strain of 19 bars. Since uneven strain lengths and the cantus firmus-like writing are common tools of Bull's craft, the presence of the piece in *Terpsichore* is alone not especially strong evidence against his authorship.

Seven more pieces in *Ant* of the alman-coranto type also lack concordances: all bear designations that could refer to models. The echolike opening of Coranto d/II appears to indicate a keyboard piece whether by Bull or not; the style is unusually naive in any case. Likewise, the lack of decorated repeats in Coranto G2, as well as the uncommonly square 4 / 4 / 4 structure, casts doubt on the claim that it is Bull's. The same might be said of the structure of Coranto a, yet the latter's music is far more engaging and its tonal structure more captivating. Initial and second strains in Coranto g3 of four bars each are also conspicuous, as is the four-plus four phrase structure of the third strain and its abundant mixture of 3/2 into the fundamental 6/4 meter. Yet the figuration is refined, varied, and takes good advantage of imitative opportunities. Coranto G1 deserves less praise as far as the keyboard writing is concerned, for the figuration is largely parallel and running rather than imitative and motivic. Though lacking decorated repeats, Coranto g2 also appears to be authentic. Like Coranto C2, its second strain begins with a registral echo and eventually veers off into a cantus firmus-like second half, forming an irregular complement to the first.

Country Dance has the character of an alman, at least if Morley's criterion is applied,[2] but the form is a special case. Vars. 1, 2, 5, and 11 treat the theme and its ground, while the others utilize the ground alone as a basis for decoration. Byrd's *Galliard Jig* represents a similar hybrid genre in which alternating materials are subject to variation. No. 86 in Vallet's *Secretum Musarum,* book I, is still more similar to the present piece.[3] Called *Branle d'Irlande,* the piece consists of four eight-bar sections, the first two of which have the same bass and the second two of which depart in their first halves, returning each time to the original bass in the second half. Dart questioned Bull's authorship of *Country Dance* in the second edition.[4] There is indeed little in this piece to recommend its attribution to any composer of reasonable sophistication, yet the style may be intentionally simple. It resembles Alman F a good deal in its swinging rhythm, longer notes at the beginning of each bar tilting the motion forward, and in the pure use of note repetition as a means of ornamentation and activity. Furthermore, the noisy eighth-note alternation of tonic and dominant in vars. 6 and 8–9 is reminiscent of *The King's Hunt,* itself a special type of variation piece. Other pieces of simple conception are also ascribed to Bull, notably Grounds 1 and 2, *Les Buffons,* and several of the preludes. *Country Dance,* like these, may well have been written for an amateur player or student.

Thematic or minor structural features invite comparison of several pairs of these dances. Almans F and D2 both exhibit a technique encountered, if rarely, in Bull's pavans, that of varying the length of a strain in its repeat (see Pavan g3). Alman F does so by compressing the fifth and sixth bars of II into one bar, while Alman D2 expands the final bar into two. The result in the former case is to create an uneven strain decorating one of even length; in the latter the opposite occurs, yet the effect is not that of righting something wrong, but rather of balancing off the three-bar segment that began the strain. Alman D2 is anonymous in both its sources, *El* and *Mo,* but is adjacent in the former to Alman D1, a somewhat undistinguished piece ascribed there to Bull. Also lacking any ascription is the *Welsh Dance.* The existing versions of the piece are analogous to those of Coranto C1, the *Bu* text in both cases representing a shortened form. Here it appears to be tonal, not metrical, structure that the composer (or arranger) is concerned with, for the text of *Bu* avoids the tonic close of I found in *P1* and *ChCh 431* by simply trimming off the strain's final two bars. In addition to this feature, which is suggestive of an arrangement, the cross-relation in the last bar of II is unusual, a detail of the accompaniment that the composer may have taken over from tradition.

Tregian ascribed Alman G1 to Farnaby while the work appears as

Bull's in *El* and *Mo* (no ascription in *Bu*). Although there is no convincing argument against Tregian's attribution, the discreet patches of imitation, the lack of caesure in III and the piece's overall quality are more indicative of Bull. In addition, Alman G2, ascribed to Bull in *El*, contains a piece of melody like the one in the first strain of Alman G1 (Ex. 5-1). Though there is no reason why Bull should not have quoted from Farnaby (or Farnaby from Bull), he in fact quoted from himself from time to time as a way of reusing material and may be doing so here. Both these almans and Alman C share limping repeated-note figuration such as that in Galliard d6/II', and tinkering triadic fillers. Alman C, though found in *Tr* (anon) in the midst of pieces by Farnaby, appears to be Bull's by virtue of these casual resemblances as well as the more important seamless quality of strain II and the plainsong settinglike figuration at the opening of III.

Coranto g1 and the *Duchess of Brunswick's Toy* similarly employ identical melodic fragments (Ex. 5-2) but without quoting an entire phrase. The resemblance is probably coincidental in this case, for pieces by other composers also begin in this manner.[5] Coranto g1 is notable for a fine balance between melodic activity and the fast harmonic rhythm in strain I and a stasis in strain II which eventually gives way to the manner of the opening. Both strains are decorated in Bull's best taste. Dart suggested in his edition that the *Duchess of Brunswick's Toy* is given in a later version by *Tr* than by *Bu*, and conveniently printed both texts. His theory is difficult to support, for there is very little difference between the two. Tregian's one notable divergence, the octave displacements in the left-hand figuration of b, 13, is neither of necessity an improvement nor a

Ex. 5-1 Bull, Alman G1/I

Bull, Alman G2/II

revision. The note repetitions at the same pitch logically echo a similar passage in the second half of the first strain, and correspond to the right-hand figuration in the subsequent two bars.

The *Duke of Brunswick's Alman* complements the *Duchess's Toy;* as such the two may be though of as an alman-coranto pair. Like Pavan a2, in the same key, the piece leans heavily toward the sharp side of the mode (transposed dorian) and in the second strain even employs a similar motive. Repeated-note decoration again lends a personal touch to the piece, pushed to its extreme in a unique extra repeat of II. Cosyn apparently transposed the alman, with considerable corruptions, in order to fit it into his collection along with d-final pieces.[6]

Two further almans in the same mode are marked by gentle and lyrical melody, are periodic, and are motivic in conception. They, like the "French" Coranto C1, may be arrangements made by Bull. Completing the a-dorian pieces in *Bu* are an alman, *English Toy,* and coranto, *Dutch Dance.* The former is another instance of casual resemblance to a well-known melody; here the first two bars recollect the Spanish Pavan.[7]

Along with *Dutch Dance, What Care You?* and *Irish Toy* are found only in *Bu.* Beautifully flowing figuration, succinct use of imitation and expressively placed rests mark the *Toy* as assuredly Bull's. *What Care You?* also poses no particular problems of authorship, though the style is again that of the blunt, bumping alman. If the title can be taken as traditional, then this is the only known setting of the tune. It may, however, be a whimsical title such as those Bull gave to several pieces discussed below.

Of greatest interest among these works are several "signature" pieces, or self portraits, each of strong character and bearing a title which refers to the composer. In composing music effectively dedicated to himself,

Ex. 5-2   Bull, Coranto g1/III

Bull, *Duchess of Brunswick's Toy* I

Bull belies the virtuosity and adventuresome experiments of his early works and focuses on a more intimate and understated side of his complex nature. Two of these pieces, *My Grief* and *My Choice I Will not Change,* consist simply of two strains without decorated repeats. The latter speaks for itself without inviting comment; the former, however, displays a remarkable melodic design in its first strain built on descending thirds. The effect is one of tearful sweetness, balanced by the placid rocking motion of the second strain that owes its rhythm to the complex textures Bull had adopted in several of his plainsong settings.[8]

Bull's original version of *My Jewel* 1 is probably that in *Tr,* also transmitted in a slightly more refined text in *Co.* It was revised and shortened for *Bu,* then later used as the basis for the text in *Ant.* The idea of inserting a variation of strain III which quotes from "The Woods so Wild" may have occurred to Bull only after writing *My Jewel* 2, which uses the popular song in the second variation of its third strain. The special harmonic quality of the piece derives from a mixture of mixolydian and ionian modes implicit in the emphasis on B flat in the first and second strains as a contrast to tonic and dominant, and in the third strain as a leaning toward the subdominant. The cantus firmus-like treatment in the final strain allows for the song quote, an afterthought, but more importantly gives perfect testament to Bull's adherence to the archaic technique as a viable means of composition (as evidenced already by many other works). Melody and figuration are in perfect balance in *My Jewel* 1; no peculiar demands are made by the symmetrically constructed strains or by their calm and well-paced harmonic rhythm.

A more telling contrast can scarcely be imagined than that between the superb *My Jewel* 1 and the second setting from some ten years later and presumed to be Bull's. The work depends successively upon strict imitation (I and I'), constant eighth-note motion (II, II', III, III') or harmonized bicinim (III''). A ceaselessly busy texture detracts substantially from the beauty of the melody—certainly, at least, by comparison to the first setting—and gives the whole a feeling of an exercise in syncopated counterpoint and routine diminution. Judging from the relative quality of these two works, Bull had not yet resolved the crisis inherent in his transition from a keyboard style that valued decorum to one that was often satisfied with decoration alone.

6

Grounds and Variations

Instrumental music of the sixteenth and seventeenth centuries that in some way utilizes the techniques of variation may be thought of in three broad categories: pieces that employ fixed melodic elements, pieces that retain only a bass or harmonic ground, and those that are a hybrid of both types. In the following list and discussion grounds appear first, then the hybrid pieces (called here variation-grounds) and finally variations on given tunes. The last group is further divided into English and Continental settings.

Ground 1	*MB* 19:102a
Ground 2	19:102b
Les Buffons	19:101
A Battle and No Battle	19:108
The New Bergomask	19:124
The King's Hunt	19:125
Quadran Pavan 1 (Pavan G3)	19:127a
Quadran Pavan 2 (Pavan G4)	19:127b & c
Quadran Galliard (Galliard G4)	19:127d, e, & f
Why Ask You? 1	19:62
Why Ask You? 2	19:63
Spanish Pavan (Pavan g2)	19:76
Bonny Peg of Ramsey	19:75
Bonny Sweet Robin	19:65 and
	24:35 (*Tr* text)
Walsingham	19:85
Rosasolis	19:122 and
	24:47 (*Tr* text)
Go from My Window	19:123
Pavan and Galliard G1	19:126a & b
St. Thomas Wake''	
(Discussed in chapter 4)	

My Self	19:138
Bull's Goodnight	19:143
Den lustelijcken Meij	14:52
Een Kindeken is ons geboren 1	14:53
Een Kindeken is ons geboren 2	14:54
Een Kindeken is ons geboren 3	14:55
Laet ons met herten reijne	14:56
Revenant	19:100

Two treble grounds, Hexachord Fantasy 2 and *God Save the King,* have been considered in chapter 3 because of their greater affinity with the works discussed there. *Een kindeken* 3 and *Laet ons met herten reijne* are properly speaking not variations, for they state the tune only once; the former, however, contains an indication for a repeat of the whole piece, and both are best considered along with the other Dutch carols. One setting of "Why Ask You?" (*MB* 19:64) has been omitted for the reasons given on p. 193.

With four exceptions the numbering of variations and bars used here follows that of the printed edition (unless otherwise noted). The arrangement of the Quadran Pavans and Galliard and the misleading labeling of their sections, as well as those of *The King's Hunt,* necessitate a different system of reference, which is as follows:

Pavan G3:	b. 1–32	= Var. 1
	"Rep." (b. 33–64)	= Var. 2
	"2" (b. 65–80)	= Rep. 1
	"Rep." (b. 81–96)	= Rep. 2
	"3" (b. 97–128)	= Var. 3
	etc.	
Pavan G4:	The numbering of sections is analogous to that of Pavan G3 except that it continues without a break from *MB* 19:127b to c; therefore, *MB* 19:127c, b. 1–32 = Var. 3	
Galliard G4:	b. 1–16	= Var. 1
	"Rep." (b. 17–32)	= Var. 2
	"2" (b. 33–40)	= Rep. 1
	"Rep." (b. 41–48)	= Rep. 2
	b. 1–16 (*MB* 19:127e)	= Var. 3
	etc.	
The King's Hunt	b. 1–8	= Var. 1
	"Rep." (b. 9–16)	= Var. 2
	"2" (b. 17–24)	= Rep. 1
	"Rep." (b. 25–32)	= Rep. 2
	etc.	

Grounds

Two rudimentary efforts in ground composition are found in weak texts ascribed to Bull in the amateurish keyboard book RCM 2093. One wonders what Bull's purpose was in writing these pieces, characterized as they are by stiff figuration, paucity of ideas, and an absence of virtuosic elements. Yet, both contain elements that figure in authentic and perhaps later works. The RCM grounds appear to be didactic pieces, like the simple prelude (G1) in Suzanne van Soldt's book, and could have been written either by Bull or by a student who chose grounds that Bull used elsewhere.[1]

Grounds 1 and 2 are built respectively on the Bergamasca bass and a bass that may be related to the "Bel fiore."[2] In the latter the two halves of the eight-bar ground differ (unlike *The New Bergomask*), producing a chord of the dominant at the caesura. In both pieces the bass is inextricably allied with root-position harmonies which govern the melodic material above or below it. The procedure was usual for Bull, even in his most sophisticated grounds, and he took little interest in reharmonizing either grounds or tunes once a pattern was established. Nor was he moved to try placing the ground elsewhere than in the bass (the two treble grounds excepted) such as in Hugh Aston's *Hornepype,* where the roughly tenor placement of the ostinato allows for some melodic and harmonic flexibility.[3] But for a single doubling of the harmonic rhythm in b. 40 of Ground 1, no contrast is offered here, even where imitation, as in var. 8 of Ground 2, might have served as a natural catalyst for reharmonizing the bass.

A further feature of these grounds, also stock in trade for Bull, is the pairing of variations either in the manner of decorated repeats or by exchanging treble for bass divisions. Both can be seen in the anonymous Romanesca variations in the *Dublin Virginal Book.*[4] There, the melodic material of var. 1 is retraced and decorated in var. 2, and the treble divisions of var. 5 are further elaborated in var. 6. After a steady stream of sixteenths in the right hand of var. 7, the left hand takes over, as if to answer its predecessor, and forms a pair with it. Though successive decoration of a melodic design and reciprocal exchange of registers (obvious means of development and contrast) figure in all of Bull's grounds and variation sets, the latter technique is particularly indigenous to keyboard music. In this respect the lute offered relatively less and the viol consort relatively more flexibility. Byrd, with his background of consort composition, may highlight the middle as well as the outer parts of the texture in the course of keyboard variations. In Bull's case, on the other hand, it is almost always the polarities of the texture that are the focus of attention.

In Ground 1, vars. 2 and 3 build speed up to the continuous eighths of var. 4, all the while decorating the rising fourth connected with the bass in the first variation. Likewise, var. 2 of Ground 2 ornaments the opening melody; var. 3 then retreats to quarter motion and less slavish melodic invention before reaching steady eighths in var. 4. In both pieces, just as in the Dublin Romanesca variations, it is the attainment of continuous eighths, the fastest values, that brings on the exchange of registers. Thus the continuous eighths of Ground 1, var. 4, afford like material in the following variation, the divisions now in the bass. Another pair, based on parallel thirds and tenths, follows straight away. Eighths reappear as a passing feature of var. 8, whose material is subsequently varied in minor detail, then answered in var. 10. This group of three variations is rounded off with a single one which returns to the descending-third idea of vars. 6–7 and is followed by three more involving continuous eighths in the right hand, left hand, and right hand again. In Ground 2 the continuous eighths of var. 4 provoke the inversion of parts in var. 5, but single variations which follow offer more in details of contrast—tripla and imitation—than do the later ones of Ground 1. The simplicity of these pieces hardly invites close critical scrutiny; yet the pairing of variations and control of rate of motion, features belonging to the tradition into which Bull came, are important in both earlier and later stages of the composer's thinking.

Two further short grounds are found in *Ant. The New Bergomask* and *Les Buffons* are constructed on eight-bar (eight-semibreve) basses which, as in the RCM grounds, dictate root-position harmonies without exception. Though the pieces are admittedly more advanced in figuration than their counterparts in the English manuscript, they offer no more harmonic variety, engage no melodic techniques to counteract the implicit foursquare phraseology, and repeatedly employ blunt registral exchange as a means of contrast. Such features may have worked to disadvantage in *The New Bergomask* because of the ground's internal repetition had Bull not chosen highly contrasting and strongly profiled ideas for each variation. In all, a lightness and grace pervades the work, itself judiciously limited to eight variations. Still, the fact that the two halves of the ground are identical could have provided the opportunity to treat them differently. Such is the case in a contemporary lute setting of the same bass by Nicolas Vallet in his *Secretum Musarum,* (no. 24). Lacking the option of the facile registral exchange ubiquitous in keyboard variations, the composer instead introduced melodic variants to mitigate the repetition (Ex. 6-1).

In his "Note to the second edition," Dart doubts the authenticity of this work; yet typical features abound. The trilling figuration of var. 1 appears in Pavan and Galliard G1 as well as var. 4 of the Quadran Pa-

Ex. 6-1   Vallet, *Les Pantalons*, var. 9

Bull, *The New Bergomask,* var. 7

van 2; the limping repeated notes of var. 4. are found in Alman C and Galliard d6 among other pieces; and the Alberti-like pattern of var. 6 is extensively used in both *Miserere* 2 and var. 27 of *Walsingham.* Closing with a flourish in toccata style is also typical: indeed, the handling of scale-figurations there is the high point of the piece.

Les Buffons offers little more in harmonic or structural variety than does *The New Bergomask,* yet it indulges in a playful display of figuration that is in keeping with its title. The bass pattern has been identified with one called *antycke* (antic), equated with *buffon* (fool or clown).[5] The bass, which is nearly identical to the passamezzo moderno, also forms the ground to "John, Come Kiss Me Now," which Bull quotes in the third variation. Although the ground of *Les Buffons* is not a repeating one like *The New Bergomask,* the sounding of the tonic on the fifth bar followed by a chord of the subdominant, rhyming with the opening, was difficult for Bull to circumvent as an obvious point of articulation in the paragraph. Where the caesura is somewhat subverted, as in var. 8 and 15, the effect is a welcomed one, providing needed relief from the predictable blocks of four bars. Just twice in this piece does Bull juxtapose variations that are reciprocal: var. 5 is paired with var. 4 and var. 10 with var. 9. Other-wise, he separates variations that deal with the same notions: vars. 2 and 11, which treat the   motive, and vars. 6 and 13, based on broken sixths. This is one of the techniques that Bull found useful in *Walsingham*.

Another technique common to the two works is that of introducing imitation near the beginning of the piece, abandoning it, and finally re-turning to it near the end. The point of var. 3, derived from "John, Come Kiss Me Now," serves as little more than a reference to the source of the ground, and is subjected to no further variation. Toward the end of the piece, however, the rattling sixteenths are arrested, and var. 14 ushers in a smooth, scalewise point for imitation followed by a quasi-imitative opening of the next variation in even slower values. The return to both slower values and imitative textures before a closing flourish reflects a concern for framing, or rounding off, a series of possibly disparate events that are tied together only by their common harmonic progression. In *Les Buffons*, as in *God Save the King* (Ex. 6-2) and to a certain extent in Hexachord Fantasy 2, imitation justifies the slower motion which in turn halts forward momentum, dampening the expectation of repetition. The technique provided a way of making an effective conclusion in what was, somewhat paradoxically, one of the most open-ended of all sixteenth cen-tury forms.

The broken figuration of var. 13 can be found in other works of Bull, such as *Walsingham* (var. 16) and *Miserere* 1 (b. 60), where it is liberally mixed with other figurations. The pure form in which it is used in *Les Buffons* resembles still more closely passages in Sweelinck's music (Ex. 6–3). Yet it seems unlikely that Bull would have composed *Les Buffons* (or *The New Bergomask*, also in the same source) during his Continental period, after the awesome Quadran variations. Such a straightforward use of the figuration as appears in Sweelinck's toccata which Tregian copied

Ex. 6-2   Bull, *God Save the King*, b. 121-

Bull, *Les Buffons*, var. 14

into his anthology (Ex. 6-3) suggests rather that its use on the Continent may have been recognized in England even before Bull left the country.

The largest of these compositions on a single bass ground, *A Battle and no Battle,* is a descriptive work in the tradition of Continental battle and hunt pieces. Though unascribed in its source, *Bu,* occasional trilling figuration (as in the Galliard "St. Thomas Wake"), continuous eighth-note motion in two voices in several variations (as in the Spanish Pavan), and an energetic thrust to the whole suggest that it is both an authentic and a youthful work. It could even have been kindled by Byrd's composition in the genre, *The Battle,* which appears already in Nevell.[6] But Byrd's work is a medley, not a ground, and describes a victory rather than a retreat. These fundamental differences engender two significant features of the composition, both designed to give shape to continuous variations: unusually extensive use of imitation for a light-weight composition, and concentration of the fastest motion in the middle of the piece rather than towards the end.

Bull plans to build urgency in the first half by beginning with motion dominated by quarters but energized with imitation (as in vars. 2, 3, 6, 7, and 8, where the point is in stretto at a minim). Faster motion gradually supplants the need for imitation, and the rapid-fire repeated notes and chords so typical of the genre take over. The tripla change just before the

Ex. 6-3 Sweelinck, Toccata in a, b. 92- (*SK* 1:16)

Bull, *Les Buffons,* var. 13

Sweelink, *Onder een linde groen,* var. 4, b. 31- (*SK* 3:8)

midpoint (var. 17) occurs here, as elsewhere, in conjunction with a slight retreat of motion before picking up again for the climax in vars. 18–19. The second half of the piece then works still harder the *stile concitato*— one might say that it is worked to death—until the quarter note motion that opened the piece returns. Then still slower are the knell and conclusion, interrupted by the bells. The piece is in some way a contest, not only between opposing forces on the field, but between the mesmerizing ground and ever-renewing animation of the accompanying figuration. When an idea has not been exhausted, Bull inverts the texture in familiar fashion to further utilize it (var. 14–15). When an idea holds little more interest, he varies it slightly (vars. 8–10) and even once introduces a counter-metrical pattern for added life (var. 20: see Ex. 6-4).

Neighbour surmises that Bull's first Quadran Pavan and Galliard date from the 1580s, following Morley's and preceding Byrd's variations on the popular ground.[7] Neighbour's chronology, based on musical evidence, looks to the Quadran variations of Morley and Bull as the intervening influence between Byrd's Passing Measures and Quadran variations that accounts for a new impetus in the latter ground (see Ex. 6-5a). Connections among these works cited by Neighbour and the present author are shown in Ex. 6-5.[8]

Certainly Bull's work is a youthful one and if, as it seems, the composer pruned and revised the pavan(s) for a definitive version in *Bu*, then he must have had the distance of some years on it when the collection

Ex. 6-4   Bull, *A Battle and No Battle,* var. 20

Ex. 6-5a   Morley, Quadran Pavan, rep. 3; Bull, Quadran Pavan 1 (G3), var. 2

Byrd, Quadran Pavan, var. 3

was compiled. The situation may be outlined as follows: Bull initially composed a pavan consisting of four variations on the main ground (A) and four on the reprise (B) grouped, as was usual for settings of the passamezzo moderno, according to the strain–plus–decorated repeat plan of freely composed pavans. The initial pavan, then, took the form of A, A', B, B', A'', A''', B'', B''', the last section ending with tripla and a one-bar tonic extension. To this was added a further set of four variations each on the main ground and reprise, set out in the same way and occupying the same space as the first set. (This has been separated into two pieces, 127b and c, in *MB*.) The galliard was also composed in the alternating scheme for a total of six variations each on the main ground and reprise, viz. A, A', B, B', A'', A''', B'', B''', A'''', A''''', B'''', B''''' (separated into three pieces in *MB*.) Only in *Tr* do both pavans appear, while the second alone is found in *Bu, Co, D2,* and *Fo*. The structure of the galliard is identical in all three of its sources (*Tr, Bu, Co*). An obvious explanation for the situation is that Bull first composed Pavan G3, then G4 later, and both were picked up by Tregian. Such is Neighbour's conclusion, based on evidence that Byrd drew only upon Bull's first pavan and the galliard rather than upon his second pavan in making his own pair. Two factors, however, propose that Pavan G4 was composed only a short while after Pavan G3. The first is the matter of content. As Ex. 6-5b and c show, Bull uses Morley's first variation at the outset of both pavans, and quotes a figure in the second which he had not used in the first. While

Bull could have been thinking in terms of revision in the former instance, it is unlikely that he would have gone all the way back to Morley for the latter figure if much time had elapsed since making his first setting—particularly if Byrd's own Quadran Pavan had been composed in the meantime. The second factor concerns the texts of Pavan G4. The large number of variants in *Tr* (and the other sources) appear not to be corruptions, but earlier versions, and imply that the piece was not new at the time *Bu* was compiled, but was being revised and improved.

The quality of his first pavan must have struck Bull as inferior when he later reviewed his work. He may have found himself impatient with the time it takes the piece to get into motion: steady sixteenths appear for the first time in rep. 2, whereas they are underway by var. 2 of the second pavan. He may also have found the slower-moving beginning wanting in either melodic richness or variety of figuration. Once the piece is in midstream, it experiences some problems of motivation and direction. The right-hand decoration of rep. 2 soon becomes repetitive; and when it is answered in the following section by similar motion in the left hand, Bull seeks to fill the void by eventually reengaging the right hand. Still, the rather long passage of sixteenths in both hands loses to aimlessness what it gains in virtuosity. Perhaps Bull also saw that the figures he chose for imitative or quasi-imitative treatment were cut from too square a mold. That of var. 4 remains locked into the semibreve until a new motive, not a variant of the old one, releases it. The second pavan is not entirely free of faltering moments, occasionally weak melodic designs, and ineffectual imitation, yet the faster overall rate of movement and lavish attention to detail, with its resulting luxuriant textures, take over the scene. Continuity is improved through the flow of one idea to another, activity is increased, and nothing is sacrificed to variety. Here, Bull must have realized, was his forte. If a choice was to be made, it was the first pavan that he would forego.

While Bull reveals the source of some of his ideas by reference to Morley's pavan, he elaborates them much more fully. In var. 1 of the first pavan, Bull puts Morley's opening material to concise use, introducing a repetition of the high note from which the descent begins in order to create a motive suitable for imitation. When Bull reuses the idea at the opening of the second pavan, he takes Morley's material more literally, retaining the characteristic interval of the sixth (Ex. 6-5b), but again makes it work more motivically than in his model. In var. 4 of the second pavan, Bull takes what was a passing idea—one which Morley returned to in a varied form in his rep. 5—and again works it through motivically, in the service of a lightly imitative texture. Imitation, in fact, is much more important in Bull's pavan than in Morley's, a surprising state of

Ex. 6-5b   Morley, Quadran Pavan, var. 1

Bull, Quadran Pavan 1 (G3), var. 1

Bull, Quadran Pavan 2 (G4), var. 1

Ex. 6-5c   Morley, Quadran Pavan, var. 4

Bull, Quadran Pavan 2 (G4), var. 2

affairs in view of the individual biases of the two men. Morley consistently embarks upon a point and quickly abandons it for decorated homophony. Bull regularly insists upon pursuing his ideas further, even if they may not always support extensive development; and in this respect Bull's work may be regarded as an attempt to perfect what Morley had begun. With the exception of the opening variations of the two pavans, most of the imitative counterpoint serves to elaborate the harmony through close imitation of a melodically neutral but rhythmically acute motive. This practice, rooted in cantus firmus setting, sets Bull's variations apart from Byrd's, which alternate imitation of a more purely melodic type—except where he appears to be drawing on Bull's vocabulary (Ex. 6-5d)—with figuration in one hand accompanied by plain chords in the other. Given a proclivity for melodic rather than rhythmic counterpoint, Bull might have eventually rethought his approach after Byrd's. Instead, he touched up the better of his pavans here and there and, as if in response to Byrd's dense variations, added imitative involvement where passive filler-figuration had existed (Ex. 6-6).

Bull let his galliard stand as it was. The extensive figuration in parallel thirds and sixths of vars. 3 and 4 may have seemed a bit old-fashioned, yet the closely paced imitations that prevail in the first two variations and reprises (Ex. 6-5e) complement well those of the pavan, and the conciseness of the whole—in part a natural consequent of working in shorter periods—is a satisfactory sequel to it. In the second pair of reprises the texture thins considerably and a rhythmic feature of the bass emerges more clearly than previously. Bull sets the first two notes of the reprise in the galliard as a hemiola, a detail which Byrd may have taken from him; it appears at the very surface of the music in rep. 1 of the older composer's galliard (Ex. 6-5f) in the first of a series of harmonizations that seem to cast a critical glance in Bull's direction. A further connection between the two composers' works appears in the third set of variations and reprises of Bull's galliard. Here the hemiola makes its impact on the main ground through a figure occupying two dotted minims that dances above the bass (Ex. 6-5g). Bull carries this on for the entire variation and derives from the four-eighths figure a texture of daunting density for the following variation and reprise. Byrd, without using tripla, takes Bull on and chooses not to use the motive in the service of hemiola, but rather to exploit an ambiguity inherent in it. First stated in an upbeat context in the treble, it is answered in the bass in a downbeat context, reversing the syntactical function of the rhythm in a manner certainly not unfamiliar to Bull (cf. Galliard a2/I' and several of the In Nomines). Byrd is amused for half a variation with the ambiguity, then goes on to normalize the rhythm. Bull, on the contrary, after sailing breathlessly through the fol-

Ex. 6-5d   Bull, Quadran Pavan 1 (G3), var. 4

Byrd, Quadran Pavan, rep. 1

Ex. 6-5e   Bull, Quadran Galliard, rep. 1

Byrd, Quadran Galliard, rep. 3

Ex. 6-5f   Bull, Quadran Galliard, rep. 3

Bull, Quadran Galliard, rep. 1

Ex. 6-5g   Bull, Quadran Galliard, var. 5

Byrd, Quadran Galliard, var. 4

Ex. 6-6   Bull, Quadran Pavan 2 (G4), var. 2

Bu

other sources:

lowing sixth variation and fifth reprise in relentless eighths, presses further
toward the edge of rhythmic dissolution in the sixth reprise with a right-
hand figure that cycles eight times in six beats (Ex. 6-7). The suspense of
momentary disorientation does not bear repetition, and the four-eighths
group alone is retained in the ensuing passagework as a means of contra-
dicting the metrical norm. Byrd chose not to develop the motive in this
manner, probably partly because he had earlier explored a different
rhythmic ambiguity and partly because such small-scale metrical asperities, routine in earlier plainsong settings and a feature of variation as early
as the *Chi passa* in *DVB,* did not appeal to him. Byrd selectively drew on
Bull for details in composing his Quadran Pavan and Galliard, but there
are signs that it was as much the spirit as the letter of Bull's work that
inspired Byrd. Byrd's pavan is marked by an unusually extensive use of

sixteenth-note movement, unprecedented polyphonic density and a continuity through figuration at cadences that is seldom found in his music. Bull's response was not to return the compliment and answer what criticism may have been implied, as he did in writing Pavan and Galliard G2 for *Parthenia,* but was rather to further refine his original statement.

Ex. 6-7   Bull, Quadran Galliard, rep. 6 (*Bu*)

Ex. 6-8   Bull, Quadran Pavan 1 (G4), final bars (*Bu*)

Two matters of text should be noted. The first concerns the penultimate bar of Pavan G4. *MB* gives the reading of *Tr,* while the still more beautiful one of *Bu* and *Co* is nowhere noted (Ex. 6-8). The first two bars of rep. 6 of the galliard are also made to read like *Tr,* with a justification in the critical note: "no ties in any source, but the cross-rhythm requires them." The corresponding place in the preceding reprise may indeed by an omission and the tie should be considered optional there. In rep. 6, however, it is likely that the composer did intend that the chord be repeated on the downbeat of the second bar in order to preserve a strong first beat against the cross-rhythms and hemiola. The passage as it appears in *Bu* is given in Ex. 6-7. Finally, the division of the pavans and the galliard into three parts each in the edition is misleading to performers. Clearly, there is only one galliard, not three, and the second pavan is one piece rather than two.

Variation-Grounds

The designation "variations" is generally taken to mean a work consisting of a series of sections that subject a given theme to decoration and alteration. In contrast to this type of composition are grounds, or pieces based on a repeating pattern of notes usually in the bass but often in the treble or elsewhere, as in Hugh Aston's *Hornepype*. Bass grounds, furthermore, were more often than not associated with a specific harmonic pattern. Bull's grounds, as noted, are no exception to this tradition. In the sixteenth and seventeenth centuries the distinction between ground and variation was not always a sharp one, and bass patterns were sometimes identified by the melodies which had come to be attached to them.[9] For example, in Playford's *Brief Introduction to the Skill of Music* (1672), a version of the passamezzo moderno bass is identified as "The Ground of John, come kiss."[10] As a corollary of this situation, variations of popular melodies may be reliant as much upon the ground as upon the tune itself. A set of variations on "Malt's come down" in *Tr* (no. [150]) abandons the tune after no more than two variations and proceeds with divisions upon the ground, which is itself a type of passamezzo moderno bass.[11] In cases such as this it may be the melody that is ostensibly the subject of variation; but in the absence of any clear reference to it, the bass/harmonic pattern is the constant. Byrd also follows this practice, as in his *Woods so Wild*. Conversely, divisions upon a ground may quote all or part of an associated

Ex. 6-9   Bull, Spanish Pavan (g2), var. 8

discant melody in the course of the work; Bull does this in *Les Buffons*. It is the former ambiguity that is found in three of Bull's works, the Spanish Pavan, *Bonny Peg of Ramsey,* and *Why Ask You?* 1.

The Spanish Pavan is a harmonic pattern to which melodies came to be attached.[12] Though no two known discants are identical, that of Bull's first variation appears to belong to the Anglo-Dutch type characterized by a note-repetition in the second (semibreve) bar.[13] This feature is preserved in the second variation but disappears thereafter, except for references to it by octave displacement in the two bars of the final variation which quote from the first (see Ex. 6-9). As the eighth-note divisions become more constant after the first variation, the contours of the original melody are gradually obscured until they are virtually absent in the fourth variation. Thereafter, a semblance of melodic variation resurfaces through reiteration of the basic descending shape of the opening melody.

Within a frame of two variations ruled by quarter-note motion, Bull proceeds according to what must have been a fixed plan. A second variation which mixes quarters and eighths is followed by the first of three in constant eighths. Divisions in the right hand and left hand are eventually combined in the fifth variation, resulting in a texture which appears to be from the 1580s (see Ex. 6-10 and p. 122). Rather than surrounding this variation with right-hand and left-hand divisions, as Philips did, Bull typically exchanges one for the other before combining them. Like Philips, however, he follows with a section in tripla, but predictably repeats the process of exchanging left-hand for right-hand decoration rather than going on to another texture. What Bull ignores here is the harmonized bicinium treatment of Philips's fifth variation, which he evidently thought more suitable for works in which some rhythmic flexibility was needed to offset the monorhythmic quality of a cantus firmus. In Hexachord Fantasy 2 and *God Save the King* Bull uses the virtuosic bicinium as a means of small-scale variety where little or no rhythmic definition was otherwise implied. Such is not the case here. When two-part or quasi two-part (harmonized bicinium) textures are used in the course of non-cantus firmus variations, such as Galliard G1 or *Go from My Window,* the movement of the free voice is more continuous, less inclined toward cellular organization and its attendant rhythmic articulations. Bull's return to note-against-note homophony in the final variation rounds off the piece in the style of the first variation, a well-worn structural principle for him, rather than introducing a new element as Philips did.

The Spanish Pavan is a work of considerable reserve, avoiding usual virtuosic figurations and tight, decorative, or motoric devices. The piece has a serious, carefully paced air which suggests Bull may have been imitating Philips (whose music is by nature rather severe by comparison to Bull's). The figurations conform neatly to the semibreve, and the early strumming filler figures in the left hand crop up more frequently than in other of Bull's works. Both features, along with a certain relationship to the Philips piece dated 1592 by Tregian, point toward the early 1590s at the latest. It was one of the early works excluded from *Bu,* while *Bonny Peg of Ramsey,* whose style belongs to about the same period, was included. Metrically confined divisions and trilling figurations in var. 8 indicate an early date for the piece, which may have been included for retrospective purposes. The Spanish Pavan was perhaps rejected for its length or its unusual sobriety. More than one type of tune is again associated with the ground of *Bonny Peg of Ramsey,* but that used by Bull is found in no other source.[14] He manages to retain the repeated g' of the third bar and/or the b'-flat—c'' ascent at the end of the tune in each variation, while casting off much of the rest of the original with the freedom allowed him by the constant bass/harmony. The approach to variation, though again schematic, involves no simultaneous activity in both

Ex. 6-10   Philips, Passamezzo Pavan, var. 4 (*FVB* no. 76, dated 1592)

Byrd, Hugh Aston's Ground, var. 10 (Nevell, 1591)

Bull, The Spanish Pavan (g2), var. 5

hands, probably because of the wide spacing involved with the low-lying bass. In place of tripla, Bull opts for increasing the motion up to the sixteenth, as in *The New Bergomask*, but ends somewhat abruptly without a flourish.

Three sets of variations called *Why Ask You* are based on an unidentified tune and its associated bass. The first half of the tune bears some resemblance to one called "Wanton Season" found anonymously in BL Add. MS 30486 in a keyboard setting and set for lute by Anthony Holborne in CUL, Dd. ix. 33 (Ex. 6-11).[15] The longest and substantially the best of the three settings is the one found in *Bu*.[16] After the initial opening variation, accompanied by plain chords that are sometimes broken with the typical strumming figure, a second variation admits right-hand, then left-hand activity. The process of repeating information already given in accordance with internal repetition of the bass continues in an exercise in thirds, then in an imitative texture in the fourth variation. Where this symmetrical response had been weakening in *The New Bergomask*, it has no such effect here, for Bull's repetitions are never literal and the ideas themselves are unmechanical. In the fourth variation, Bull breaks into a quasi-imitative homophony identical to that in var. 2 of the Quadran Galliard (Ex. 6-12). Metrical ambiguity, again similar to that in the Quadran Galliard (Ex. 6-13) enlivens the tripla, which in due course reworks the fourth variation by reinstating quarter motion.[17] The set is rounded off, exactly as in the Spanish Pavan, by a return to common time with a new discant to the bass. Again, the role of the melody here is to establish certain melodic goals and points of departure and occasionally, as in var. 4, to serve as the source for quotation; the role of the bass/harmony, on the other hand, is that of governing the whole.

Why Ask You? 2 is unascribed in *D2* but given to Bull in its other source, *We*. It is a typical smaller-scaled composition that shows, by reference to the *Bu* setting, the same contrast in approach that can be seen in a comparison of *Bonny Peg of Ramsey* with the Spanish Pavan: unmitigated increase in motion up to the end versus acceleration to the tripla followed by a capitulation to quarters. The third setting appears to be spurious. The absence of decorated repeats in all but the sixth variation is anomalous, as is the exceptionally stodgy figuration and lack of participation of the left hand in the activity of the right. Unlike the other two sets, a third (*MB* 19:64) at one point, var. 5, bluntly decorates the original tune; the following variation looks suspiciously like a plagiarism of var. 2 of the second variation set. This apparent misattribution is likely the doing of the scribe, who mistakenly attributed another setting (immediately preceding this one in *P1*) and identified in *Co* as Cosyn's.

Variations

The two most important composers for keyboard in England at the end of the sixteenth century left not only rival settings of the passamezzo moderno but also large variation sets on the "Walsingham" tune.[18] Neighbour has dated Byrd's *Walsingham* from "toward the end of the 1570s", or from around the same time as his consort variations, *Browning*.[19] Bull's variations owe little to Byrd's yet must have been written a decade or more later, given the style of his pieces which appear to date from the 1580s and the advances over them achieved in *Walsingham*. Ward noted in his *Lives*: "This tune, which begins, 'As I went to Walsingham,' was first composed by William Birde, with twenty-two variations; and afterwards thirty others were added to it, at different times, by Dr. Bull."[20] Ward does not give the source of his information, and the statement is likely to have been speculation on his or Pepusch's part; yet the sequence, corroborated by Neighbour's dating of Byrd's *Walsingham,* seems right.

In Neighbour's discussion he points out that Byrd's plan for the set

Ex. 6-11   *Why Ask You?* (treble and bass reduction)

Wanton Season, Add. MS 30486 (treble and bass)

Ex. 6-12   Bull, *Why Ask You?* 1, var. 4

Bull, Quadran Galliard, var. 2

Ex. 6-13   Bull, *Why Ask You?* 1, var. 5

Bull, Quadran Galliard, var. 5

was based, like that of *Browning,* on groups of variations. An original conception of four groups of five variations was eventually altered by the insertion of two extra ones in the middle of the piece, upsetting the symmetry by giving a false start to the increase in rate of motion that in part determines each group. Bull adopted a similar plan on a broader scale, yet rejected the other determining factor of Byrd's groups, that of rotating the melody from part to part. In the framing groups of Byrd's set, the melody moves from part to part between variations, changes octave for a note here and there within variations, and even appears to change parts in the course of a phrase as a consequence of the broken keyboard style. Assuming that Bull had the occasion to know Byrd's variations before writing his own, he must have decided against the procedure. For Byrd, it was part and parcel of his experience as a composer of consort variations; Bull had evidently had little or no such experience. The lesson of one early piece with a migrating cantus firmus, *Miserere* 1, had perhaps not proven sufficiently fruitful in his eyes to bear further exploration.

The two composers' variation sets typically find them at opposite ends on a continuum which at one extreme is concerned with broad musical criteria and at the other with display and invention. For Byrd several factors—among them the placement of the melody, density of imitation, and registral color—play a part alongside that of rate of motion in regulating the form. For Bull it is primarily the desire to create a mosaic of figurations within a scheme of variation groups controlled by increasing motion that sets the sequence of events. Such priorities clearly stemmed as much from his experience in plainsong setting as from his observation of Byrd's variations. The resulting plan was one consisting of groups of nine, ten and eleven variations, the middle group divided symmetrically, the outer ones in subgroups of four plus five and five plus six, respectively.

The first four variations are marked by the most active counterpoint and densest textures of the set, clearing the way for the more important exercises in figuration to follow. To this end Bull lunges into four full parts in the second variation after a slightly thinner initial statement that acknowledges Byrd with the single-voice opening phrase. Byrd, who is as anxious to pace the stages of his four-part polyphony as Bull is to dispense with such textures, delays completion until the third variation. Only twice more in the course of the work does Bull return to polyphonically involved variations; at the end of the second third of the piece, in vars. 18 and 19, he relieves the driving sixteenths momentarily, then for a whole variation in preparation for the change of motion at the tripla which begins in var. 20; in var. 30 he finishes with a typical return to the opening texture and rate of movement. After steady eighths have been well established in vars. 3 and 4, Bull retreats to slower values, as he would do from time to time in marking off the stages of the work. Var. 5, a reworking of the second variation with the inner parts inverted and slightly altered (Ex. 6-14), offers a feeling of new beginning both by a reinstatement of quarter note motion and by reference to counterpoints heard earlier in the piece. Here is also heard the first of two minor melodic variants, an arch through g'' in the fifth bar. Bull states his next goal in var. 6, combining it with new melodic initiative in the third-fourth bars, but without involving the sixteenths in anything more substantial than trilling figuration. Rather, he insists in such a large-scale work on proceeding patiently again in the following variation through eighths, this time leaping eighths, before finally admitting sixteenths at full tilt. A pair of variations involving respectively right-hand and left-hand divisions (the second restoring the original form of the tune) predictably mark the definitive arrival of the established goal of rhythmic rate.

Var. 10 again steps back before releasing the motion that will carry the middle of the piece. Here Bull's mosaic begins to unfold: var. 11 recalls the character of var. 9, while var. 15 will in turn intensify that of var. 11. Var. 13 provides some lightness in the midst of the churning textures by referring back to the events of var. 6. The triadic figuration in both hands from the first half of var. 12 is the consequent of broken triads in the left hand of var. 9, but its second half, marked by the upward-rushing ♪♪♪♪♪ figure, anticipates a fuller development in var. 14 where the figure appropriately reaches for a'' in response to the g'' of the fifth bar (heard also in vars. 7, 8, 9, and 12). The midpoint of this central section is marked by a further stepping up of density through involvement of a third voice. Up to this point the highly figured variations could all be easily reduced to melody plus divisions. Now, however, the alto is in-

Ex. 6-14   Bull, *Walsingham,* var. 2

Ibid., var. 5

volved, in the manner of a three-voice plainsong setting with running bass
(Ex. 6-15). Subsequent variations likewise catalogue figurations familiar
from elsewhere in Bull's music, such as the broken sixths of var. 16 (c.f.
Ex. 6-3) and the zig-zag figure in vars. 17–18 (Ex. 6-16).

A change of pace offered by the mixed values of var. 19 and its
particularly strong emphasis on a'' open the way for the first of the tripla
variations, placed at the two-thirds point in the work, about where Byrd
had placed his. In Byrd's variations, the tripla form part of an increase
of speed from vars. 13–17, for sixteenths play no major part in the rate

Ex. 6-15   Bull, *Walsingham,* var. 15

Bull, *Miserere* 1, var. 2

Bull, *The King's Hunt,* rep. 6

Ex. 6-16   Bull, *Walsingham,* var. 17

Bull, *Miserere* 1, var. 2

of motion in his composition. In Bull's variations, however, the first tripla variation marks the beginning of the final drive of the work, one which will reach still higher levels of activity. The two composers are remarkably similar in their tripla settings, derived from instances of mixed meter in earlier organ and consort music (Ex. 6-17). Yet Bull abandons the two-against-three more quickly and engages a favorite rocking figure which sails eventually into the subdivided tripla of vars. 22–24. Here is the climax of the work: constant divisions of 12 to the minim stretching over three full variations in right hand, left hand, and right again, with repeated melodic arrivals on a" rather than a'. The settling effect rendered by the tinkering var. 25 is similar in quality and origin to that of var. 10, which follows the first two consecutive variations of continuous sixteenths. Bull has four more ideas to display before drawing his conclusion: an extension in var. 26 of the texture of var. 15, comparable to that of his In Nomine a6 (Ex. 6-18), the Alberti-like pattern of var. 27, crossed hands and repeated-note figuration in vars. 28–29. In spite of its slower motion, the final variation maintains intensity, rather than relaxing the forward drive, by focusing on a hitherto ignored element of composition. Bull has through-out retained essentially the same harmonization of the tune and a constant rate of harmonic change. By a return to the contrapuntal involvement of the earlier variations, Bull doubles and even quadruples the harmonic rhythm, effectively building a crescendo into the excitement rather than dissolving it into pure melody and predictably paced harmony.

If Bull's *Walsingham* is seen as a rival to Byrd's, it will be accorded only partial success, for the older master accommodated elements of variety—particularly as regard melodic placement and harmony—that are lacking in the younger's work. Also, figuration remains in finer balance with imitation in the shorter set. Bull's variations may best be regarded as a complement to those of Byrd. In them are displayed at once Bull's preference for a conservative approach to variation and his rich creativity for the keyboard.

On a much smaller scale and probably dating from some years after *Walsingham* is an appealing variation set, *The King's Hunt*. Like the Quadran variations, Bull's descriptive piece is organized as a set of double variations in the form A, A', B, B', A", A''', etc., each strain consisting of two four-bar phrases. A slow harmonic rhythm allows for a maximum of flexibility in elaboration, yet Bull still chooses in each variation to retain the melody, decorated or undecorated, as if to elicit a mood of jovial simplicity. All imitation is banned, unlike *A Battle and no Battle,* for it is the ear, not the mind, that the composer wishes to delight.

Off-beat chords, broken octaves, and rapid-fire repeated notes are stock in trade of the genre, yet a feature in each strain of the present

Ex. 6-17 Bull, *Walsingham*, var. 20

Byrd, *Walsingham*, var. 16

Ex. 6-18 Bull, *Walsingham*, var. 26

Bull, In Nomine a6

piece provided Bull special opportunities for exploiting them. The octave-echo of the first strain is first ornamented (var. 1), then accompanied by a corresponding octave displacement in the left hand (var. 3 and 4), decorated differently at statement and echo (var. 5), and finally becomes part of an uninterrupted descent in the accompanying voice (var. 6). Still more interesting is Bull's treatment of the second strain, which is devised so that the harmonic rhythm counters the symmetrical structure of the strain itself. Three bars of subdominant followed by three bars of dominant help to undercut the predictable caesura at b. 4–5 and provide long pedals for the vivid trumpetlike accompaniment first heard in rep. 1, then elaborated in reps. 2 and 3 in a texture that is found as early as *The Crocke* in Roy. App. 58 (Ex. 6-19). It comes as no surprise that the last word on this material is the same texture found in many cantus firmus settings, a playfully disjunct bass against a slower melodic voice with an inner line of intermediate motion (see, for example, Ex. 6-15).

Two further variation sets, both apparently postdating *Walsingham*,

Ex. 6-19   Anon., *The Crocke,* Roy. App. 58

Bull, *The King's Hunt,* rep. 3

show the two sides of Bull's thinking about variation principles that must have emerged by the time he had tried some of his own and studied some of Byrd's. In *Go from My Window* the melody rotates from part to part both between and within variations—in the manner of Byrd—and the figuration accompanying each variation unfolds freely, with little visible motivic organization.[21] In *Bull's Goodnight,* by several indications also a relatively late English work, Bull sticks to his former norm of retaining the melody in the cantus and adopting one specific type of figuration to do duty in each variation.

As in the early Spanish Pavan and elsewhere, Bull builds a frame for his variations on *Go from My Window* out of two statements dominated by slower movement, the latter providing a new discant to both bass and melody which appears in all three octave registers. It is perhaps this displacement of the melody from the top of the texture (which takes place in the second, fourth, and sixth variations) that led Bull to return to the plan of variation pairs, a procedure he had only occasionally used in Walsingham and which seems to disappear almost entirely in *Bull's Goodnight.* It must have seemed natural to fall back on a proven device in the interest of structural cogency when trying something new in another realm of the composition. Thus, within the framing variation, two move in eighths and two in sixteenths, the second of each pair replacing left-hand for right-hand divisions. The trade-off is a straightforward one in the case of var. 4, where the melody is unambiguously in the tenor. In var. 2, however, the tenor seems to begin each phrase, but it is the descent of the right hand at the close of the phrase that brings the melody to rest. In Bull's final variation tenor and bass trade off, then the cantus pipes in briefly before returning the tune to the tenor.

Such flexible treatment can be seen as a corollary of the priority accorded figuration. However, the singular freedom in Bull's handling of the melody and the supple polyphony of the last variation appear to betray as well a consideration of Byrd's methods. Whether Byrd's variation set did in fact precede Bull's is not explicit, for Byrd had used migrating melodies as early as *The Maiden's Song.* Bull, while now willing to try something he hadn't risked in *Walsingham* and earlier works, still opted for decoration (rather than imitation) and for harmonic repetitions (rather than variety) as underlying principles. Only once does Bull give an alternative to the standard harmonization of the tune: in the first variation the A which begins the second verse is harmonized with a chord of F major. Byrd, by contrast, uses chords of both d and a minor at that point in the tune, and closes the verse with D major as well as the usual A major. As much as Bull may have felt himself straying from his normal way of doing things in *Go from My Window,* harmonic experimentation was yet too far afield, a curious attitude for a composer sometimes intensely interested in harmonic color.

Bull's Goodnight is presumably based on a simple quatrain of the composer's invention. As in *Go from My Window,* the harmonization is rigid, but here Bull makes no effort to move the melody about. Instead, it adheres to the top voice, decorated to a greater or lesser extent, but returns from time to time to its original quarters when decoration begins to obscure the contours. Such is the alternative to passing the melody to another voice when the decorated line waxes elaborate. The figuration can then move fluidly from one part of the texture to the other, obviating the schematic alternation of bass and treble that tended to split variations down the middle, as in *The New Bergomask,* or pair them together, as in *Go from My Window* (and elsewhere). This manner of composing variations, which seems to be characteristic of Bull's English maturity, can also be found in other "signature" works which depend upon variation principles, *My Self* and *My Jewel.* In addition to balancing the roles of melody and figuration in *Bull's Goodnight,* the composer also finds the right amount of counterpoint to motivate the variations in which pure figuration does not yet take over—counterpoint that is only as imitative as it needs to be, never asserting its own self-importance to the detriment of the melody. Finally, Bull is poised in his *Goodnight* somewhere between the polarities of ever-increasing motion and cycles of increasing motion punctuated by periodic retreats. Thus his tripla variations change the quality of the motion, in fact slowing it down a bit by reference to the preceding sixteenths, but are not succeeded by either further increases, which usually included a toccatalike flourish, or by an imitative variation in striding motion. The composer seems to have sensed that the simplicity of the material here demanded no such dramatic handling.

Equally refined is Bull's *My Self,* a tune of three strains, the outer ones decorated, followed by one variation. The supertonic cadence in the second phrase of the first strain, a common feature of popular tunes like "Go from My Window," and the fact of a setting with the same title by Cosyn in his virginal book point toward the possibility that the melody was traditional and not necessarily of Bull's own invention. It remains otherwise unidentified, however, and the setting is wholly characteristic of Bull's maturity as represented in other "signature" pieces, *My Jewel* 1 and his *Goodnight.* One of Bull's most thoroughly relaxed works, *My Self* neither attempts to compensate with cleverness for the lack of variety in placement or harmonization of the tune nor forces virtuosity and imitation for the sake of interest. The figurations of the variations grow naturally out of the slight increase in speed that marks the decorated repeats of the first half of the piece, and pass with remarkable grace from hand to hand.

The one patch of imitation, at the beginning of the third strain of the variation, is a spontaneous consequence of the figuration itself and dissolves as easily as it coalesced.

From the conflicting ascriptions in their sources, it appears that Giles Farnaby had a hand in two variation sets, *Bonny Sweet Robin*[22] and *Rosasolis*.[23] The first is ascribed to Farnaby in *Tr* (no. [128]), to Byrd in *D2*, and to Bull in *Ant* and *Ly A1* ("D.B."). In the final and most important source, *Bu*, the work is given without ascription. The texts themselves are also at variance. Those of *Bu, Ant, Ly A1,* and *D2* are essentially the same except that the last of these orders the sections 1–4–3–2 (with respect to the order in *MB* 19, which follows *Bu/Ant/Ly A1*). The order in *Tr* conforms with that of *D2*, except that it is decidedly more elaborate in detail and has an extra variation at the end.[24] Instead of the closing variation of the other sources, governed by an eighth-note movement which balances the first (but here transposed to second place and dressed up with sixteenths), that of *Tr* goes from the duple-division bicinium of the penultimate variation into a tripla bicinium during which the parts are exchanged so that the melody lies in the tenor for the fourth phrase. The halting style and cell-like structure of this bicinium are quite unlike the flowing sixteenth motion of the previous variation, and are features Bull tended to avoid in secular variations.

Certainly, the ascription to Byrd can be rejected; there is nothing whatever in the style of this piece to suggest his manner of variation. Dart's thoughts on the situation, with which Richard Marlowe did not take issue in preparing his edition of Farnaby's keyboard music,[25] are as follows:

> The explanation of the conflicting attributions might be that Bull composed the piece more less as it stands in *Bu*, and that Farnaby then re-arranged (and slightly re-worked) the variations, adding a fifth variation of his own.[26]

No argument based on external evidence can be advanced against this theory, for any work appearing in *Tr* could theoretically postdate one in *Bu*. The opposite often appears to be the case, however, and such a sequence seems at least as plausible in this case. Bull, finding Farnaby's piece an attractive but defective one, may have rearranged the variations, cleaned up the figuration here and there, and replaced the closing tripla bicinium with a variation that hearkens back to the first—a usual touch for him. Conversely, it is hard to imagine another composer transforming the fine fourth variation in *Bu/Ant/Ly A2* into the dull second variation of *Tr*. Since Farnaby's figuration so often resembles if not actually imitates Bull's, observation of details provides no conclusive evidence with respect to the priority of the revisions. Yet it seems likely that we are dealing with a piece by Farnaby arranged by Bull. Be that as it may, we may safely assume the *Tr* version to be Farnaby's and that of the other sources to be Bull's.

The situation for *Rosasolis* is analogous in several respects. *Tr* again ascribes the piece to Farnaby, while the other source, *Ant,* claims it as Bull's. The ascriptions in *Ant* are of little value in themselves, and Dart's and Marlowe's observation that the style of the piece is closer to that of Farnaby than Bull is well taken. Again, the texts differ in matters of detail as well as structure. *Tr* states the unidentified theme straight through (AB) and follows it with a decorated repeat in each variation, while *Ant* introduces the decoration after each two-bar half, resulting in an AA'BB' rather than ABA'B' scheme. The order of the material also differs considerably in the two texts. *Tr* again has a final variation in a principally two-voice texture with tripla, replaced in *Ant* with a variation more faithful to the style of the rest of the piece. It therefore seems that a similar explanation to the one we have advanced for *Bonny Sweet Robin* is in order: Bull took a piece of Farnaby's that appealed to him, changed the internal structure as well as the overall order of variations (conforming, in fact, with that of *Bonny Sweet Robin*), and substituted for the last variation a new one which treated only the first half of the theme and then went on to tonicize the dominant in a brief coda.

Bull's variations *Revenant* are found solely in *Vi,* yet the international distribution of its tune, "More Palatino," precludes labeling Bull's set exclusively English or Continental. The title in *Vi* refers to the French *contrafactum* of the tune, which is known in at least sixteen vocal and instrumental settings in Continental sources and in a setting by Gibbons or Robert Johnson.[27] The manner in which Bull set the tune also involves a number of contradictions which frustrate any attempt to date the work. The variations are strictly paired in a manner suggestive of both the early grounds and the rather later *Go from My Window.* Vars. 1 and 2 treat the cantus melody in a three-voice texture first simply, then adorned with an eighth note counterpoint; vars. 3 and 4 are respectively in two and three parts, the latter utilizing a tenor cantus firmus (cf. vars. 4 and 5 of *Go from My Window*); var. 5 balances in tripla var. 3, and var. 6 expands upon it in four-part texture, this time without dislodging the tune from the top part. The mixed duple-triple figuration of the final variation is an early feature, occuring just once in secular variations (var. 20 of *Walsingham*); yet Bull fails to resolve the metrical contradiction in either of his usual ways. He neither increases the motion toward the end nor concludes with imitation in slower values. Instead, he preserves the metrical conflict right up to the final cadence, producing an effect that could be used to advantage by a good player.

The most striking feature of Bull's *Revenant* is the unusual uniformity of texture within variations. Parts do not drop in and out in the accustomed manner of the English variations, and the polyphony retains a linear quality that is uninterrupted by any virginalistic filler figures. Particularly uncharacteristic for virginal music is the treatment of the final bars of each variation, which appear to strive toward a more melodic extension of the cadence rather than a purely harmonic or rhythmic one (Ex. 6-20). These uncommon features may point toward the work's having been planned for organ rather than harpsichord or virginals. The coexistence of the early mixed tripla and the apparently later tenor placement of the tune for one variation would have been less anomolous in an organ setting.

Bull's Dutch carol variations also are in a comparatively conservative style, yet here the explanation is a dual one, for the pieces are both intended for audience (rather than player) and undoubtedly conceived for organ. Bull himself made a vocal setting of the carol "Den lustelijcken Meij," which appeared in the 1629 and 1648 editions of a collection of sacred vocal music for use at Vespers, the *Laudes Vespertinae* printed by Phalesius at Antwerp.[28] The pair of keyboard variations on the tune in *Ant* are in fact intabulations of this setting. Though polyphonic settings of "Een kindeken is ons geboren" and "Laet ons met herten reijne" are not known, the keyboard variations on those melodies, which likewise would have been used at Vespers in the Antwerp cathedral, may also be related to vocal models by him or known to him. Bull would have conceived such variations to serve as a prelude to or even replacement for the singing of the carols at Vespers.

The carol "Den lustelijcken Meij" is in the familiar AABB form, which naturally evoked an alternation between statement and decoration. Thus the first verse (A) of var. 1, virtually a transcription of Bull's vocal setting (Ex. 6-21) is followed by coloratura of average quality that decorates treble, then bass. The second verse is also based on the vocal model and is varied with quiet eighth note motion. Var. 2 follows a similar plan, incorporating a typical bicinium in the first half and further coloratura in

Ex. 6-20   Bull, *Revenant,* var. 2, final bar

Bull, *Walsingham,* var. 10, final bar

the second half. Bull's earlier music brings little to bear on an appreciation of this work, for here are to be found neither the traditional figurations of his English plainsong settings nor the luxuriant decoration of his secular variations, pavans, and galliards. Also absent is the highly individual and imaginative passagework of his *Salve Regina* settings. In *Den lustelijcken Meij* Bull has simply arranged his vocal setting for organ, using the popular techniques of intabulation practice. Bull showed himself master of this style in his fantasies on *Vestiva i colli,* yet the Dutch carol variations in no way exhibit the involvement with materials and the effort to build from them an independent musical structure that Palestrina's madrigal inspired.

Similar in intent to *Den lustelijcken Meij,* yet employing a greater range of figuration and keyboard textures, are the three sets of variations on "Een Kindeken is ons geboren." Especially noteworthy are the twisting treble decoration in *Een Kindeken* 1 (var. 1) so typical of Cornet, the Alberti-like left-hand pattern in *Een Kindeken* 2 (var. 2), and the off-beat chordal punctuation in both (Ex. 6-22). In this passage a virginalistic device is happily transferred to the organ for the sake of a shaking effect. No two of the variation sets treat the melody in the same form. The first two, which are both in the missing manuscript of Vincentius de la Faille (*Fa*), are related by key, details of harmony (particularly in the first variation), and use of the off-beat chords. They evidently are based on the same model, or one is a second version of the other. The parts of the tune appear in slightly different sequence, however, and the second setting lacks decoration in the first variation:

Een kindeken 1	A	A'	B	B'	C	/	A	A'	B	C		
Een kindeken 2	A	A	B	B	C	C	A	A'	B	B'	C	
Een kindeken 3	A	A'	B	B'	C	C	A					

The third setting differs from the other two in that it is in a different key, is in two parts throughout, and is rounded off with a repetition of the A section with the tune in the tenor. The printed edition omits an added bar in the manuscript, which indicates that the piece is to be repeated.

Laet ons met herten reijne is substantially the most appealing of the Dutch carols. The tune and its refrain, beginning with the bicinium, are set only once, and a four-bar coda restores the tonic tonality. The setting is preceded in its source by a prelude which is intended to accompany it, for both are based on the opening point of the carol. Unlike *Den lustelijcken Meij* and *Een Kindeken, Laet ons* begins with the air of a serious instrumental composition: the imitations, continuing in the manner established in the prelude, would appear to speak more strongly in favor of a polyphonic model than a homophonic one such as that implied in the

Ex. 6-21 Bull, *Den lustelijcken mey,* vocal setting

Ibid., keyboard setting

Ex. 6-22   Bull, Galliard G6, final bars

Bull, *Een kindeken,* var. 2

second carol and known in the first. Yet here is not to be found a systematic series of points upon the phrases of the melody, but a fluid keyboard texture incorporating both imitation and figures of passing interest.

Consideration must be given in a performance of *Laet ons* to the registrations as they appear in *Ant:* b. 36, above the upper staff, "Cornet"; b. 42, above the upper staff, "chromhorne"; b. 43, between the staves, "cornet alleen"; b. 48; between the staves, "Voll register." The indications appear to mean that the duo beginning in b. 37 is to be played with the right hand on the cornet and the left hand on the chromhorne (not indicated at this point). The hands would then reverse in b. 42–43, so that the right hand plays on the chromhorne and the left hand on the cornet. So far, all would be possible on a two-manual organ; yet the cornet normally did not sound below middle C, and a third manual (not known at the Antwerp cathedral at the time) is implied by the sudden appearance of the plenum in the left hand at b. 48. There is no satisfactory explanation of the situation, but the indication "cornet alleen" may be an erroneous direction for removing the cornet, leaving just the foundation stops. At "Voll register" the stops of the plenum could then be added.

The Dutch carols are an admittedly weak indication of the path of Bull's thought in his Antwerp period. That the late work of the composer of *Walsingham* and the Quadran variations should survive in these unpretentious pieces is disappointing. Destined more for a practical than an aesthetic function, they are conceived in an intentionally and appropriately simple style. The absence from Continental sources of variation sets comparable to those in the English sources of course raises the question whether Bull in his later years continued to be interested in the genre. The requirements of ecclesiastical service were indeed quite different from the opportunities provided by noble patronage; Bull's responsibilities in Antwerp may not have encouraged his returning to variations of the size and scope of those he had written while still in England. The burden of any evaluation must therefore rest with the English works.

The techniques of decoration Bull used in his grounds and variations are the same that did service in the pavans and galliards and in the plain-song settings. After the relative stiffness of early works like the Spanish Pavan and the earlier Quadran, the free reign granted the composer by the open-ended nature of the variation eventually provided him with much stimulation in the invention and application of keyboard ideas. This is especially true in *Walsingham,* where he constructed a virtual mosaic of interrelated figurations. Variation did not, on the other hand, give Bull the impetus to undertake new formal experiments, as the pavan and galliard had done, nor did they often uproot him from his conservative preferences regarding placement and harmonization of melody, limited use of imitation, and schematic planning. Except in *Go from My Window,* which Bull probably wrote in response to Byrd's music, the composer stands even further from his elder than he does in pavan and galliard composition. Bull repeatedly proceeded from the obvious exigencies of the instrument or (less often) with an abstract formal idea, and not with the always broader but occasionally less adventuresome musical values of Byrd.

Conclusion

In the course of our study we have seen that there are numerous obstacles that stand in the way of defining a canon of Bull's authentic works, and an equal number that frustrate attempts to establish definitive texts of his music. Nevertheless, priority can be accorded some ascriptions over others, and the relative integrity of certain sources by comparison to other ones becomes increasingly clear. More importantly, the music itself often provides important clues as to authorship and frequently furnishes its own guiding principles for textual choices. The result of this situation, which is by no means restricted to Bull's music, is that the authority often granted a monumental complete works edition must be moderated and new consideration of its every detail given. Therefore, a complete redoing of *MB* 14 is in order, while only small revisions, additions and deletions in *MB* 19 are called for.

On the basis of external evidence, a small handful of pieces can be dated precisely and a larger number more generally, yet such evidence, when it exists at all, is subject to varying interpretations and apt to be misleading. Fantasy a4 "on a theme of Sweelinck" was certainly written in 1621, the year of the Dutchman's death and the date given to the piece in its manuscript source. Pavan and Galliard G2 date from 1612 when the print for which they were written appeared, yet most of Bull's other works in *Parthenia* are earlier. Further ambiguities obtain in the case of dedicatory pavans which, as Dart believed, could have been written as *tombeaux,* or could equally well have been conceived as pieces in honor of a living person or in remembrance of someone who had died several years previously. Given the variables of competing theories such as these, lack of firm dates for many of the sources, and scanty biographical information, it is again the music itself which furnishes the most concrete evidence for a chronology. Such chronology as can be constructed is, however, only relative and gives at best an idea of Bull's development as a composer rather than firm dates for every piece.

Bull's earliest works are those based on plainsongs which had become by the third quarter of the century commonplace vehicles for free composition in England. The tradition, in which Bull took special interest, furnished the composer with two guiding principles: prosaic phrase and metrical structure as a corollary of cantus firmus setting; and structural articulations that are made by cadences and changes of rhythmic speed, usually allied with changes in texture and figuration. These features, already strong in the keyboard music of Tallis and Blitheman, remained present in Bull's thinking with few interruptions throughout his life. They made possible works of Bull's maturity such as the extraordinary 11/4 In Nomine as well as the earlier two-part fantasies written in imitation of sixteenth-century organ faburden settings. Uneven and irregular structures also figure heavily in early pavans and galliards, particularly Galliards d6 and d7, the latter containing a strain actually built on a cantus firmus. Unlike Byrd, Bull neither soon forsook plainsong setting nor opted for more global compositional principles. Rather, he remained faithful to the methods of his forebears and sought to breath new life into them with brilliantly inventive figurations and artful proportions.

Bull's early short grounds and the Spanish Pavan betray none of his propensity for irregular structures. Instead, they follow closely the units predicated by the given material, a very traditional approach in itself, and sometimes suffer as a result. In the mature grounds and variations such as the Quadran and *Walsingham,* however, any stiffness implicit in this one-to-one relationship between theme and variation is mitigated by the variety of ideas and sheer weight of the virtuosity. Bull's notion is to create a mosaic of interrelated figurations which, first conceived as old-fashioned variation pairs, eventually yields a complex pattern of reminiscences and development. Still, the fundamental thrust is a conservative one, for the composer maintains a single harmonization and rarely allows the theme to migrate. Only in the graceful *Go from My Window* can Byrd's influence in this respect be seen, though even here the planning is somewhat schematic and imitation curtailed.

The greatest achievements of Bull's maturity, roughly the last 15 years before he departed England, are the pavans and galliards. The composer eventually abandoned his early experiments in uneven strain lengths, but continued to manifest an interest in assymetrical internal structuring. Although the outcome was frequently to limit small-scale rhythmic and metrical flexibility—the late Galliard g1 is an important exception—the effect was otherwise an intensely expressive one. Likewise, Bull's idosyncratic themes could prove difficult to decorate in the repeats, yet their essence was highly personal. Seeking to counterbalance the eccentricities of his language, Bull discovered several ways to instill unity in the midst of diversity. In a good half of the pavans he related the outer strains through some small melodic or rhythmic device and sometimes, as in the powerful "Queen Elizabeth's" Pavan, tapped deeper motivic currents to draw the composition together. Pavan and Galliard a3 are even more tightly organized from this motivic point of view, but in general Bull's goal was to heighten interest through focusing on the intrinsic melodic, rhythmic, and sonic effect of his ideas rather than to give first priority to overall cohesiveness. In a few works, notable among them the "Prince's" Galliard, he managed to achieve both at once.

Bull's late works are marked by two fundamental changes: they exhibit a turning away from player's music toward audience music, and they are involved with the current genres and styles of Continental keyboard music. His fantasies on *Vestiva i colli* show how well he was able to synthesize the routine techniques of intabulation with his English background. The later of his two settings of *My Jewel,* on the other hand, proves that his own material could be ill-adapted to the newer, more contrapuntal demands. The influence of Cornet is strong in Bull's finest works from the period, the *Salve Regina* settings which combine English virginalistic figuration with a Continental type of alternatim verset that had been dead in England for half a century or more. One wonders whether there might have been other similar works written during Bull's considerable tenure at the Antwerp cathedral. While the absence of large-scale variation works other than the utilitarian Dutch carol settings and a setting of "More Palatino" is understandable, the lack of liturgical settings is not and demonstrates the losses that seem likely to have been incurred over time. The same might be said of fantasies from the earlier period, for it seems that we should have more works of this genre from so prolific a composer. Yet the bulk of the music preserved does date from the English period. Given the comparatively small number of works from Bull's Continental period and the somewhat mechanical demands of ecclesiastical service as opposed to the freedom when he enjoyed in England, it appears that an assessment of Bull's aesthetic achievement and historical contribution must rest with his English works. Interesting and occasionally significant as the late works are, it is those of the middle maturity that carry the most weight and made the strongest impression on the Continent, even before Bull went there to live and work.

The virtuosic elements in this music deserve some final comment. The most striking of these are rhythmic complexity, relentless figuration, a high percentage of fast notes with an unusually wide range of values within a single piece, and an often awkward disposition of the notes between the hands. Examples of each of these can be found in music before Bull, yet none of his contemporaries chose to exploit them to the extent that he did. A few composers in England—Lugge and Tomkins in particular—followed Bull's lead and in doing so contributed little that he had not. Byrd, at the other extreme, sought altogether different ends through a fresh interest in melody, particularly periodic melody, and through an infusion of imitation which was reaped not from the stoic mid-century organ style but from the background of his and others' consort and vocal music.

If traditional virtuosity could be pushed to its limits in the service of forging a new kind of keyboard piece, Bull tried to do it. It had to have been this that appealed on the Continent, judging from the significant shift around 1600 in the music of Sweelinck and others who were in contact with English keyboard music. Before this time the most virtuosic element traceable in keyboard music is the scalar figuration of the Venetian toccata; after 1600 the interest of the figuration itself becomes a primary concern to composers from Sweelinck to Bach. Frescobaldi had set the pattern for seventeenth-century keyboard music in Italy—albeit a short-lived one—with his fusion of Venetian and Neapolitan elements to the rhetorical aims of the new monody. Byrd's style, which had an even shorter life, was in response to very different, highly personal goals. Yet it was Bull's music—marked by a duality of conservatism and virtuosity—that would occupy a more central position in the development of Northern keyboard music throughout the Baroque.

Appendix I

The Sources of Bull's Keyboard Music Described

Manuscripts, Including Those Surviving Only in Photocopy or Transcription

Siglum*	Description**
Ant *(=Me)*	London, British Library, Add. MS 23623 See chapter 1.
Be	London, British Library, Add. MS 31403

The earlier layer of this manuscript was probably written in the 1630s and contains music of Bull, Gibbons, Blitheman, Byrd, Tallis, Edward Bevin (who may have been the compiler) and Emanuell Soncino. The second layer, which is written on the same paper, contains music of Corelli, Blow, Locke and others, and was completed much later. In the earlier part of the collection (f. 3-31) is a "Preludium" by Soncino, the last 28 bars of which are identical with the corresponding bars of the *Cromatica* by the same composer in *Tu*. Although Soncino's piece is dated 1633, most of the pieces in this part of the manuscript seem older. *Be* shares with *We* a number of variants in its two common pieces by Byrd, *The Carman's Whistle,* and *The Woods so Wild.* Both are in *My Ladye Nevells Booke,* and therefore date from before 1591. Notable features of *Be* are a profusion of ornaments and a generous amount of fingering. On f.5 is found "Graces in play," the only ornament table in an English source of the period (printed in *Early English Keyboard Music,* vol. 2, ed. Howard Ferguson [London 1971], p. 11). *Be* is the unique source of the Canon 4 in 2, ascribed to Bull, and also ascribes to him the Canon 2 in 1, with a running bass. (See p. 77.)

bibliography: *MB* 14, p. 159.
                MB 27, p. 169.
                Augustus Hughes-Hughes, *Catalogue of Manuscript Music in the British Museum,* 3 vols. (1906-1909), 3, pp. 90-91.

---

*Except where equivalents are noted, the *sigla* from *MB* 14 and 19 have been adopted.
**Unless otherwise noted, all sources employ 6-line, 2-staff (Anglo-Dutch) notation.

Siglum	Description

Bu

Paris, Bibliothèque Nationale, Fonds du Conservatoire, Rés. 1185: See chapter I.

ChCh 431

Oxford, Library of Christ Church College, Music MS 431

A small manuscript of 22 folios, containing pieces by Bull, Byrd, Gibbons, Dowland and Lugge. Stubs at the end of the manuscript indicate it may have originally been a larger collection. *ChCh 431* dates from about 1625 and gives no unique texts of Bull.

bibliography: *MB* 19, p. 225.
MB 20, p. 91.

Co

London, British Library, RML MS 23.1.4—"Benjamin Cosyn's Virginal Book"

The index of this large manuscript (146 folios) is dated 1620 and signed by Benjamin Cosyn. Thus *Co* was written during Bull's lifetime, but after he departed England. It contains works of Cosyn and Bull, and is the most important manuscript source for the keyboard music of Gibbons. In addition, Tallis and Byrd are each represented by one piece. Cosyn's source for Bull's pieces may have been *Bu,* which he owned, but his ascriptions are not always reliable. Cosyn's texts are profusely ornamented and often appear to be considerably rewritten.

bibliography: *MB* 14, p. 159.

Cp

Berlin, Deutsche Staatsbibliothek, Mus. MS 40316

Lost since 1945, this keyboard collection of 85 folios is preserved on microfilm at Cambridge, Mass., Isham Memorial Library of Harvard University. The music is written partly in 5-line staff notation and partly in score. It is the largest source of Cornet's music, and also contains works of G. Gabrieli, Orazio Vecchi, Quagliati, Frescobaldi, James, P. Philips, William Brown, Bull, Sergeant-Major Kennedy, Luyton, C. Erbach, H. L. Hassler, Sweelinck and Abraham Strauss. Of the three hands which made the collection, the first two completed their work by 1626, and the second (not the first, as Dart has it) refers to Cornet as "mio maestro"; hence the *siglum Cp* for "Cornet's pupil" whom Dart thought might be Abraham Strauss. Only one piece of Bull's is contained in the collection, a galliard on f. 11', also found in *Tr* and *Du.*

bibliography: *MB* 19, p. 225.
SK 1, p. xxi.
Lydia Schierning, *Die Ueberlieferung der deutschen Orgel- und Klaviermusik aus der ersten Hälfte des 17. Jahrhunderts* (Kassel, 1961), pp. 84-86.

Dd

Cambridge, University Library, MS D. 4.22.

A lute-book of 83 folios, 70 of which are blank. Six lute pieces occupy f. 1-12, and the keyboard pieces, Bull's Prelude G1 and a 4-bar didactic piece

Siglum	Description

(both fingered) are found on f. 28'-27', written upside down and from the back to the front of the book. The prelude is also found in *So, Be, RCM,* and *Musicks Hand-Maide.*

bibliography: *MB* 19, p. 225.
                 T. Dart, "New Sources of Virginal Music," *M&L* 35 (April, 1954), p. 99.

D2   New York City, New York Public Library, Drexel MS 5612

One of two large manuscripts of keyboard music owned by the NYPL, this volume of 114 folios dates from 1620-1660. The majority of the ascribed pieces in the collection are from Bull, Byrd and Gibbons, but there are also works of G. Farnaby, Tomkins, Weelkes, and a large number of shorter pieces associated with the masque and broadside ballad. Seven different hands can be discerned in the collection, which was originally organized by mode; hands I and II were responsible for the 21 pieces of Bull's recorded, of which Galliard G9 is the only one unique to this source. *D2* gives some fingerings, but ornaments are scarcer than in most other contemporary sources.

bibliography: *MB* 14, p. 159
                 Hilda F. Gervers, "A Manuscript of Dance Music from Seventeenth-Century England," *Bulletin of the New York Public Library* 80 (1977), pp. 503-52.

Du   Uppsala, Universitetsbiblioteket, Instr. mus. handskr. 408

A carefully written manuscript in German organ tablature of 44 folios containing 20 pieces. Composers named in the collection include Sibern, Scheidemann, Bull, Tomkins, P. Philips, Byrd, Sweelinck, Scheidt, Schildt, Anerio, Striggio and Frescobaldi. The two pieces by Bull are also found in other sources. The original layer of the manuscript was completed by Gustav Düben in 1641 and added to as late as 1653.

bibliography: *MB* 19, p. xx and 225.
                 SK 1, p. xxii.
                 Schierning, p. 95-98.
                 Bruno Grunsnick, "Die Dübensammlung: Ein Versuch ihrer chronologischen Ordnung," *Svensk tidskrift for musikforskning* 48 (1966), pp. 177-86.

El   Oxford, Library of Christ Church College, Music MS 1113

Dart took the initials on the binding of this manuscript, W.E., to be those of William Ellis, composer and organist of St. John's College, Oxford, from 1639 to 1646. Caldwell however, rejects this identification and believes the manuscript to have been compiled as early as 1620. It contains music of Bull, Byrd, Cosyn, Frescobaldi, Gibbons, Johnson, P. Philips, Tomkins and Sweelinck. Like *Co, El* has a large number of concordances with *Bu,* but unlike *Co,* it gives plain, unornamented texts. Ascriptions here are sometimes wrong or suspect. Three pieces (Fantasy, g, Alman D1 and Prelude G2) ascribed to Bull are unique to this source.

Siglum	Description

bibliography: *MB* 14, p. 159.
                  MB 20, p. 92.
                  John Caldwell, *English Keyboard Music before the Nineteenth Century* (Oxford, 1973) p. 151.

Fa   manuscript of Vincentius de la Faille

The whereabouts of this manuscript, formerly in the collection of M. Jules Ecorcheville, is not known. A transcription of it made by Charles van den Borren resides in the library of the Brussels Conservatoire. It is dated 1625 and gives the unique text of *Een Kindeken is ons geboren* 1.

bibliography: *MB* 14, p. 159.
                  Charles van den Borren, "Le Livre de clavier de Vincentus de la Faille (1625)," in *Mélanges de musicologie offerts à M. Lionel de Laurencie* (Paris, 1933), pp. 85-96.
                  Bruce Gustafson, *French Harpsichord Music of the Seventeenth Century,* 3 vols. (Ann Arbor, 1979), 1, pp. 77-78.

Fo   London, British Library, RML MS 24.d.3.—"Will Forster's Virginal Book"

The index of this manuscript is dated 31 January 1624/5. It is a major source for the keyboard music of Byrd, and also contains pieces by Tallis, Morley, Ward, Inglott, Bull and Cosyn. Of Bull's music *Fo* provides neither unique texts nor texts of independent value. One piece, no. 72 in the collection, is misattributed to Bull.

bibliography: *MB* 19, p. 225.
                  Neighbour, *Byrd*, p. 23.

Ly A1   Berlin, Deutsche Staatsbibliothek, Lübbenauer Orgeltabulaturen, MS Lynar A 1

An important source of Sweelinck's keyboard music, this manuscript of 331 folios was long thought to be an autograph of Matthias Weckmann. Curtis refuted this theory and proffered Jan Reinken as the probable scribe. Breig, however, argued against this, maintaining that the manuscript must be the work of a south German. It appears to have been compiled not before the 1630s. Among other composers represented in the collection are Bull, G. Gabrieli, P. Philips, Giles and Richard Farnaby, and Cornet. *Ly A1* is the only manuscript source for *God Save the King,* ascribed there to Sweelinck. The literature on this manuscript is large, but see especially the sources below.

bibliography: *MB* 19, p. xxi.
                  SK 1, p. xxii.
                  A. E. F. Dickinson, "A Forgotten Collection: A Survey of the Weckmann Books," *The Music Review* 17 (1956), pp. 97-109.
                  A. E. F. Dickinson, "The Lübbenau Keyboard Books: A Further Note on Faceless Features," *The Music Review* 27 (1966), pp. 270-86.

Siglum	Description

Schierning, pp. 66-80.

A. Curtis, "Jan Reinken and a Dutch Source for Sweelinck's Keyboard Works," *TVNM* 20 (1964-65) pp. 45-51.

W. Breig, "Die Lübbenauer Tabulaturen Lynar A1 und A2," *AfMW* 25 (1968), pp. 96-117 and 223-36.

Ly A2   Berlin, Deutsche Staatsbibliothek, Lübbenauer Orgeltabulaturen, MS Lynar A2

This manuscript was compiled by the same hand as *Ly A1* and includes music of C. Erbach, G. Gabrieli, T. Merula, Byrd, Bull and Gibbons. Twelve pieces, two of which are Bull's, were copied from *Pa* and are therefore of no independent value as texts.

bibliography: Schierning, pp. 81-84
W. Breig, "Die Lübbenauer Tabulaturen."

Ma   "Clement Matchett's Virginal Book"—from the library of Lord Dalhousie, on loan to the National Library of Scotland, Edinburgh

A manuscript of 32 folios in oblong quarto format containing 12 pieces and dated 1612. Besides anonymous pieces and pieces ascribed to Byrd, *Ma* gives texts for two of Bull's works; one, *My Choice,* is unique to this source. *Ma* is also the only known source for the one virginal piece of John Wilbye.

bibliography: *MB* 19, p. 225.
Dart, "New Sources."
Clement Matchett's Virginal Book, ed. T. Dart (London, 1957).

Mo   Oxford, Library of Christ Church College, Music MS 1003

A small book of keyboard music, compiled for or by C. Morgan, a pupil of Ellis, around 1650. Its 13 pieces of Bull's are copied from *El* and therefore are of no value as independent texts.

bibliography: *MB* 19, p. 225.
MB 20, p. 93.

P1   Paris, Bibliothèque Nationale, Fonds du Conservatoire, Rés. 1186.

A collection of 200 pieces of which 5 are variously dated 1635, 1636 and 1638. The repertoire includes not only larger keyboard pieces, but sacred and secular part music in transcription, simple dance settings, ballads, masque tunes and transcriptions of lute music. "R. Cr.," initials on several pieces, is presumed to be the writer, possibly Robert Creighton. The same hand affixed the dates, but no positive identification has been made. The collection dates from 1630-40. The manuscript belonged at one time to Pepusch (see Appendix II).

bibliography: *MB* 14, p. 159.
M.-L. Pereyra, "Les Livres de virginal de la Bibliothèque du Conservatoire," *Revue de Musicologie* 11 (1927), pp. 205-13, 12 (1928), pp. 235-42, and 13 (1929), pp. 32-39.

| Siglum | Description |

Martha Maas, *Seventeenth-Century English Keyboard Music: A Study of Manuscripts Rés. 1185, 1186 and 1186bis of the Paris Conservatory Library* (Ph.D. diss., Yale University, 1968).
English Pastime Music, 1630-1660: An Anthology of Keyboard Pieces, ed. Martha Maas (Madison, 1974).

P2   Paris, Bibliothèque Nationale, Fonds du Conservatoire, Rés. 1186bis

This is actually two separate manuscripts. The first contains music from Bull and Gibbons to Blow, Purcell and Croft. The second appears to be earlier—one piece is dated 1635—and consists of simple dances and vocal transcriptions in addition to independent keyboard pieces.

bibliography: *MB* 14, p. 159.
Pereyra, in *Revue de Musicologie* 10 (1926), pp. 204-9, 11 (1927), pp. 36-39.
Maas, *Seventeenth-Century English Keyboard Music.*
Maas, *English Pastime Music.*

RCM   London, Royal College of Music, MS 2093

Formerly in the library of Richard Clark, this small book of keyboard music is in oblong format and dates from the second half of the seventeenth century. Its amateurish contents, mostly preludes, give the appearance of a teaching collection, perhaps made by a student. Two pieces, Grounds 1 and 2, are unique to this source.

bibliography: *MB* 19, pp. xxi and 225.

So   London, British Library, Add. MS 29485—"Suzanne van Soldt's Keyboard Book"

This small volume, which contains 33 pieces on 27 folios, belonged to the daughter of a wealthy merchant and Protestant refugee from the Netherlands. The manuscript may have been originally written in the Netherlands, brought to England later and added to there. The date of 1599 on the title page, however, is not too early for the music in the later, English hand. The collection consists mainly of dance tunes and psalm settings, and is the only significant record of Dutch keyboard music before Sweelinck. No. 30 is Bull's Prelude G1.

bibliography: *MMN* 3.

To   Paris, Bibliothèque Nationale, Fonds du Conservatoire, Rés. 1122.

A holograph collection of Thomas Tomkins written in the second quarter of the seventeenth century. It contains, in addition to his own music, works of Byrd and Bull. The chief importance of *To* as a source for Bull's music lies in the fact that it gives unique texts for three In Nomines, a7, a8 and a10. Tomkins also gives the only attribution to Bull of a plainsong setting found

Siglum	Description

in five other sources. The texts of *To* tend to be the most intricate, and may corrupt in the direction of complexity rather than simplicity.

bibliography: *MB* 5, pp. 155-62.

Tr   Cambridge, Fitzwilliam Museum, Music MS 32.G.29.

See chapter 1.

Tu   London, British Library, Add. MS 36661

Dart believed that the earlier section of this manuscript was compiled during the 1630s by Thomas Tunstall, whose signature is found on f. 63. However, the signature appears to have been added, along with the titles on f. 63 and 60', at a later date. The manuscript contains music of Gibbons, Hugh Facy, Soncino, Bevin and Bull, whose Fantasy d2 is unique to this source. Soncino's *Cromatica* is printed in *Tarquinio Merula: composizioni per organo e cembalo,* ed. Alan Curtis (Brescia and Kassel, 1961).

bibliography: *MB* 14, p. 160.
         See also *Be,* above.

Vi   Vienna, Oesterreichische Nationalbibliothek, Cod. 17771

See chapter 1.

We
(=Wr)   London, British Library, Add. MS 30485

This collection was very likely compiled by Thomas Weelkes and is an important source for the keyboard music of Byrd. It also contains works by eleven other named composers, including Alwood, Blitheman, Bull, Weelkes and Tallis. On the basis of a comparison of the music of Byrd in *We* with that in *My Ladye Nevells Booke,* it appears that this manuscript was begun after 1591. Its contents cover a wide time span but, with the exception of Byrd's music, are largely retrospective. It was probably finished by 1610. *We* gives the only text for Bull's Prelude a3 and for a galliard "St. Thomas, Wake!" (*MB* 19:126c) which was once ascribed by Dart to Bull. The style of the latter piece, however, suggests a younger and less sophisticated composer.

bibliography: *MB* 14, 0. 160
         MB 28, p. 192.
         Neighbour, *Byrd*, p. 20.

Lost Manuscript Sources

Siglum	Description

Pe 16   Pepusch's collection, Number 16

This manuscript and the following one, *Pe 18,1,* are among those listed in Ward's *Lives* as belonging to Dr. Pepusch. The list in Ward gives the titles

Siglum	Description

of compositions by Bull in the manuscripts, but does not provide a complete index. *Pe 16* was written by Gulielmus à Messaus. See *Pe 18,1*.

bibliography: Ward, *Lives*, pp. 204-5. Reproduced in Appendix II.

Pe 18, 1
(= Clark)

Pepusch's collection, Number 18, Volume I

This is the first of two numbers under Volume 18 in Pepusch's catalogue. The second was *Ant*. There appears to be no justification for Dart's claim that they were written by Messaus, as *Pe 16* in fact was. *Pe 18, 1* may have passed from Pepusch's hands to Edward Jones, who provided a transcription of *God Save the King* which appeared in *Ki*, then to Richard Clark, who is said to have owned *Pe 16* and *RCM*.

bibliography: *MB* 19, p. 225.
                 Ward, *Lives*, p. 205. Reproduced in Appendix II.

NOTE: Several other manuscripts are listed on p. 207 of Ward, but the above two and no. 34, Rés 1186, are the only ones that have been identified.

Printed Sources

Cummings   W. H. Cummings, *God Save the King* (London, 1902)

This book provides a transcription of one piece from *Pe 18, 1*, an "air" (*MB* 19:91); see p. 121.

bibliography: *MB* 19, p. 232 (critical note to no. 91).

Ki   William Kitchiner, *The Loyal and National Songs of England* (London, 1823)

Through this source survives the text of Jones's transcription from *Pe 18, 1* of *God Save the King*.

bibliography: *MB* 14, p. 160.

Pa   *Parthenia, or the maydenhead of the first musicke that ever was printed for the virginalls*...(London, [1612/13])

This volume of 21 pieces—8 by Byrd, 7 by Bull and 6 by Gibbons—was engraved as a wedding present to princess Elizabeth, daughter of James I, and Frederick V, Elector Palatine of the Rhine. Only one copy of the original small issue survives (Huntington Library, San Marino, California), but it was immediately reprinted for public sale and again reissued in 1646, 1651, 1655 and 1659. According to Dart, it was Gibbons who was responsible for the editing of the volume.

bibliography: *Parthenia*, ed. T. Dart (London, 1960).
                 Facsim. ed., London, 1942.

Pal   *Parthenia In-Violata, or mayden-musicke for the virginalls and bass-viol*...
        (London, [c. 1625])

Siglum	Description

Twenty anonymous duets engraved as a wedding present for Prince Charles of England and Princess Henrietta Maria of France. Two pieces can be established through concordances to be Bull's and a third, the *Welsh Dance*, is attributed to him on grounds of style.

bibliography: *Parthenia In-Violata,* ed. T. Dart (New York, 1961).
Facism. ed. New York, 1961, with introduction by T. Dart, bibliographical note by Richard Wolfe and foreword by Sidney Beck.

Musicks Hand-Maide (London, 1663)

Published by John Playford, this is a collection of 58 keyboard pieces, including psalm tune settings. The opening piece is a late, anonymous text of Bull's Prelude G1.

bibliography: *The First Part of Musick's Hand-Maid, published by John Playford* (London, 1969).

Appendix II

List of Pieces by Bull in Pepusch's Manuscript Collection

MVSIC PROFESSORS.

have feen another edition dated 1659, with the words *cum privilegio* un-derneath, tho' the two laft figures feem to have been altered; nor was that time at all fuited to publifh works of this kind, while the affairs of the nation were in fuch diforder. The collection contains twenty one leffions, of which thofe from nine to fifteen inclufive were made by Dr. Bull.

2. *The firft book of felected church mufick, confifting of fervices and an-thems, fuch as are now ufed in the cathedrall, and collegiat churches of this kingdom: Never before printed: Collected out of divers approved authors by* John Barnard, *one of the minor cannons of the cathedrall church of St. Paul,* London: London 1641. folio.

In this collection the anthem, *Deliver me, O God,* folio 123, is afcrib-ed to Dr. Bull.

3. *The divine fervices and anthems ufually fung in the cathedrals, and collegiate choirs, in the church of* England: *Collected by James Clifford:* London 1663. folio.

Some peices of Dr. Bull are put into this collection, at p. 36, 137, 187, *etc.* as Mr. Wood relates, for I have not feen the book.

But befides thefe there is extant a large number and variety of Dr. Bull's peices in manufcript, that make a part of the curious and valua-ble collection of mufic, now repofited in the library of Dr. Pepufch; of which I fhall here add the following account, as communicated to me by the doctor.

For the organ or harpficord.

A large *folio* neatly writen, bound in red Turkey leather, and guilt, but not entered in the catalogue.

Page.
1. Walfingham [a].
27. *Galliard to My lord Lumley's pavan.*
30. *Pavan.*
34. *Galliard.*
49. *The quadran pavan.*
54. *Variation of the quadran pavan.*
59. *Galliard to the quadran pavan.*
63. *Pavan.*
66. *Galliard to the pavan.*
67. *St. Thomas Wake.*
69. *In nomine.*
70. *Fantafia upon a plain fong.*
76. *Pavan of My lord Lumley* [b].
80. *Praeludium to* Gloria tibi Trinitas.
81. Gloria tibi Trinitas.
82. Salvator mundi, Domine.
86. *Galliard.*
87. *Variatio.*

[a] This tune, which begins, *As I went to Walfingham,* was firft compofed by William Birde, with twenty two variations; and afterwards thirty others were added to it, at different times, by Dr. Bull.

[b] *Vid.* the galliard to this pavan, p. 27, above.

89. *Galli-*

204 ## MVSIC PROFESSORS.

Page.

Number 16 in the catalogue. *A large quarto.*

Folio.

---

[a] This peice is not the fame with any other on this fubject.

77. *Prae-*

MVSIC PROFESSORS.   205

Folio.

77. *Praeludium voor de fantafia octavi toni, fopra fol, ut, mi, fa, fol, la.*
78 *Fantafia fopra fol, ut, mi, fa, fol, la.*
80. *Fantafia cromatica primi toni, contraria al' altra.*
85. *Ricercata fopra ut, re, mi, fa, fol, la.*
92. *Ricercata primi toni, a 4.*
93. *Ricercata altra primi toni, a 4.*
95. *Ricercata quinti toni, a 4.*
96. *Fantafia fecundi toni.*
99. *Toccata fecundi toni.*
100. *Fantafia fexti toni, a 4.*
107. *Fantafia fexti toni, fopra* A leona.
161. Salve, regina, 1.
162. Ad te clamamus, 2.
163. Eja ergo advocata noftra, 3.
164. O clemens, 4.
165. O dulcis virgo, Maria, 5.
166. Regina caeli, 1.
168. Quia quem meruifti, 2.
169. Ora pro nobis Deum.
172. Vexilla regis prodeunt [a].

Number 18, 11 Vol. *quarto.*

Volume 1.

1. *Praeludium to the fantafia,* Felix namque offertorium.
1. *Fantafia,* Felix namque offertorium.
8. *Galliard, Madamoyfelle Charlotte de la Haye.*
15. *Tres voces in unum,* Salvator mundi.
56. God fave the king.
63. Gloria tibi, Trinitas.
77. *Fantafia on a chromatic fubject, a 4 v.*
86. *Door Dr. Bull gemaekt, ter eeren Van Goduart Van Kappell.*
88. *Dr. Bull voor my gemaekt,* En revenant.
92. Levez vous coeur.
98. *Air.*
101. *Ballet, die partyen door Dr. Bull op fuperius gemaekt.*
102. Philis heeft myn hert geftoolen, *voor my gamaekt.*
103. *Gemaekt op * **
105. *Courante de chapelle primi toni,* ann. 1619.
105. *Courante de chapelle.*
106. *Galliard op die eerfte courante.*
107. *Almand de chapelle primi toni.*
109. *Galliard de chapelle primi toni.*
110. *Galliard.*
111. *Almand op die voorgaende galliard.*
113. *Fantafia.*
114. *Fantafia.*
116. *Den luftelycken Mey.* Imperfect.

[a] At the end of this book is writen the follow-   1628. *Scribebat Gulielmus a Meſſaus, Divæ*
ing note. *Incepit 6 Apr. 1628, finivit 20 Oct.   Walburgis Antverpienfis phonafcus.*

206   M V S Í C   P R O F E S S O R S.

Volume ii.

Folio.

27. Bonny well Robin.
33. Rofa folis.
35. *Praeludium octavi toni* [a].
37. *Praeludium in c, fol, fa, ut.*
38. *Les buffons.*
44. *Den luftelycken Mey,* quod fecit 30 Maii 1622.
53. *Fantafia fuper* Veftiva i colli.
56. *Fantafia fecunda fuper* Veftiva i colli.
58. *Fantafia.*
61. *Pavana finfonia,* ann. 1622.
64. *Galliard.*
65. *Het juweel,* quod fecit anno 1621, 12 Decemb.
68. *Fantafia op de fugue Van Mr. Jan. Pieterfs,* fecit 1621, 15 Decemb.
70. *Pavana finfonia.*
73. *Galliard voor de voorgaende pavana.*
74. *Fantafia op de fugue Van la Guamina.*
77. Een kindeken is ons geboren.
79. Een kindeken is ons geboren, *in d, la, fol, re.*
81. *Praeludium voor* Laet ons met herten reyn.
81. Laet ons met herten reyn.
84. *Het nieu Bergomafco.*
86. *Courante, Juweel.*
91. *Courante, Bataille.*
93. *Courante, Alarme.*
95. *Courante, Joyeufe.*
97. *Courante, Brigante.*
98. *Courante, The princes.*
99. *Courante,* Adieu, *of,* The vaerwel.
100. *Courante, A round.*
101. *Courante, Kingfton.*
104. *Courante prima in a, la, mi, re.*
105. *Courante fecunda in a, la, mi, re.*
106. *Courante tertia in a, la, mi, re.*
107. *Courante quarta in a, la, mi, re.*
108. *Courante quinta in a, la, mi, re.*
109. *Boeren dans.*
112. *Pavana fecundi toni.*
120. *Praeludium pour la fantafia fopra re, re, re, fol, ut mi, fa, fol.*
121. *Fantafia fopra re, re, re, fol, ut, mi, fa, fol.*
129. *Fantafia fexti toni, a 4 v.*
138. *Fantafia fexti toni, fopra* A leona.
142. *Ricercata fexti toni, a 4 v.*
144. *Praeludium voor de fantafia quinti toni.*
145. *Fantafia quinti toni.*
168. Vexilla regis prodeunt, 1. *a 3 v.*

---

[a] This *praeludium* is printed in the *Parthenia* in manufcript, which have all Dr. Bull's name N. xxi, and there afcribed to Orlando Gib- to them. bons; but Dr. Pepufch has feveral copies of it

170. Vexil-

MVSIC PROFESSORS.   207

Folio.

170. Vexilla regis prodeunt, 11. *a* 4 *v.*
172. Vexilla regis prodeunt, 111. *a* 4 *v.*
175. Vexilla regis prodeunt, 1v. *a* 4 *v.*
177. Jam lucis orto fidere, 1. *a* 3 *v.*
179. Jam lucis orto fidere, 1. *a* 4 *v.*
181. Te lucis ante terminum, *a* 4 *v.*
182. Alleluja, *a* 4 *v.*
183. Veni, redemptor gentium, *a* 4 *v.*
185. Salvator mundi Deus, *a* 4 *v.*
186. Telluris ingens conditor, 1. *a* 4 *v.*
188. Telluris ingens conditor, 11. *a* 4 *v.*
189. Telluris ingens conditor, 111. *canon a* 4. *in fuper diateffaron,* 2 *in una.*
190. Telluris ingens conditor, 1v. *canon a* 4. *in fuper diateffaron,* 2 *in una.*
191. Telluris ingens conditor, v. *canon a* 4. *in fub diateffaron,* 2 *in una.*
193. Telluris ingens conditor, v1. *canon a* 4. *in fuper diapafon,* 2 *in una.*
194. Telluris ingens conditor, v11. *canon a* 4. *in fub diapafon,* 2 *in una.*
195. Alleluja *canon, a* 4, 2 *in una.* Imperfect.

Number 26. *folio.*

347. *Galliard.*
447. *The king's hunt.*
458. *Praeludium.*
460. Watkins ale. *With feveral others unnamed to the end of the book.*

Number 34. *folio.*

56. *The king's hunting jig.*
108. Why afk you?
111. Why afk you? *paulo aliter.*
122. Little Pegge of Ramfie.

Number 37. *folio.*

Page.

15. Robin Hood.
40. *A ground, with* 15 *variations* [a].

Number 102. 1v Vol. *folio.*

Two Mifereres, *one with two parts, the other with three.*

Number 103, v Vol. *folio.*

A prelude.

Number 131. *folio.*

Folio.

21. *An ofitary.*

For inftruments.

Fantafias and *In nomines.*

Number 8. 1v Vol. *quarto.*

In nomine, *the* 18 *in number.*

Number 61. *folio.*

Duo, *for two bafs viols, the* 4 *in number.*

[a] There is another *ground* extant of Dr. Bull with 45 divifions, not in the library of Dr. P. and likewife an anthem, *In thee O Lord.* Which latter is (with other mf. peices) added to the printed treatife mentioned above, intitled, *The firft book of felected church mufick,* at pag. 189.

Number

208 MVSIC PROFESSORS.

Number 61, v Vol. *oblong quarto.*

Folio,

45. In nomine [a].

Number 75, v Vol. *oblong quarto.*

52. In nomine, *a* 5 *v.*

Motetti and *Madrigali.*

Number 5, vi Vol. *folio.*

16. Fraile man defpife, *a* 4 v.
20. In the departure of the Lord.
21. Attend unto my tears, o Lord.
136. Almighty God, *a* 5 *v.*
270. Almighty God, *a* 6 *v* [b].

Curiofities in mufic.

Number 13. *folio.*

Deus omnipotens, *a* 5 *v.*
A peice for three voices.

The eminent abilities of Dr. Bull in his profeffion, and the great regard which was fhewn to his compofitions, may in fome meafure appear from the number and variety of his peices contained in this catalogue, that are yet preferved.

There is likewife extant a *folio* volume, handfomly bound, in red Turkey leather, and gilt, with the following words ftamped on the cover.

IOHN. BVLL.
DOCTER. OF.
MVSIQVE. ORGA
NISTE. AND. GENT
ELMAM. OF. HER. MAIES
TIES. MOSTE. HONORABLE.
CHAPPELL.

Befides this infcription, the ruled paper fhews, that the book was made at that time, by the letters T. E. marked upon every fheet, which ftand for *Thomas Eaft,* who printed mufic under the patent of Thomas Tallis and William Birde, granted them in 1575 by queen Elizabeth for 21 years. However, few of the tunes have the words put to them, or the name of the compofer; and Dr. Bull's name is not to any of them, but only thofe of other perfons; fo that whether any of them were really made by him, or not, is uncertain [c].

II.

THOMAS CLAYTON was firft of Glocefter hall, and afterwards of Balliol college, in Oxford [d], where he proceeded mafter of

[a] Here he is called *Mr. Bull,* which fhews, that this peice was compofed very early, before he was created a doctor.

[b] A copy of this peice for five voices was communicated to me by Mr. Richard Goodfon, batchelor of mufic, and profeffor of that fcience at Oxford.

[c] This manufcript is now in the poffeffion of Mr. Ames; who has alfo a printed book intitled, *The*

Pfalmes of David in Englifh meter, with Notes of foure partes fet unto them, by Guilielmo Daman, *for* John Bull, *London* 1579: *an oblong quarto.* But this John Bull being in the *Preface* called *citezen and goldfmith of London,* and faid to have collected and publifhed thefe *Pfalms*; he could not have been the profeffor, who was then but fixteen years of age.

[d] *Hift. et ant. Ox.* L. 11, p. 40.

arts.

Appendix III

Bull's Pavan g1 (*Co*, p. 166)

Notes

Foreword

1. See the list of works given by Susi Jeans in her article on Bull for the sixth edition of *Grove's Dictionary of Music and Musicians*, with the following additions: a three-part fantasy and a five-part In Nomine in *MB* 9, and a four-part fantasy (also ascribed to Coprario) in *Nine Fantasias in Four Parts by Byrd, Bull, Ferrabosco, Jenkins and Ives*, ed. Sydney Beck (New York, 1947); the Dutch carol *Den lustelijcken Meij* in *Six Seventeenth-Century Carols from the Netherlands*, ed. Frits Noske (Oxford, 1965); two short pieces, *Bull's Toye* and *The Bull Masque*, in *Four Hundred Songs and Dances from the Stuart Masque*, ed. Andrew J. Sabol (Providence, R.I., 1978); and Pavan g1 in Appendix III of this volume.

2. For an overview of the critical literature, see the author's Ph.D. dissertation, *The Keyboard Music of John Bull* (University of California, Berkeley, 1981), pp. 2–6 (hereafter cited as Cunningham).

Chapter 1

1. See Johann Mattheson, "Beytrag zu des Hrn. Professor Delrichs historischen Nachricht von den academischen Würden in der Musik," published in *Beitrag zu Die Hamburgischen Nachrichten aus dem Reiche der Gelehrsamkeit* (Hamburg, 1759–63) and quoted by Friedrich Wilhelm Marpurg in his *Historisch-kritische Beyträge zur Aufnahme der Musik*, 5 vols. (Berlin, 1754–78), 4, pp. 413–18; Sir John Hawkins, *A General History of the Science and Practice of Music* (London, 1776); Charles Burney, *A General History of Music from the Earliest Ages to the Present Period*, 4 vols. (London, 1776–89), 3; Johann Gottfried Walther, *Musicalisches Lexikon oder musicalische Bibliothec* (Leipzig, 1732); and Ernst Ludwig Gerber, *Historisch-biographisches Lexikon der Tonkünstler*, 2 vols. (Leipzig, 1790–92), 1—this entry for Bull is expanded in Gerber's *Neues historisch-biographisches Lexikon der Tonkünstler*, 4 vols. (Leipzig, 1812–14), 1.

2. Seiffert, *Die Geschichte der Klaviermusik*, p. 88.

3. Unless otherwise noted, the following biographical sketch is based on Thurston Dart's "Calendar of the Life of John Bull," *MB* 14, pp. xxi–xxvi; and on Susi Jeans's article in *Grove 6*. The present account expands upon several facets of Bull's life not detailed in these two sources.

4. Thurston Dart, "Search for the Real John Bull," *New York Times,* 1 November 1959, sec. 2, p. 1.

5. Bull's appointment to Hereford would seem to lend support to the theory that he was born there, for it was customary under Elizabeth for organists (Byrd and Morley, for example) to return to their home cathedrals after completing their training in London.

6. Caleb Willis probably did not read beyond the inaugural lecture, and was succeeded by Richard Ball. Matthew Gwinne, like Thomas Campion, was a physician and musician. He had formerly been associated with St. John's, Oxford, where he was a scholar, fellow, regent master and was appointed to read on music. His lecture at Oxford of 15 October 1582, "Oratio in laudam musices," is printed in the Appendix to John Ward's *The Lives of the Professors of Gresham College* (London, 1740).

7. Alec Hyatt King, "Fragments of Early Printed Music in the Bagford Collection," *M&L* 40 (1959), pp. 270–71.

8. Most authors have relied upon an entry in *The Old Cheque-Book* referring to the appointment of Arthur Cock as a "gentleman in ordinary and organiste (without pay) in her Majestes saide chapple, untill an organiste place shalbe come voyde, and the saide Arter Cocke (by his Honor's appointment) to his attendaunce, and to supplye the wantes of organistes which may be through sicknes or other urgent causes. . . ." (Edward F. Rimbault, ed., *The Old Cheque-Book* (1872, reprint ed., New York, 1966), p. 37.

9. Dart, "Search for the Real John Bull."

10. See Wilibald Gurlitt, *Michael Praetorius* (1915, reprint ed., Hildesheim, 1968), pp. 94–138; A. H. J. Knight, *Heinrich Julius, Duke of Brunswick* (Oxford, 1948), pp. 7–17; and Martin Ruhnke, *Beiträge zu einer Geschichte der deutschen Hofmusik-kollegen im 16. Jahrhundert* (Berlin, 1963), pp. 61–87.

11. See Thomas Birch, *The Life of Henry Prince of Wales* (London, 1760), p. 189.

12. Anthony à Wood, *Athenae Oxoniensis* (Oxford, 1691), *Fasti*, col. 758.

13. Alan Curtis, *Sweelinck's Keyboard Music* (Leiden and London, 1969), pp. 26–27.

14. For further information about de Caus, see Cunningham, pp. 223–26.

15. John Nichols, *The Progresses, Processions, and Magnificent Festivities of King James the First,* 4 vols. (London, 1828), 2, pp. 138–39. Also present were Nathaniel Giles, then Master of the Children in the Chapel Royal, William Byrd, William Lawes, Elway Bevin and Orlando Gibbons.

16. *The Old Cheque-Book,* pp. 163–66.

17. Burney, *History of Music,* 3, p. 108.

18. See letters from William Trumbull, Ambassador at Brussels, to King James, 31 March 1614 (below) and from Robert, Earl of Somerset to Trumbull, 26 May 1614 in Historical Manuscripts Commission, *Report of the Marquess of Downshire,* 4 vols. (London, 1940), 4, pp. 355 and 411–12.

19. Squire erroneously gives the date of the letter as 30 May 1614.

20. Thurston Dart, "An Unknown Letter from Dr. John Bull," *Acta Musicologica* 32 (1960), p. 175.

21. *Downshire Papers* 4, pp. 270–71. Quoted in part in G. A. Philipps, "Crown Musical Patronage from Elizabeth I to Charles I, *M&L* 58 (1977), pp. 37–38.

22. Jeannine Lambrechts-Douillez, Secretary of the Ruckers-Geenootschap and Curator of the Vleeshuis Museum in Antwerp, claims that recent researches on musicians and instrument builders in City and Cathedral archives have uncovered no documents that were not known to Dart. (Conversation between the author and Mme. Lambrechts-Douillez, Antwerp, 27 July 1979.)

23. See especially Thurston Dart, "English Music and Musicians in 17th-Century Holland," *Kongress-Bericht, Internationale Gesellschaft für Musikwissenschaft, Utrecht 1952* (Amsterdam, 1953), pp. 139–45; Curtis, *Sweelinck's Keyboard Music*, pp. 10–34; and Werner Braun, *Britannia Abundans* (Tutzing, 1977), passim.

24. The account of the four main sources given here may be found in a more complete form in Cunningham, pp. 33–91. A brief description of all other sources is given in Appendix I of this volume.

25. A complete inventory of the manuscript, including watermarks and foliation, may be found in Cunningham, Appendices II and IV.

26. The later music is discussed by Martha Maas in *Seventeenth-Century English Keyboard Music: A Study of Manuscripts Res. 1185, 1187 and 1186 bis of the Paris Conservatory Library* (Ph.D. diss., Yale University, 1968), pp. 149ff.; and by Bruce Gustavson in *French Harpsichord Music of the Seventeenth Century*, 3 vols. (Ann Arbor, 1979), 1, pp. 58–60.

27. According to Susi Jeans, Benjamin Cosyn did not write *Co.* To my knowledge, she is alone in that opinion.

28. See especially *Orlando Gibbons: Complete Keyboard Works*, 5 vols., ed. Margaret H. Glyn (London, [1925]), 1, p. i; *John Bull: Selected Edition*, 2 vols., ed. Margaret H. Glyn (London, [1928]), 1, p. iii; M.-L. Pereyra, "Les Livres de virginal de la Bibliothèque du Conservatoire," *Revue de Musicologie* 15 (1931), pp. 22–32; 16 (1932), pp. 86–90; 17 (1933), pp. 24–27; John Steele, "English Organs and Organ Music from 1500 to 1650" (Ph.D. diss., Cambridge University, 1959), Appendix, p. 17; *MB* 14 (1st ed.), p. 159; *MB* 19 (both eds.), p. xvi; and *MB* 14 (2nd ed.), p. 159.

29. The pieces are discussed by Hugh Miller in "Sixteenth-Century English Faburden Compositions for Keyboard," *MQ* 26 (1940), pp. 50–64.

30. See *Altenglische Orgelmusik*, ed. Denis Stevens (Kassel, 1953), p. 21; Stevens's entry in *MGG*, s.v. "Thomas Preston"; and Oliver Neighbour, *The Consort and Keyboard Music of William Byrd* (London, Berkeley and Los Angeles, 1978), p. 103 (hereafter cited as *Byrd*).

31. The author is grateful to Susi Jeans for pointing these out.

32. Reproduced in *Grove* 6, vol. 3, p. 442.

33. Reproduced in *MB* 14, p. xxviii. Kindly offering her advice on the SP specimens, Pamela Willets, Deputy Keeper, Department of Manuscripts, British Library, observes that such monogram-type signatures occasionally occur in copyists' hands, but they are not very common. (Pamela Willets to the author, 31 March 1980.)

34. Professor Anthony Petti, Department of English, University of Calgary, generously

gave his time to examine the writing samples and concluded that "there is a good chance that [the SP parts are] holograph and a moderate chance that [*Bu*] is." (Anthony Petti to the author, 1 May 1980.) Susi Jeans accepts the SP parts unequivocally as holograph in her article on Bull for *Grove 6*.

35. *MB* 14, p. xxiv.

36. *MB* 19, p. xvi.

37. The hymn verse is transcribed in full in Cunningham, Appendix V.

38. See especially T. Dart and Betram Schofield, "Tregian's Anthology," *M&L* 32 (1951), pp. 205–16 and two articles by Elizabeth Cole, "In Search of Francis Tregian," *M&L 33* (1952), pp. 28–32 and "L'Anthologie de madrigaux et de musique instrumentale pour ensembles de Francis Tregian," in *La Musique instrumentale dans la Renaissance*, ed. Jean Jacquot (Paris, 1955), pp. 115–26. Stages in solving the puzzle of the virginal book can be traced through *FVB*, pp. v–ix; E. W. Naylor, *An Elizabethan Virginal Book* (London, 1904); Elizabeth Cole, "Seven Problems of the Fitzwilliam Virginal Book," *Proceedings of the Royal Music Association* 79 (1952–53), pp. 51–64; Richard Marlow's note on the manuscript in *MB* 24, p. 139; and Jerry C. Persons, "The Sambrooke Book: Drexel 4302" (M.Mus. thesis, Wichita State University, 1969), pp. 24–28.

39. Persons, "The Sambrooke Book," p. 26.

40. A complete inventory of the manuscript, including watermarks and foliation, may be found in Cunningham, Appendices II and IV.

41. Attempts to formulate an early history of the manuscript have been made by Augustus Hughes-Hughes, *Catalogue of Manuscript Music in the British Museum*, 3 vols. (1906–09), 3, pp. 82–83; Hugh Miller, "John Bull's Organ Works," *M&L* 28 (1947), pp. 25–35; Thurston Dart, "John Bull's Chapel," *M&L* 40 (1959), pp. 279–82; see also Dart's comments in *MB* 14, p. 159.

42. Reprinted from Ward's *Lives* in Appendix II.

43. Hugh Miller ("John Bull's Organ Works," p. 26) says that *Ant* was "copied apparently by some student or admirer soon after the master's death." Dart ("John Bull's Chapel," p. 281) then attributes the manuscript to Messaus without further ado. All subsequent writers on Bull's music and on this manuscript have accepted this attribution unquestionably.

44. *Harpsichord Pieces from Dr. John Bull's Flemish Tabulatura*, ed. H. F. Redlich (Wilhelmshaven, 1958), p. [17].

45. Dart, "John Bull's Chapel," p. 281–82.

46. Ibid., p. 281n.

47. Jost Harro Schmidt, "Eine unbekannte Quelle zur Klaviermusik des 17. Jahrhunderts," *AfMW* 22 (1965), pp. 1–11; Curtis, *Sweelinck's Keyboard Music*, pp. 76–77.

48. Hans Redlich published two of the former under Bull's name in 1958 (*Harpsichord Pieces from Dr. John Bull's Flemish Tabulatura*, pp. 2 and 6) and Jost Harro Schmidt published the allemande as Sweelinck's in 1965 (*Jan Pzn. Sweelinck: Werken voor orgel of clavecimbel uit het "Celler Klavierbuch 1662,"* Exempla Musica Neerlandica, vol. 2 [Amsterdam, 1965], p. 20).

49. Frits Noske, "Een apocrief en een dubieus werk van Sweelinck," *Mededelingenblad VNM* 20 (1966), pp. 27–30; English version under "Music Reviews," *MLA Notes* 24 (1967), pp. 134–35.

50. See *Luitmuziek van Emanuel Adriaenssen, MMB* 10, ed. Godelieve Spiessens (Antwerp, 1966), pp. xiii and 29.

51. The pavan, galliard, and fantasy are transcribed in Cunningham, Appendix V.

52. See du Caurroy's *Fantasies à iii. iiii. v. et vi. parties* (1610) in *Les Oeuvres complètes de Eustache du Caurroy*, ed. Blaise Pidoux (Brooklyn, 1975); three fantasies from le Jeune's *Second Livre des meslanges* (1612) in *Claude le Jeune: Trois fantaisies instrumentales*, ed. J. Bonfils (Paris, 1956); and Guillet's *Vingt-quatre fantasies, à quatre parties, disposées selon l'ordre des douze modes* (1610) in *MMB* 4.

53. In Paris, Bibliothèque Nationale, Fr. 9152; see the detailed discussion of the piece and transcription in Irving Godt, *Guillaume Costeley: Life and Works* (Ph.D. diss., New York University, 1969), pp. 239–83 and 269–70.

54. Modern edition in *Les Maîtres français de l'orgue*, vol. 2, ed. Felix Raugel (Paris, 1959), p. 6.

55. For further discussions of *Vi* see *SK* 1, p. xviii; Lydia Schierning, *Die Ueberlieferung der deutschen Orgel- und Klaviermusik aus der ersten Hälfte des 17. Jahrhunderts* (Kassel, 1961), p. 62–63; and J. H. van der Meer, "The Keyboard Works in the Vienna Bull Manuscript," *TVNM* 18 (1957), pp. 72–105.

56. Ascribed to Sweelinck in *Ly A1* and Berlin, Stadtbibliothek, Gymnasium zum Grauen Kloster, MS HB 103; anonymous in Berlin, Deutsche Staatsbibliothek, MS 340 and Vienna Musikarchiv im Minoritenkonvent, MS 714.

57. The chromatic hexachord fantasy in *Tr, The King's Hunt* in *Bu*, "The Prince's" Galliard in *D2*, and *Revenant* in *Pe 18,1*.

Chapter 2

1. A *Qui tollis* by Philip ap Rhys and an anonymous *Iste confessor* (*EECM* 10:1 and 6:46II) in Add. Ms 29996 (first compiled ca. 1547–49), and an *Agnus Dei* by Redford (*EECM* 10:4) in ChCh 371 (early 1560s). On the basis of the repertoire of the *Mulliner Book*, this author agrees with John Ward's proposed dating: "Je suggère que le *Mulliner Book* a été commencé autour de 1560 . . . et terminé en moins de dix années, bien qu'il n'existe aucune raison qui nous oblige à supposer que la copie fut faite en plus d'une année ou deux." ("Les Sources de la musique pour clavier en Angleterre," in *La Musique instrumentale dans la Renaissance*, p. 230.)

2. These are two *Miserere*, the *Pleni sunt* of Blitheman's *Te Deum*, his second *Gloria tibi Trinitas*, a *Christe Redemptor omnium*, and Carleton's *Gloria tibi Trinitas* (*MB* 1:7, 8, 77, 92, 108, 3). No. 9, Tallis's *Natus est nobis*, is not included here since the cantus firmus is not monorhythmic.

3. Mulliner's taste as reflected by the pieces he chose to copy is stressed by Neighbour, *Byrd*, p. 105.

4. *MB* 28:68.

5. Neighbour, *Byrd*, pp. 107–8.

6. Except in instances where the nature of the proportion is at issue, the term *tripla* is used here to mean both *tripla* (3:1) and *sesquialtera* (3:2). This usage was acknowledged, but not condoned, by Morley. See Thomas Morley, *A Plain and Easy Introduction to Practical Music* (1597), ed. R. Alec Harman (New York, [1952]), pp. 133–34.

7. Sweelinck's adoption of this rhythmic feature is discussed by Alan Curtis in *Sweelinck's Keyboard Music*, pp. 103–4.

8. *SK* 1:9 and 2:12.

9. *EECM* 10:10 and 11.

10. See Neighbour, *Byrd*, p. 104.

11. *EECM* 10:12, *MB* 1:13, and *EECM* 10:13.

12. Neighbour, *Byrd*, p. 106n.

13. *EECM* 6:11 and 20.

14. Two consort In Nomines by Tye, "Farwell my good 1. for ever" and "Rachell's weeping" (*Christopher Tye: The Instrumental Music*, ed. Robert Weidner [New Haven, 1967], pp. 10 and 13), never quite achieve this texture, though their repeated-note and triadic motives are kin to those of Parsons. White's (?) second In Nomine (*MB* 44:28) provides another example of this stock textural device, which can also be seen in numerous consort works of the period, and eventually finds its way into noncantus firmus works such as Philips's Pavan in *Tr* (no. 85) and Bull's Galliard d7.

15. For an example of the texture in a vocal setting, see the "Osanna" from the *Sanctus* of Taverner's Mass *The Western Wynde* (*TCM*, vol. 1, p. 19).

16. *EECM* 10:10.

17. *EECM* 10:12.

18. Neighbour's designations for Byrd's consort and keyboard music are used here throughout.

19. Textual corrections suggested always refer to the second edition of *MB* 14 and 19.

20. Parallels such as this between motives in instrumental music of the period can frequently be drawn. The initial point of Bull's *Salvator mundi* 2, for instance, appears closely related to that of Byrd's In Nomine 5/5, owing to the common distinctive sixth leap.

21. Perhaps Lugge had Bull's examples in mind when he composed the In Nomine in ChCh 49, which states the plainsong through twice.

22. For instance, in Psalm 36, var. 1, in *SK* 2:10.

23. *Tye: The Instrumental Music*, p. 27.

24. See Key, *Instrumental Ensemble Music*, pp. 257–77.

25. See Neighbour, *Byrd*, p. 27.

26. The contents of Add. MS 31390 and Bodley D. 202–16 may be compared in Key, *Instrumental Ensemble Music*, pp. 31–45. Note also the relative paucity of In Nomines in the repertoire represented in *MB* 9 (*Jacobean Consort Music*) as compared with *MB* 44.

27. See especially Thomas Morley, *The First Book of Consort Lessons* (1599), reconstr. and ed. Sydney Beck (New York, 1959), and *MB* 9.

28. Morley, *Introduction,* p. 296.

29. In Roy. App. 56 and Add. MS 29996; all are printed in *EECM* 10:10–21. For further details, see John Caldwell, "Keyboard Plainsong Settings in England, 1500–1660," *Musica Disciplina* 19 (1965), pp. 136–37.

30. Pepusch lists a "Fantasia, Felix namque offertorium" (see Appendix II), but we cannot be sure it was Bull's work.

31. *Tr* is the only source for Tallis's first *Felix namque,* but the second setting appears additionally in *We, Fo, Be* and RML 24.1.4.

32. The date of two anonymous settings in ChCh 1142A (ca. 1640, according to Steele, "English Organs and Organ Music," Appendix, p. 15) is unknown.

33. With regard to the evolution of the keyboard In Nomine, Denis Stevens emphasizes that it was the organists who were in a position to develop cantus firmus composition; see "Les Sources de l'*In nomine,*" in *La Musique instrumentale dans la Renaissance,* pp. 85–90.

34. The use of the organ at offertory for the "princely comminge of her Majestie to the Holy Communion at Estre" and for the Queen's churching is described in *The Old Cheque-Book,* pp. 150 and 169–70.

35. Hawkins gave the following description of Mass in the Chapel Royal: "The alter was furnished with rich plates, with two gilt candlesticks, with lighted candles and a massy crucifix in the midst; and the service was sung not only with organs, but with artificial music of cornets and sackbuts on solemn festivals . . . in short, the service performed in the Queen's chapel, and in sundry cathedrals, was so splendid and showy, that foreigners could not distinguish it from the Roman, except that it was performed in the English tongue." (*A General History,* vol. 3, p. 484.)

36. Neighbour, *Byrd,* p. 106n.

37. Jean Jacquot puts it slightly differently: "En Angleterre, la chanson spirituelle n'a pas fourni en abondance de nouveaux *cantus firmi,* ce qui explique la longue prolifération des *In nomine.*" ("Sur quelques formes de la musique de clavier élisabéthaine [d'après des oeuvres inédites de John Bull]" in *La Musique instrumentale dans la Renaisaance,* p. 247.)

38. The lavish use of the organ and other instruments on a state occasion in 1601 is described by Peter Le Huray in *Music and the Reformation in England 1549–1660* (New York, 1967), p. 77; and the playing of the organ for processions is recounted in *The Old Cheque-Book,* pp. 152–53.

39. See Morley, *Introduction,* p. 136.

40. Denis Stevens theorizes that the purpose of placing a cantus firmus in the tenor in post-Reformation music was to make it less noticeable. ("Les Sources de l'*In nomine,*" p. 88.) This interpretation seems somewhat misguided in view of the ends to which pre-Reformation composers went to obscure the identity of a plainsong through ornamentation and faburden.

41. Two of Strogers's In Nomines are quoted in Key, *Instrumental Ensemble Music,* pp. 271

and 274; Bull's single surviving consort setting (*MB* 9:50) uses this principle of successive contrasting motives.

42. Edward Lowinsky interprets these pieces as a cycle in "English Organ Music of the Renaissance," *MQ* 39 (1953), pp. 543–44, but the notion of a set is more appropriate to the English tradition. Preston's *Felix namque* settings in Roy. App. 56 (*EECM* 10:12–19), though apparently not conceived with the unity of Blitheman's In Nomines, are yet a group of pieces by one composer on a single plainsong.

43. The author is grateful to Davitt Moroney for his observations on Tudor vocal music and the technique of "rhythmic imitation."

44. Taverner's source for the chant may well have included the two extra notes. However, it is noteworthy that the number 54 is a powerful one in Christian-Cabalist terms. It can be factored by two (Christ's dual nature, implicit in his taking human form to come "in Nomine Domini") and by three (the Trinity, explicit in the words of the antiphon): $2 \times 3^3 = 54$. Can it be that this esoteric aspect of the structure of Taverner's passage had something to do with the fascination of other composers with it?

45. See Neighbour, *Byrd*, p. 35. The occurrence of n. 23' in Bull's In Nomines a1, a2, a3, a4, a11 and d corresponds to none of the groupings in the sources and gives no clue to the chronology of the works.

46. See Byrd's two *Salvator mundi* settings and his second *Miserere* in particular (*MB* 28:68, 69, 67).

47. Such offsetting, accomplished through dotting, had been used by Tye in his In Nomine "Seldom sene" (*Tye: The Instrumental Music*, p. 59).

48. Misquoted in the critical note to the piece (*MB* 14, p. 165).

49. See the discussion of Fantasy d1 in chapter 3.

50. *EECM* 10:10.

51. *Early Tudor Masses: I*, pp. 56–60; *Tye: The Instrumental Music*, p. 39; the first seven bars of Strogers's In Nomine are given in Key, *Instrumental Ensemble Music*, p. 257.

52. *MB* 44:42. Making the plainsong "five minims and a crotchet" is one of the options mentioned by Morley for "driving some note or rest through your plainsong" (*Introduction*, p. 169).

53. Preceded by a prelude in d, which is printed with the In Nomine in *MB* 14. There is nothing, however, besides their contiguity in *Tr* to connect the two pieces. The prelude stands independently in *Bu*.

54. *EECM* 10:8.

55. *Pe 16* and *Pe 18,1* (see Appendix II) contained both pieces for Roman use and pieces based on Netherlandish secular tunes.

56. A two-verse and a five-verse *Salve Regina* orginally in *Ant* (according to its "Register") may have been the same as these pieces. *Pe 16* also contained a five-verse setting.

57. Guido Persoons, "John Bull, organist te Antwerpen, 1614–1628," *Musica Sacra "Sancte Sancte"* 64 (1963), p. 42.

58. An entry in the Household Account Books of the Archduke and Archduchess for the

second "tercio," or four-month period, of 1613 shows payments to "maestro felipe, Geri Gersem, Juachin^a Zacarias, P^o Cornetto" and "Vinzencio Guami." Bull's name is added (and Cornet's temporarily disappears) for the third tercio. Cornet's name reappears in the first tercio of 1614, and all six are paid up to the third tercio of 1614, when Bull's name is no longer entered. Guami's name is dropped in the first tercio of 1615. (*Chambre de Comptes* [1837], f. 146', 197' and 385'-388.)

59. All the music in ChCh 89 is transcribed in Raymond Harrison Kelton, *Christ Church Music Ms. no. 89: A Seventeenth-Century Organ Book,* 2 vols. (Ph.D. diss., Boston University Graduate School, 1974), 2. Philips's *Veni Creator Spiritus* (p. 22 in the ms.) is found in vol. 2, p. 46.

60. *CK*, pp. 57 and 68.

61. Thurston Dart, "An Early Seventeenth-Century Book of English Organ Music for the Roman Rite," *M&L* 52 (1971), pp. 27–38.

62. ChCh 89 contains a short toccata (p. 1) with this ascription and another toccata, "a 3" (p. 200), which is a version of the fantasy ascribed to "Wilhelmo Brouno" in Liège, Bibliothèque de l'Université, MS 888 (*Liber Fratrorum Cruciforum*, Archives des Maîtres de l'Orgue, vol. 10, ed. A. Guilmant and A. Pirro [Paris, 1909], p. 88). Dart has identified this person, whose keyboard works are also found in *Cp*, as the Englishman William Browne, "principal benefactor in founding the Jesuit College at Liège in the early seventeenth century" (Dart, "Organ Music for the Roman Rite," pp. 33–34).

63. On pp. 147 and 181; Kelton, *Christ Church 89*, vol. 2 pp. 285 and 333.

64. Two-manual instruments in the Antwerp Cathedral are cited by Dart (*MB* 14, p. xviii) and Persoons ("John Bull," p. 41).

65. On pp. 34, 64, 119; Kelton, *Christ Church 89*, pp. 65, 127, 238.

66. J. H. van der Meer, "The Keyboard Works in the Vienna Bull Manuscript," *TVNM* 18 (1957), p. 99.

67. The complete lack of affinity with the *Salve Regina* verses is overlooked by Wilfred Mellers in his estimation of the position of the *Ant* verses in Bull's oeuvre: "The wild figurations and harmonic adventures of Bull's earlier work are discarded in favor of a texture of the utmost sobriety, recalling Cabezon in its grave restraint. It is probable that during these years Bull became familiar with the Spanish organ school as well as with the Flemish school of Sweelinck, and that he found the mystical fervor of the one as congenial as the earthier vigor of the other." ("John Bull and English Keyboard Music, I," *MQ* 40 [1954], p. 379).

68. *TK,* p. 42.

69. In the preface to *Elizabethan Virginal Music.*

70. Neighbour, *Byrd,* p. 105n.

71. As, for example, in an anonymous three-voice *Audi benigne conditor* (*EECM* 6:30II) and an anonymous four-voice *A solis ortus cardine* (*EECM* 6:24III).

72. *MB* 14, p. 162. See the discussion of this piece on pp. 87-88.

73. *Thomas Tallis,* (London, 1928), p. 214.

74. *EECM* 6:31 and 32; see also ibid., p. 160.

75. John Caldwell, "Keyboard Plainsong Settings in England, 1500–1660," *Musica Disciplina* 19 (1965), p. 150n.

76. Ibid., p. 141n.

77. Since the English organ of the sixteenth century and earlier is so poorly documented, the best record of compass probably lies in the music. Steele observes that "notes above a'' are never required until the seventeenth century, and even as late as this alternatives [e.g., John Lugge's voluntaries] are sometimes provided for instruments adhering to the old, restricted compass." ("English Organs and Organ Music," p. 2.)

78. Examples may be seen in *EECM* 6:4; 10:22, 24, 27; and *MB* 1:36, 48. See also John Caldwell, "The Pitch of Early Tudor Organ Music," in *M&L* 40 (1970), pp. 156–63 and "The Organ in the British Isles until 1600," *The Organ Yearbook* 2 (1971), p. 7.

79. See *MB* 14, pp. xviii–ix.

80. *EECM* 10, p. 28.

Chapter 3

1. In addition to the sources cited in *MB* 14, Prelude a1 is also in Wolfenbüttel, Herzog August Bibliothek MS Helmstedt 1055, a keyboard book containing simple pieces, many of them fingered. (See Willi Apel, *The History of Keyboard Music to 1700*, trans. and rev. Hans Tischler [Bloomington, 1972], p. 381).

2. For instance, Hexachord Fantasy 2, the Quadran Pavan 2 and its Galliard, pavan and galliard pairs G5, G6, and G7, *The King's Hunt, My Jewel* 1, *My Self*, or *My Grief;* Cosyn placed this prelude before the Quadran Pavan 2 in his collection.

3. Charles Butler, *The Principles of Musik in Singing and Setting,* (London, 1636), p. 1.

4. John Dowland, trans., *Andreas Ornithoparcus his Micrologus, or Introduction: Containing the Art of Singing* (London, 1609), p. 36. Ornithoparcus's original treatise was published in Cologne in 1533.

5. Gerald Hendrie shares this author's opinion in part: "It seems highly probable that both pieces [Preludes a4 and a5] are by the same composer, but whereas the first could be by Gibbons, the second is uncharacteristic of him" (*MB 20*, p. 103).

6. Similarly, an F-major prelude attributed to Byrd by Neighbour is related through its harmonic scheme to his Pavan and Galliard F2. See Neighbour, *Byrd*, pp. 210, 221, 222.

7. Caldwell, *English Keyboard Music*, p. 58. The lute fancy is published in *An Anthology of English Lute Music*, ed. David Lumsden (London, 1954), no. 23. Only the first 18 bars of the organ piece actually correspond to the lute model.

8. Fantasy C4 (*MB* 27:28).

9. *TK*, p. 32; *MB* 28:66, 47, and 50.

10. *MB* 24:55; *SK* 1:10.

11. The frequency with which this proportion occurs in music (see especially J. H. Douglas Webster, "Golden-Mean Form in Music," *M&L* 31 [1950], pp. 238–48) does not necessarily imply an intentional use of it in all cases, for the Golden Section occurs as a

virtually universal phenomenon of nature, and very early became a recognized principle in design (see H. E. Huntley, *The Divine Proportion: A Study in Mathematical Beauty* [New York, 1970]). However, studies of its use by some composers show that it can play such a significant role in the structure of the music as to be unmistakably planned (see M. van Crevel's introductions to the masses *Sub tuum praesidium* and *Maria zart* in *Jacobus Obrecht: Opera omnia,* vols. 6 and 7 [Amsterdam, 1959 and 1964]; and two works of Ernö Lendvai, *Béla Bartók: An Analysis of His Music* [London, 1971] and *Bartók and Kodály,* 3 vols., rev. ed. [Budapest, 1979], passim.). The present case, an isolated one in Bull's music, may or may not be of great meaning.

12. The structural proportion is obscured by the rebarring in ¾ of the ostinato section in the *MB* transcription. It can only be arrived at on the basis of the real length of the piece, 134 semibreves, not on the basis of 122 bars of varying length.

13. Apel (*Keyboard Music to 1700,* p. 306) cites the *Gloria* (b. 104ff.) of Ockeghem's Mass *De plus en plus* as an early example, followed by Obrecht and Issac.

14. See Tientos 2 (b. 45–57), 10 (b. 125–40) and 13 (b. 69–87) in *The Collected Works of Antonio de Cabezón,* ed. Charles Jacobs (Brooklyn, 1972).

15. *FK,* p. 57.

16. *Tutte le opere di Claudio Monteverdi,* vol. 14, ed. G. Francisco Malipiero (Bologna, 1932), 14, p. 250.

17. *John Taverner* (London, 1923), p. 16.

18. *BW* 17, no. 11; see Neighbour, *Byrd,* pp. 64–65.

19. Neighbour, *Byrd,* p. 226, and Dart in *MB* 14, p. 162.

20. *MB* 27:27.

21. *BW* 17, no. 34; see Neighbour, *Byrd,* p. 92. Examples of this type of bilateral theme can be found in *O salutaris hostia* or *Felix es sacra Virgo* (*William Byrd: Gradualia, Books I and II* [London, 1927], pp. 129 and 28).

22. See Morley, *Introduction,* pp. 24 and 26.

23. *MB* 18:53, 53a, 20.

24. *Altenglische Orgelmusik,* pp. 13 and 15.

25. *MB* 5:21; possibly based on the Offertory *Exsultant Sancti* (tune in *EECM* 10, p. 135) or *Benedictus sit Deus Pater,* on which Philip ap Rhys's Offertory is based, but there are other plainsongs as well from which the ostinato could have been derived.

26. Morley, *Introduction,* p. 249.

27. *J. P. Sweelinck: Werken voor orgel en clavecimbel,* ed. M. Seiffert (Amsterdam, 1943), no. 12.

28. Curtis, *Sweelinck's Keyboard Music,* pp. 61–64. Thurston Dart had earlier recognized the correspondence between the three pieces and accepted the ascription of *God Save the King* to Bull as correct. However, he took Seiffert's no. 13 to be the work of Sweelinck. See "Sweelinck's 'Fantasia on a theme used by John Bull'," *TVNM* 18 (1959), pp. 167–69.

29. *SK* 1, 1:5; *CW,* no. 5; *FK* 2, pp. 3 and 10; see also an anonymous lute fancy in

Lumsden, *An Anthology of English Lute Music,* no. 24. A hexachord fantasy in ChCh 89 (p. 181; Kelton, *Christ Church 89,* vol. 2, p. 347) also belongs to this second species, though it, like Byrd's second hexachord fantasy, ends with figuration and tripla. A number of its figurations as well as an overall plainsong-setting approach speak in favor of an English attribution of this anonymous piece.

30. Another hexachord fantasy is given in Pepusch's list. Folio 53 of his Number 16 was "Fantasia sopra ut, re, mi, fa, sol, la, a.2. a.2, 3, et 4, diversis modis." A footnote in Ward's *Lives* states, "This piece is not the same with any other on this subject," meaning not the same as either of those in *Tr,* which Pepusch owned (see Appendix II).

31. *FK* 5, p. 44.

32. Among those who talk about equal temperament for lutes and viols are Francisco Salinas, Vincenzo Galilei, Nicola Vicentino, Marin Mersenne and Pietro Aron (see J. Murray Barbour, *Tuning and Temperament: A Historical Survey,* 2d ed. [East Lansing, Michigan, 1953], passim. and pp. 11–12 where iconographical evidence is cited; and Edward Lowinsky, "Echoes of Willaert's Chromatic 'Duo' in Sixteenth and Seventeenth-Century Compositions," in *Studies in Music History: Essays for Oliver Strunk,* ed. Harold Powers [Princeton, 1968], p. 211). Isaac Newton, too, is quoted on the subject by Mark Linley in "Instructions for the Clavier Diversely Tempered," *Early Music* 5 (1977), p. 18.

33. Barbour, *Tuning and Temperament,* pp. 190–91.

34. Steele, *English Organs and Organ Music,* p. 202.

35. Lowinsky, "Echoes of Willaert's Chromatic 'Duo'." For present purposes the composer of the ensemble fantasies in question will be called simply Alfonso.

36. *MB* 9:39 and "Echoes of Willaert's Chromatic 'Duo'," pp. 213–18. The four-part version is found in *MB* 9:23 and Ernest Walker, "An Oxford Book of Fancies," *The Musical Antiquary* 3 (1912), pp. 70–73. Lowinsky gives a complete list of sources and examines the ascriptions on pp. 223–25 of his article (see also *MB* 9, pp. 221 and 222). Keyboard transcriptions are in Add. MS 29996 (Tomkins's hand) and ChCh 436.

37. Apel, *Keyboard Music to 1700,* p. 307.

38. See the *Correspondance du P. Marin Mersenne,* vol. 1 (Paris, 1932), pp. 75, 79–80, 223. Mersenne gives plates of keyboards with split keys in the *Traité des consonances, Livre troisiesme des genres de la musique* and in the *Traité des instrvmens, Livre troisiesme des orgues* of the *Harmonie universelle.* For a fairly complete discussion of split key instruments, see Frank Hubbard, *Three Centuries of Harpsichord Making* (Cambridge, Mass., 1965), pp. 32–36.

39. Curtis, *Sweelinck's Keyboard Music,* p. 146.

40. Several from Italy do exist. See Hubbard, *Harpsichord Making,* pp. 134ff. and 36.

41. Barbour gives the following information about organs with split keys in *Tuning and Temperament,* p. 108: "Handel played on English organs with split keys [Helmholtz, *Sensations of Tone,* p. 434]. Father Smith's Temple Church organ in London, constructed in 1682–83, had the same pairs of divided keys as the Lucca organ, G-sharp – A-flat and D-sharp – E-flat, and so did Durham Cathedral." Certainly, either split keys or some form of equalized temperament is required by two pieces of Nicholas Carleton (d. 1630), *A Verse of Four Parts* and *Upon the Sharp (Pieces from the Tomkins*

Manuscript, ed. Frank Dawes [London, 1951], nos. 4 and 5). Indirect evidence for the existence of split-key instruments may be found in a work of Salomon de Caus (1576–1626), one of Bull's colleagues under Prince Henry. His *Institution Harmonique* (Frankfurt, 1615) contains a description of an expanded Pythagorean tuning which requires four extra keys. Per se, however, de Caus's system does not render Bull's piece playable.

42. *MB* 14, p. 160. Dart's list of the copies attributed to Poglietti is incomplete. They are given as follows in Friedrich Wilhelm Riedel, *Quellenkundliche Beiträge zur Geschichte der Musik für Tasteninstrumente in der zweiten Hälfte des 17. Jahrhunderts* (Kassel, 1960), pp. 149–50, 145–46, 142: In keyboard tablature in Vienna, Musikarchiv des Minoritenkonventes XIV 710; Berlin Deutsche Staatsbibliothek Mus. MS 17670 (b) (now in Marburg); and Munich, Bayerische Staatsbibliothek MS 4495 (Beiband 3); in score for four-part strings in Berlin, Deutsche Staatsbibliothek Mus. MS 17670 (c) and Vienna, Bibliothek der Gesellschaft der Musikfreunde IX 6809. In addition, the piece appears twice as a didactic example: in Poglietti's *Musica aulica,* formerly owned by the Minoritenkonvent but now, according to Curtis (p. 63), in Vienna, Stadtbibliothek Musiksammlung MS 10074 (according to Riedel, "verschollen") and in Poglietti's *Compendium oder kurtzer Begriff, und Einführung zur Musica* (1676), owned by the Benediktinerstift Kremsmünster, Regenterei (L 146).

43. Gerd Zacher, "Frescobaldi und die instrumentale Redekunst," *Musik und Kirche* 45 (1975), pp. 54–64. Warren Kirkendale discusses movements of the *Fiori musicali* as *principium* and *insinuatio* in "Ciceronians versus Aristotelians on the Ricercar as Exordium from Bembo to Bach," *JAMS* 32 (1979), pp. 41–42. See also Ursula Kirkendale's valuable study, "The Source for Bach's *Musical Offering:* The *Institutio Oratoria* of Quintilian," *JAMS* 33 (1980), pp. 88–141.

44. Facsim. ed. Gainesville, Florida, 1962.

45. See William Crane's introduction to the facsimile edition of Henry Peacham's *Garden of Eloquence* (Gainesville, Fla., 1954), p. 7.

46. Thomas Wilson, *The Arte of Rhetorique* (London, 1553), p. 7.

47. Ibid., p. 99. The identification of opening imitation with *insinuatio,* as opposed to *principio,* or the straightforward beginning, has been amply documented by W. Kirkendale, in "Ciceronians versus Aristotelians."

48. Nicola Vicentino, *L'Antica musica ridotta alla moderna* (1555), passage quoted and translated by Claude Palisca in "*Ut oratoria musica:* The Rhetorical Basis of Musical Mannerism," in *The Meaning of Mannerism* (Hanover, N.H., 1972), p. 39.

49. Wilson, *The Arte of Rhetorique,* p. 106.

50. Francis Bacon, *Sylva Sylvarum: or a Naturall Historie In Ten Centuries* (London, 1627), p. 38.

51. Wilson, *The Arte of Rhetorique,* pp. 109, 112, 113.

52. Butler, *The Principles of Musick,* p. 90. Butler's treatise *Rhetoricae, libri duo* (London, 1598) was frequently reprinted in the seventeenth century.

53. Wilson, *The Arte of Rhetorique,* pp. 114 and 123.

54. Palisca, "Ut oratoria musica," and Willem Elders, "Humanism and Early-Renaissance

Music: A Study of the Ceremonial Music by Ciconia and Dufay,'' *TVNM* 27 (1977), pp. 65–101.

55. Reprint, ed. Edward Arber (London, 1869). See also the analogy of tropes and figures with musical devices in Henry Peacham's *The Garden of Eloquence* and *The Compleat Gentleman*.

56. Morley, who tried to comprehensively cover the subject of composition, nowhere suggests that there is any correlation between the two disciplines.

57. See note 11, above.

58. Frances Yates, *The Occult Philosophy in the Elizabethan Age* (London, 1979).

59. One English composer of the sixteenth century did write about his interest in astrology. See *The Autobiography of Thomas Whythorne,* ed. James M. Osborn (Oxford, 1961), pp. 59 and 204–6.

60. A useful introduction to this topic is Gregory Butler's "Music and Rhetoric in Early Seventeenth-Century English Sources," *MQ* 66 (1980), pp. 53–64.

61. Richard S. Sprague, ed., *The Rule of Reason, Conteinying the Arte of Logique by Thomas Wilson* (Northridge, Ca., 1972), p. 10.

62. See, for example, the fantasy in the fifth tone and the fantasy in the eighth tone (*CK,* pp. 42 and 46–47).

63. In Liège 888 (*Archives des maîtres de l'orgue,* vol. 10, p. 11).

64. See Luyton's ricercar no. 7 (*MMB* 4, p. 89) and four fantasies of Cornet (nos. 2 and 5 in *CK,* plus the two ascribed to him in ChCh 89 [Kelton, *Christ Church 89,* vol. 2, pp. 525 and 530]); also two fantasies and two toccatas of Sweelinck (*SK* 1:3, 5, 18, 19), to mention but a few examples.

65. Dart's list of the sources of the canzona is incomplete. The fuller version is found in *Partidura per sonare delle canzonette alla francese, del Sig. Giuseppe Guami* (Venice, 1601) and in *Canzonette francese a quattro, cinque, et otto voci . . . del Signor Gioseppe Guami* (Antwerp, 1612); the second version is found in Adriano Banchieri's *Canzoni alla francese a quattro voci per sonare . . . libro secondo* (Venice, 1596), Johann Woltz's *Nova musices organicae tabulatura* (Basel, 1617), and in two manuscript sources, Verona, Biblioteca Capitolare Cod. MCXXVIII and Vienna, Musikarchiv des Minoritenkonvents XIV 714. Both versions are published in *Giuseppe Guami: Canzoni da sonare,* ed. I. Fuser and O. Mischiati (Florence, 1968), pp. 47 and 99.

66. Neither the *La Leona* of Gussago (*Sonate a quattro, sei et otto,* Venice, 1608) mentioned by Dart nor a nine–part canzona of the same name by Pietro Lappi (*Canzoni da suonare . . . libro primo,* Venice, 1616) is the basis of this composition.

67. The madrigal first appeared in *Il desiderio, il libro de madrigali* (Venice, 1566). It is published in *Le Opere complete da Giovanni Pierluigi Palestrina,* vol. 9 (Rome, 1940), p. 117. The *prima parte* appeared with an English text in *Musica transalpina* (London, 1588). *Vestiva i colli* was ornamented, parodied, and adapted by numerous Italian composers, including Bassano, Orazio and Orfeo Vecchi, Banchieri, Monte, G. Maria Nanino, Ruggero Giovanelli, and Palestrina himself (see Gustave Reese, *Music in the Renaissance,* rev. ed. [New York, 1959], pp. 403, 435, 490, 437, 703, 465, 471, and *Le Opere complete da Palestrina,* vol. 9, p. x), and is the basis of two recently discovered

masses given anonymously in a Berkeley manuscript (see John Emerson, "Manuscripts of the U.C.B. Music Library: MS 798, The Folario Massbook," *Cum notis variorum*, no. 13 [June, 1977], p. 7). The madrigal is also intabulated anonymously for keyboard in *El*. A "Capriccio sopra Vestiva i Colli" ascribed to Frescobaldi in Rome, Biblioteca Vaticana, Chigi Q. IV 25 appears mistitled, for it bears no resemblance to the madrigal (*Keyboard Compositions Preserved in Manuscript*, ed. W. R. Shindle, 1968). As cited by Dart (*MB* 14, p. xx), Vincenzo Giustiniani reports having heard *Vestiva i colli* played (in Bull's arrangement?) "on the bells of the campanile of the principal church in Antwerp" (Nigel Fortune, "Giustiniani on Instruments," *Galpin Society Journal*, no. 5 [1952], p. 51).

68. *MMB* 2, p. 69.

69. *Archives des maîtres de l'orgue*, vol. 10, p. 146.

70. Many of Du Caurroy's fantasies in the 1610 publication are based on tunes from the 1551 Genevan Psalter. Number 37 is a monothematic composition on the same point as that which opens Bull's Fantasy d4.

71. Steele, *English Organs and Organ Music*, pp. 209–10.

72. The style of Philips's piece suggests that it is Continental and postdates Byrd's, where he probably got the theme (Neighbour, *Byrd*, p. 234).

73. *Les Maîtres français de l'orgue*, vol. 2, ed. Felix Raugel (Paris, 1949), p. 6.

74. *SK* 1, p. liii–liv. No. 14, not no. 13, is obviously meant here.

75. *MB* 19, p. 223.

76. Curtis, *Sweelinck's Keyboard Music*, pp. 133–43.

77. *Nine Fantasias in Four Parts*, p. 5, in short score in *MB* 14:58a. On the question of attribution of the work, see Gordon Dodd, "Coperario or Bull?" *Chelys* 1 (1969), p. 41.

Chapter 4

1. Pavan and Galliard d3 and Galliard g3 are preserved only in *Ant*, and two galliards, D and G10, are found in *D2*. The former of these two also appears in *Vi*, in a somewhat different text, and is probably by chance or accident absent from the major English manuscripts. In addition, Pavan gl is unique to *Co*.

2. Perhaps the "Mlle de la Haye" whose name appears in the list of Elizabeth's train; see Green, *Elizabeth, Electress Palatine*, pp. 415–17.

3. Morley, *Introduction*, pp. 296–97.

4. BL, Egerton 3665, pp. 1028–29; see also Neighbour, *Byrd*, pp. 181 and 189.

5. *MMN* 3, p. 53.

6. The parody was discovered by Neighbour, *Byrd*, pp. 206ff.

7. See Curtis, *Sweelinck's Keyboard Music*, pp. 99ff.

8. "Harding's Galliard" (*MB* 28:55), an arrangement, and Galliard C4 (*MB* 27:34), a

special instance related to Bull's Galliard D (see the discussion below), are his only examples.

9. Neighbour, *Byrd,* p. 21f.

10. Namely, Richardson's galliard and its variation, nos. 29–30, and the variation of his galliard no. 6; Tisdale's galliard, no. [295].

11. Neighbour, *Byrd,* pp. 210ff; see also the discussion of Pavan and Galliard G2, below.

12. For the sake of convenience, the bar numbering of *MB* is used throughout in referring to matters concerning its text.

13. Neighbour, *Byrd,* pp. 182ff.

14. The intermediate cadence on the supertonic in a strain firmly anchored in the tonic is not part of Bull's usual vocabulary (*My Self* is a notable exception). Tonal emphasis on the second degree in the major mode is, however, idiomatic to much popular music, such as "Voice of the Earth" (set by Byrd as *The Ghost*), "Go from my Window" and "The Woods so Wild." Byrd seems to have taken a stronger liking to the inflection than Bull; see his consort ground, *Browning* and *The Hunt's Up.*

15. Neighbour, *Byrd,* p. 217.

16. Frits Noske mentions the connection in his critical note to Sweelinck's variations on the tune (*SK* 1, 3, p. xxiv), but Warren Kirkendale maintains that Bull's piece is not related to the popular harmonic ground (*L'Aria di fiorenza, id est, Il ballo del granduca* [Florence, 1972], p. 17).

17. The wife of Sir Thomas Lucy (1532–1600) died in 1595/6. Their eldest son, Thomas, was knighted in 1593 and married twice, but died in 1605. Two of his sons, a third Thomas and a Richard, were knighted only after Bull left England. (*Dictionary of National Biography,* s.v. "Sir Thomas Lucy.") It is more likely, however, that the dedicatee was Lady Lucy, masquer and countess of Bedford, who appeared frequently on the Jacobean stage. (See Sabol, *Four Hundred Songs and Dances,* p. 580.)

18. Note that only in *Co* is the piece connected with Queen Elizabeth; for Dart's theory, see *MB* 19, p. 231.

19. Neighbour, *Byrd,* p. 188. Philips's piece is called "Cromatica Pavana" in its lute version; see Curtis, *Sweelinck's Keyboard Music,* p. 136.

20. Neighbour, *Byrd,* pp. 252–53.

21. The pattern is fairly widespread in instrumental and vocal music in England and on the Continent. But two disparate examples are found in a Fantasy in d by Gibbons (*MB* 20:8) and in the "Gloria Patri" from the smaller Magnificat setting of Monteverdi's *Vespro della beata Virgine* (1610).

22. Morley, *Introduction,* p. 296.

23. The same doleful associations later became attached to the allemande, as Froberger's laments attest.

24. See Lawrence Babb, *The Elizabethan Malady: A Study of Melancholia in English Literature form 1550 to 1642* (East Lansing, Michigan, 1951); Raymond Klibansky, Erwin Panofsky and Fritz Saxl, *Saturn and Melancholy* (London, 1964); and especially Yates, *The Occult Philosophy in the Elizabethan Age.*

25. See Klibansky, et al., *Saturn and Melancholy,* pp. 46, 85, 267, 268.

26. James Cleland, *The Institution of a yovng noble man* (Oxford, 1607), p. 225; facsim. ed. Max Molyneux (New York, 1948).

27. There is no evidence to suggest which of the Barons Hunsdon the dedication refers to. The first, Henry Carey, died in 1596; the second, George Carey, died in 1603; and the third, John Carey, in 1617. (*Dictionary of National Biography,* s. v. "Hunsdon.")

28. In the revised edition of *MB* 19, Dart noted, "The titles of nos. 126a and 126b have hitherto been read as 'Sir Thomas Wake' and I am now inclined to think that this reading is more likely to be correct than my suggestion of 'St. Thomas, Wake!' " I can see no reason for such a conclusion, as the titles in both *Tr* and *Pa* read "St." not "Sir." In all likelihood the title refers to a song associated with a vigil or festival (such as a parish fair) of the saint.

29. Neighbour, *Byrd,* pp. 210–14.

30. The subdominant opening of Galliard G6/II is apparently intended as a preparation for the dominant third strain, which effectively develops the material of the former on a plane one tone higher.

31. Peculiar keyboard requirements in both the d3 and g3 Pavans further set them apart from the pavans and galliards in other sources. Pavan d3 calls for an instrument with a short-octave C compass (see. b. 8, 24 and 32), and Pavan g3 demands a c'''. Such requirements would appear to indicate that the pieces were conceived for a different instrument than were those in the English sources, which nowhere require a note above a'' but often need AA.

Chapter 5

1. Such as Byrd's Corantos a1, a2 and a3 (*MB* 27:21a, b and c); see Neighbour, *Byrd,* p. 170.

2. "The Alman is a more heavy dance than [the galliard], (fitly representing the nature of the people whose name it carrieth) so that no extraordinary motions are used in dancing it." (Morley, *Introduction,* p. 297.)

3. Nicolas Vallet, *Secretum Musarum,* ed. André Souris (Paris, 1970).

4. *MB* 19, p. xv.

5. See a masque by Adson in Sabol, *Four Hundred Songs and Dances,* no. 136, and one in Thomas Robinson's *The Schoole of Musicke,* ed. David Lumsden (Paris, 1971), no. 6.

6. A setting in Lüneburg, Ratsbücherei MS KN 146, called "Ein Englischer Bauern Dantz," is by a younger composer.

7. No. 5 in Brade's *Newe lustige Volten,* 1621 (Wilhelmshaven and New York, [1963]) and *Brabansche Ronden* in *So* also begin this way.

8. The variation to *My Grief* printed in *MB* 19 cannot be by Weckmann, as the editor suggests, since the German organist and composer had nothing to do with the collection from which it comes.

Chapter 6

1. Dart cites the existence of seven further variations on Ground 1 in Oxford, Bodleian Mus. Sch. 217, for a total of twenty-one variations, and identifies this fuller form of the piece with one praised by Charles Butler in his *Principles of Music* (1636): "Sometime one Part singeth Plain-song, and the rest do discant upon it: as in D. *Bulls* Ground: the which upon 4 Plain Sembriefs [the first in *C–fa–ut,* the 2 in *F–fa–ut,* the 3 in *G–sol–re–ut,* and the 4 in *C–fa–ut,*] hath 21 several Discants, all conjoined in one sweete Lesson; and in the excellent Musik of the *In-nomines* of Parsons, Taverner, D. Ty, &c." Whether the work in question and that to which Butler refers are the same is doubtful, for it is strange that a scholar of Butler's erudition would have singled out such an undistinguished work as an example of skillful discanting upon a ground. Furthermore, Butler speaks of a ground of four semibreves, and the present one occupies *eight* semibreves.

2. This author is grateful to Lawrence Moe for pointing out to me that this bass resembles the first and last thirds of that of a version of the "Bel fiore" in *Intabolatura de leuto de diversi autori* (Milan, 1536); see Howard Mayer Brown, *Instrumental Music Printed before 1600* (Cambridge, Mass., 1965): 1536₉.

3. *Ten Pieces by Hugh Aston and Others,* ed. Frank Dawes (London, 1951), no. 2.

4. *DVB,* no. 9.

5. John M. Ward, "Apropos 'The British Broadside Ballad and Its Music,' " *JAMS* 20 (1967), p. 54; the piece in question is printed in Sabol, *Four Hundred Songs and Dances,* no. 214 (see also "Buffons," no. 216).

6. Bull's use of the theme in "The March of the Horsemen" from Byrd's piece add weight to the connection; however, see other thematic resemblances in lute music cited by Diana Poulton, *John Dowland: His Life and Works* (Berkeley and Los Angeles, 1972), pp. 172–73.

7. Neighbour, *Byrd,* p. 141–43; *MK* 1:3; *MB* 28:70a and b.

8. There are notable similarities between the music in Ex. 5b and c and that of the first and fourth variations of a Quadran pavan ascribed to Sweelinck in a source from the second half of the seventeenth century, Budapest, Nemseti Museum, Ms. BS Bartfa 27. (See *SK* 1, 3, p. xx and 59, where the work is printed as an *opus dubium* of Sweelinck.) Clearly, English composers had no patent on these discants.

9. The matter of the identification of one such harmonic-bass pattern is taken up in detail in Warren Kirkendale's *L'Aria di fiorenza.*

10. Quoted in Ward, "Apropos," p. 52. For further discussion of the particular importance of the passamezzo moderno, see Otto Gombosi, "Stephen Foster and 'Gregory Walker,' " in *MQ* 30 (April, 1944), pp. 133–46.

11. Tregian's ascription of the piece to Byrd is rejected by Neighbour, pp. 115–16.

12. For sources of the Spanish Pavan and other settings, see the following: Florimond van Duyse, *Het oude nederlandsche lied,* 3 vols. ('s-Gravenhage, 1903–8), 1, p. 610ff. and 2, p. 1101ff; William Chappell, *Popular Music of Olden Time* (London, [1855–59]), pp. 240–41; W. Chappell, *Old English Popular Music,* new ed. by H. E. Wooldridge, 2 vols. (1893; reprint ed. New York, [1961]), pp. 251–52; Claude M. Simpson, *The*

British Broadside Ballad and Its Music (New Brunswick, 1966), pp. 678–81; Ward, "Apropos," p. 75; Curtis in *MMN* 3, p. xxxviii; and Diana Poulton, "Notes on the Spanish Pavan," *The Lute Society Journal* 3 (1961), pp. 5–16.

13. Poulton, "Notes on the Spanish Pavan," p. 7. Considering the pavan to be sixteen bars, a setting in Thomas Robinson's *The Schoole of Musicke* (1603; ed. David Lumsden [Paris, 1971], no. 27) follows closely Bull's var. 1, with the exception of b. 10 and 13–16.

14. See Chappell, *Popular Music of Olden Time*, pp. 218–19; Chappell, *Old English Popular Music*, pp. 248–49; Simpson *The British Broadside Ballad*, pp. 570–71; Ward, "Apropos," p. 65; and Sabol, *Four Hundred Songs and Dances*, p. 620.

15. The two settings are cited in Chappell, *Old English Popular Music*, p. 272; that of Add. MS 30486 is transcribed in Dawes, *Seven Virginal Pieces*, no. 5.

16. Two further concordances may be added to Dart's list (*MB* 19, p. 227). Maas (*English Pastime Music*, p. xix) cites a second copy of *Pl*, f. 111 in Drexel 5609, p. 85, and a second copy of *Pl*, f. 108'/*Co* p. 59 in Drexel 5609, p. 81. Both pieces are ascribed to Bull in the Drexel manuscript.

17. The shape of Bull's motive opening var. 5 and its echo-like restatement after two bars are strongly suggestive of the echo passage in keyboard settings of "Moll Sims," a tune which resembles in part "Wanton Season"; see Curtis, *Sweelinck's Keyboard Music*, p. 117.

18. See Chappell, *Popular Music of Olden Time*, pp. 121–23; Chappell, *Old English Popular Music*, pp. 69–71; Simpson *The British Broadside Ballad*, p. 741; Ward, "Apropos," pp. 79–83.

19. Neighbour, *Byrd*, p. 154.

20. In his critical note to *Walsingham*, Dart observes that the omission of 13 of the variations in *El* may explain Ward's qualification, "at different times." This seems improbable, however, since *El* postdates both Bull's departure from England and the compilation of *Tr* and *Bu*. In addition, the ordering in *El* makes little sense, even as a preliminary version, and probably represents Ellis's own cuts.

21. See Chappell, *Popular Music of Olden Time*, pp. 121–23; Chappell, *Old English Popular Music*, p. 146; Simpson, *The British Broadside Ballad*, pp. 257–59. Bull's fine set of variations did not find its way into *Tr* or *Bu*, strongly implying that it was written very late in Bull's English career.

22. The tune is also known as "My Robin Is to the Greenwood Gone." See Chappell, *Popular Music of Olden Time*, pp. 233–34; Chappell, *Old English Popular Music*, p. 153; Simpson, *The English Broadside Ballad*, pp. 59–64; Ward, "Apropos," p. 31; and Frederick W. Sternfeld, *Music in Shakespearean Tragedy* (London, 1963), pp. 68–78.

23. The current author knows of only one other setting of this tune (mentioned by Braun, *Britannica Abundans*, pp. 246–47), an arrangement by Samuel Scheidt called "Canzon a 5 voc. ad imitationem Bergamas. Angl.," no. 26 in his *Paduana, galliarda, couranta, alemande, intrada, canzonetto* (1621), published in *Samuel Scheidt: Werke*, vol. 2/3 (Hamburg, 1928), p. 36.

24. A similarly confusing situation arises in two sets of variations on "Go from My Window" in *Tr* (nos. 9 and 42). Ascribed respectively to Morley and Munday, the pieces

are identical except that the latter set has an extra variation added at the end. Curiously, that variation is wholly typical of Morley.

25. *MB* 24, p. 143.

26. *MB* 19, p. 227.

27. The tune is called "En revenant de Saint-Nicholas" in a setting for three lutes by Besard in *Novus Partus sive Concertationes Musical* (1617), published in O. Chilesotti, *Lautenspieler des XVI. Jahrhunderts* (Leipzig, 1929), p. 212. The keyboard setting by Gibbons or Johnson is ascribed to the former composer in *Bu* (Cosyn's hand), *D2*, *El* and *Tu* and to the latter in *Elizabeth Rogers' Virginal Book* and *Dl*. Gerald Hendrie accepts the Gibbons ascription and prints the text from *Bu* in *MB* 20:27.

28. Frits Noske, "John Bull's Dutch carol," *M & L* 44 (October, 1963), pp. 326–33.

Bibliography

I. Printed Music

Luitmuziek van Emanuel Adriaenssen. Edited By Godelieve Spiessens. Monumenta Musicae Belgicae, vol. 10. Berchem-Antwerp: De Ring, 1968.

Altenglische Orgelmusik. Edited by Denis Stevens. Kassel: Bärenreiter, 1953.

An Anthology of English Lute Music. Edited by David Lumsden. London: Schott, 1954.

Banchieri, Adriano. *Canzoni alla francese a quattro voci per sonare . . . libro secondo.* Venice, 1596.

Bermudo, Juan. *Declaración de Instrumentos Musicales.* Edited by Pierre Froidebise. Orgue et Liturgie, vol. 47. Paris: Schola Cantorum, [1960].

Brade, William. *Newe lustige volten, couranten, balleten, paduanen, galliarden und masqueraden.* Wilhelmshaven: Heinrichshofen, [1963].

Harpsichord Pieces from Dr. John Bull's Flemish Tabulatura. Edited by Hans F. Redlich. Wilhelmshaven: Otto Heinrich Noetzel, 1958.

John Bull: Keyboard Music I. 2d rev. ed. Edited by John Steele and Francis Cameron. Musica Britannica, vol. 14. London: Stainer and Bell, 1967.

John Bull: Keyboard Music II. 2d ed. Edited by Thurston Dart. Musica Britannica, vol. 19. London: Stainer and Bell, 1970.

John Bull: Selected Edition. Edited by Margaret H. Glyn. 2 vols. London: Stainer and Bell [1928].

Byrd, William. *Consort Music.* Edited by K. Elliot. The Byrd Edition, vol. 17. London: Stainer and Bell, 1971.

William Byrd: Gradualia, Books I and II. Tudor Church Music, vol. 7. Edited by P. C. Buck et al. London: Oxford University Press, 1927.

William Byrd: Keyboard Music. 2d rev. ed. Edited by Alan Brown. Musica Britannica, vols. 27 and 28. London: Stainer and Bell, 1976.

The Collected Works of Antonio de Cabezón. Edited by Charles Jacobs. 3 vols. Brooklyn: Institute of Mediaeval Music, 1967–76.

Casteliono, Giovanni Antonio. *Intabolatura de leuto de diversi autori.* Milan, 1536.

Les Oeuvres complètes de Eustache du Caurroy. Edited by Blaise Pidoux. Brooklyn: Institute of Mediaeval Music, 1975.

Consort Songs. Edited by Philip Brett. Musica Britannica, vol. 22. London: Stainer and Bell, 1967.

Pieter Cornet: Collected Keyboard Works. Edited by Willi Apel. Corpus of Early Keyboard Music, vol. 26. n.p.: American Institute of Musicology, 1969.

Benjamin Cosyn. *Three Voluntaries for Organ.* Edited by John Steele. London: Novello, 1959.

Twenty-five Pieces for Keyed Instruments from Benjamin Cosyn's Virginal Book. Edited by J. A. Fuller-Maitland and W. Barclay Squire. London: J. and W. Chester, 1924.

The Dublin Virginal Manuscript. Edited by John Ward. Wellesley, Mass.: Wellesley College, 1954.

Dutch Keyboard Music of the 16th and 17th Centuries. Edited by Alan Curtis. Monumenta Musica Nederlandica, vol. 3. Amsterdam: Vereniging voor Nederlandse Muziekgeschiedenis, 1961.

Early English Organ Music. Edited by Margaret H. Glyn. London: The Plainsong and Medieval Music Society, 1939.

Early Tudor Masses: I. Edited by John D. Bergsagel. Early English Church Music, vol. 1. London: Stainer and Bell, 1962.

Early Tudor Organ Music I: Music for the Office. Edited by John Caldwell. Early English Church Music, vol. 6. London: Stainer and Bell, 1965.

Early Tudor Organ Music II: Music for the Mass. Edited by Denis Stevens. Early English Church Music, vol. 10. London: Stainer and Bell, 1967.

Elizabethan Consort Music: I. Edited by Paul Doe. Musica Britannica, vol. 44. London: Stainer and Bell, 1979.

English Pastime Music, 1630–1660: An Anthology of Keyboard Pieces. Edited by Martha Maas. Madison: A-R Editions, 1974.

The Eton Choirbook: I. Edited by Frank L. L. Harrison. Musica Britannica, vol. 10. London: Stainer and Bell, 1956.

Giles and Richard Farnaby: Keyboard Music. Edited by Richard Marlow. Musica Britannica, vol. 24. London: Stainer and Bell, 1965.

The Fitzwilliam Virginal Book. Edited by J. A. Fuller-Maitland and W. Barclay Squire. 1899. Reprint. New York: Dover, 1963.

Girolamo Frescobaldi: Orgel- und Klavierwerke. Edited by Pierre Pidoux. 5 vols. Kassel: Bärenreiter, 1949–54.

Girolamo Frescobaldi: Keyboard Compositions Preserved in Manuscript. Edited by W. R. Shindle. Corpus of Early Keyboard Music, vol. 30. n.p.: American Institute of Musicology, 1968.

Girolamo Frescobaldi: Il primo libro di toccate d'intavolatura. Edited by Etienne Darbellay. Monumenti Musicali Italiani, vol. 4/2. Milan: Zerboni, 1977.

Girolamo Frescobaldi: Il secondo libro di toccate d'intavolatura. Edited by Etienne Darbellay. Monumenti Musicali Italiani, vol. 5/3. Milan: Zerboni, 1979.

Orlando Gibbons: Complete Keyboard Works. Edited by Margaret H. Glyn. 5 vols. London: Stainer and Bell, [1925].

Orlando Gibbons: Keyboard Music. 2d rev. ed. Edited by Gerald Hendrie. Musica Britannica, vol. 20. London: Stainer and Bell, 1967.

Graduale Sarisburiense. Edited by Walter Howard Frere. Facsimile. London: The Plainsong and Mediaeval Music Society, 1894.

Giuseppe Guami: Canzoni da sonare. Edited by I. Fuser and O. Mischiati. Florence: Le Monnier, 1968.

Charles Guillet, Giovanni (de) Macque, Carolus Luyton: Werken voor orgel of voor vier speeltuigen. Edited by J. Watelet. Monumenta Musicae Belgicae, vol. 4. Berchem-Antwerp: De Ring, 1938.

Gussago, Cesario. *Sonate a quattro, sei et otto.* Venice, 1608.

Jacobean Consort Music. 2d rev. ed. Edited by Thurston Dart and William Coates. Musica Britannica, vol. 9. London: Stainer and Bell, 1962.

A. van den Kerckhoven: Werken voor orgel. Edited by Jos. Watelet. Monumenta Musicae Belgicae, vol. 2. Berchem-Antwerp: De Ring, 1933.

Lappi, Pietro. *Canzoni da suonare . . . libro primo*. Venice, 1619.

Lautenspieler des XVI. Jahrhunderts. Edited by Oscar Chilesotti. Leipzig: Breitkopf und Härtel, [1891].

Leighton, William. *The Tears or Lamentations of a Sorrowful Soul*. Edited by Cecile Hill. Early English Church Music, vol. 11. London: Stainer and Bell, 1970.

Claude le Jeune: Trois fantaisies instrumentales. Edited by J. Bonfils. Orgue et Liturgie, vol. 39. Paris: Schola Cantorum, 1956.

Liber fratrum cruciferorum Leodiensium. Edited by A. Guilmant and A. Pirro. Archives des Maîtres de l'Orgue, vol. 10. Paris: Durand, 1909.

John Lugge: Three Voluntaries for Double Organ. Edited by Susi Jeans and John Steele. London: Novello, 1956.

Les Maîtres français de l'orgue, vol. 2. Edited by Felix Raugel. Paris: Schola Cantorum, 1952.

Clement Matchett's Virginal Book. Edited by Thurston Dart. London: Stainer and Bell, [1957].

Mediaeval Carols. Edited by John Stevens. Musica Britannica, vol. 4. London: Stainer and Bell, 1952.

Tarquinio Merula: Composizioni per organo e cembalo. Edited by Alan Curtis. Brescia: L'Organo; Kassel: Bärenreiter, 1961.

Merulo: Toccate per organo. Edited by Sandro Dalla Libera. Milan: Ricordi, 1959.

Tutte le opere di Claudio Monteverdi. Edited by G. Francisco Malipiero. Vol. 14. Bologna: E. Venturi, 1932.

Thomas Morley. *The First Book of Consort Lessons*. Reconstructed and edited by Sidney Beck. New York: Peters, 1959.

Thomas Morley: Keyboard Works. Edited by Thurston Dart. 2 vols. London: Stainer and Bell, 1959.

Music at the Court of Henry VIII. 2d rev. ed. Edited by John Stevens. Musica Britannica, vol. 18. London: Stainer and Bell, 1969.

The First Part of the Musick's Hand-Maid, Published by John Playford. London: Stainer and Bell, 1969.

Nine Fantasias in Four Parts by Byrd, Bull, Ferrabosco, Jenkins and Ives. Edited by Sidney Beck. New York: New York Public Library, 1947.

Le Opere complete da Giovanni Pierluigi Palestrina. Edited by Raffaele Casimiri. Vol. 9. Rome: Fratelli Scalera, 1940.

Parthenia. Edited by Thurston Dart. London: Stainer and Bell, 1960.

Parthenia In-Violata. Edited by Thurston Dart. New York: Peters, [1961].

Thomas Robinson. *The Schoole of Musicke*. Edited by David Lumsden. Paris: Editions du Centre National de la Recherche Scientifique, 1971.

Four Hundred Songs and Dances from the Stuart Masque. Edited by Andrew J. Sabol. Providence, R. I.: Brown University Press, 1978.

Samuel Scheidt: Werke. Vol. 2/3. Edited by Gottlieb Harms. Hamburg: Ugrino, 1928.

Seven Virginal Pieces (from BM Add. 30486). Edited by Frank Dawes. London: Schott, 1951.

Six Seventeenth-Century Carols from the Netherlands. Edited by Frits Noske. Oxford: Oxford University Press, 1965.

J. P. Sweelinck: The Instrumental Works. Edited by Gustav Leonhardt, Alfons Annegarn and Frits Noske. Opera Omnia, vol. 1/1-3. Amsterdam: Vereniging voor Nederlandse Muziekgeschiedenis, 1968.

J. P. Sweelinck: Werken voor orgel en clavecimbel. 2d rev. ed. Edited by Max Seiffert. Amsterdam: G. Alsbach, 1943.

Jan Pzn. Sweelinck: Werken voor orgel of clavecimbel uit het "Celler" Klavierbuch 1622." Edited by Jost Harro Schmidt. Exempla Musica Neerlandica, vol. 2. Amsterdam: Vereniging voor Nederlandse Muziekgeschiedenis, 1965.

Thomas Tallis. Tudor Church Music, vol. 6. Edited by P. C. Buck et al. London: Oxford University Press, 1928.

Thomas Tallis: Complete Keyboard Works. Edited by Denis Stevens. New York: Peters, 1953.

John Taverner. Tudor Church Music, vol. 1. Edited by P. C. Buck et al. London: Oxford University Press, 1923.

Ten Pieces by Hugh Aston and Others. Edited by Frank Dawes. London: Schott, 1951.

Tisdale's Virginal Book. Edited by Alan Brown. London: Stainer and Bell, 1966.

Thomas Tomkins: Keyboard Music. 2d rev. ed. Edited by Stephen D. Tuttle. Musica Britannica, vol. 5. London: Stainer and Bell, 1964.

Pieces from the Tomkins Manuscript. Edited by Frank Dawes. London: Schott, 1951.

Christopher Tye: The Instrumental Music. Edited by Robert Weidner. New Haven: A-R Editions, 1967.

Oeuvres de Nicolas Vallet pour luth seul. Edited by André Souris. Paris: Centre National de la Recherche Scientifique, 1970.

Robert White: The Instrumental Music. Edited by Irwin Spector. Madison: A-R Editions, 1972.

Woltz, Johann. *Nova musices organicae tabulatura.* Basel, 1617.

Yonge, Nicholas. *Musica transalpina.* London, 1588.

II. Books and Articles

Adams, Robert Lee. "The Development of a Keyboard Idiom in England during the English Renaissance." 3 vols. Ph.D. dissertation, Washington University, 1960.

Apel, Willi. *The History of Keyboard Music to 1700.* Translated and revised by Hans Tischler. Bloomington: Indiana University Press, 1972.

Arnold, Denis. "Guami." *Die Musik in Geschichte und Gegenwart.*

Babb, Lawrence. *The Elizabethan Malady: A Study of Melancholia in English Literature from 1550 to 1642.* East Lansing: Michigan State College Press, 1951.

Bacon Francis, *Sylva Sylvarum: or a Natural Historie in Ten Centuries.* London, 1627.

Barbour, J. Murray. *Tuning and Temperament: A Historical Survey.* 2d ed. East Lansing: Michigan State College Press, 1953.

Birch, Thomas. The Life of Henry Prince of Wales. London, 1760.

Borren, Charles van de. "Le Livre de clavier de Vincentus de la Faille (1625)." In *Mélanges de musicologie offerts à M. Lionel de Laurencie.* Paris, 1933.

──────. *Les Origines de la musique de clavier en Angleterre.* Brussels: Groenveldt, 1912.

Braun, Werner. *Britannia Abundans.* Tutzing: Schneider, 1977.

Breig, Werner. "Die Lübbenauer Tabulaturen Lynar A1 und A2." *Archiv für Musikwissenschaft* 25 (1968), pp. 96–117 and 223–36.

Brown, Howard Mayer. *Instrumental Music Printed before 1600.* Cambridge, Mass.: Harvard University Press, 1965.

Bryden, John R., and Hughes, David G. *An Index of Gregorian Chant.* 2 vols. Cambridge, Mass.: Harvard University Press, 1969.

Burney, Charles. *A General History of Music from the Earliest Ages to the Present Period.* Vol. 3. 1789. Reprint. New York: Dover, 1935.

Butler, Charles, *The Principles of Musik in Singing and Setting.* London, 1636.

Butler, Gregory. "Music and Rhetoric in Early Seventeenth-Century English Sources." *The Musical Quarterly* 66 (1980), pp. 53–64.

Caldwell, John. *English Keyboard Music before the Nineteenth Century.* Oxford: Basil Blackwell, 1973.

————. "Keyboard Plainsong Settings in England, 1500–1660." *Musica Disciplina* 19 (1965), pp. 129–54.

————. "The Organ in the British Isles until 1600." *The Organ Yearbook* 2 (1971), pp. 156–63.

Caus, Salomon de. *Institution harmonique.* 1615. Facsimile. New York: Broude, 1969.

————. *Les Raisons des forces mouvantes.* 1615. Facsimile. Amsterdam: Fritz Knuf, 1973.

Chappell, Paul. *A Portrait of John Bull.* Hereford: Hereford Cathedral, 1970.

Chappell, William. *Old English Popular Music.* New edition by H. E. Wooldridge. 2 vols. 1893. Reprint (2 vols. in 1). New York: J. Brussel, [1961].

————. *Popular Music of the Olden Time.* 2 vols. [1855–59]. Reprint with new introduction by Fredrick W. Sternfeld. New York: Dover, 1965.

Cleland, James. *The Institution of a Young Noble Man.* 1607. Facsimile. New York: Scholars' Facsimiles and Reprints, 1948.

Cole, Elizabeth. "L'Anthologie de madrigaux et de musique instrumentale pour ensembles de Francis Tregian." In *La musique instrumentale dans la Renaissance,* edited by Jean Jacquot. Paris: Editions du Centre National de la Recherche Scientifique, 1955.

————. "In Search of Francis Tregian." *Music and Letters* 33 (1952), pp. 28–32.

————. "Seven Problems of the Fitzwilliam Virginal Book." *Proceedings of the Royal Music Association* 79 (1952–53), pp. 51–64.

Crevel, M. van. Introductions to *Missa sub tuum praesidium* and *Missa Maria zart.* Jacobus Obrecht: Opera Omnia, vols. 1/6 and 7. Amsterdam: Vereniging voor Nederlandse Muziekgeschiedenis, 1959 and 1964.

Cummings, W. H. *God Save the King.* London, 1902.

Cunningham, Walker. *The Keyboard Music of John Bull.* Ph.D. dissertation, University of California at Berkeley, 1981. Ann Arbor: University Microfilms.

Curtis, Alan. "Jan Reinken and a Dutch Source for Sweelinck's Keyboard Works." *Tijdschrift van de Vereniging voor Nederlandse Muziekgeschiedenis* 20 (1964–65), pp. 45–51.

————. *Sweelinck's Keyboard Music.* Leiden: At the University Press, London: Oxford University Press, 1969.

Dalton, James. Review of *John Bull: Keyboard Music I. Music and Letters* 41 (1960), pp. 389–91.

Dart, Thurston. "John Bull." *Die Musik in Geschichte und Gegenwart.*

————. "John Bull's Chapel." *Music and Letters* 40 (1959), pp. 279–82.

————. "An Early Seventeenth-Century Book of English Organ Music for the Roman Rite." *Music and Letters* 52 (1961), pp. 27–38.

————. "English Music and Musicians in 17th-Century Holland." In *Kongress-Bericht, Internationale Gesellschaft für Musikwissenschaft, Utrecht 1952.* Amsterdam: Vereniging voor Nederlandse Muziekgeschiedenis, 1953.

————. "A Letter of Recommendation Written for John Bull in 1617." *Revue Belge de Musicologie* 17 (1963), pp. 121–24.

————. "New Sources of Virginal Music." *Music and Letters* 35 (1954), pp. 93–106.

————. "The Organ-Book of the Crutched Friars of Liège." *Revue belge de musicologie* 17 (1963), pp. 21–28.

————. "Purcell and Bull." *Musical Times* 104 (1963), pp. 30–31.

————. "Search for the Real John Bull." *New York Times,* 1 November 1959, sec. 2, p. 1.

————. "Sweelinck's 'Fantasia on a theme used by John Bull'." *Tijdschrift van de Vereniging voor Nederlandse Muziekgeschiedenis* 18 (1959), pp. 167–69.

————. "An Unknown Letter from Dr. John Bull." *Acta Musicologica* 32 (1960), pp. 175–77.

Dart, Thurston, and Schofield, Betram. "Tregian's Anthology." *Music and Letters* 32 (1951), pp. 205–16.

Dickinson, A. E. F. "A Forgotten Collection: A Survey of the Weckmann Books." *Music Review* 17 (1956), pp. 97–109.

————. "The Lübbenau Keyboard Books: A Further Note on Faceless Features." *Music Review* 27 (1966), pp. 270–86.

Dodd, Gordon. "Coperario or Bull?" *Chelys* 1 (1969), p. 41.

Duyse, Florimond van. *Het oude Nederlandse lied.* 3 vols. s'Gravenhage: Nijhoff, 1903–8.

Edwards, Allen. *Flawed Words and Stubborn Sounds: A Conversation with Elliot Carter.* New York: Norton, 1971.

Eitner, Robert. *Quellen-Lexikon.* Vol. 10. Leipzig: Breitkopf und Härtel, 1904.

Elders, Willem. "Humanism and Early-Renaissance Music: A Study of the Ceremonial Music by Ciconia and Dufay." *Tijdschrift van de Vereniging voor Nederlandse Muziekgeschiedenis* 27 (1977), pp. 65–101.

Emerson, John. "Manuscripts of the U.C.B. Music Library: MS 798, The Folario Massbook." *Cum notis variorum,* no. 13 (1977), p. 7.

Fortune, Nigel, "Giustiniani on Instruments." *Galpin Society Journal* 5 (1952), pp. 48–53.

Gerberg, Ernst Ludwig. *Historisch-biographisches Lexikon der Tonkünstler.* Vol. 1. Leipzig: Breitkopf, 1790.

————. *Neues historisch-biographisches Lexikon der Tonkünstler.* Vol. 1. Leipzig: A. Kühnel, 1813.

Gevers, Hilda F. "A Manuscript of Dance Music from Seventeenth-Century England." *Bulletin of the New York Public Library* 80 (1977), pp. 503–52.

Glyn, Margaret H. *About Elizabethan Virginal Music and Its Composers.* 2d ed. London: W. Reeves, 1934.

Godt, Irving. *Guillaume Costeley: Life and Works.* Ph.D. dissertation, New York University, 1969. Ann Arbor: University Microfilms.

Gombosi, Otto. "Stephen Foster and 'Gregory Walker'." *Musical Quarterly* 30 (1944), pp. 133–46.

Green Mary Anne Everett. *Elizabeth, Electress Palatine and Queen of Bohemia.* Revised edition by S. C. Lomas. London: Methuen, 1909.

Grusnick, Bruno. "Die Dübensammlung: Ein Versuch ihrer chronologischen Ordnung." *Svensk tidskrift for musikforskning* 48 (1966), pp. 177–86.

Gurlitt, Wilibald. *Michael Praetorius.* 1915. Reprint. Hildesheim: G. Olms, 1968.

Gustafson, Bruce. *French Harpsichord Music of the Seventeenth Century.* 3 vols. Ann Arbor: UMI Research Press, 1979.

Hawkins, Sir John. *A General History of the Science and Practice of Music.* 1776. Reprint of 1875 edition, edited by Othmar Wesseley (5 vols. in 2). Graz: Akademische Druck- und Verlagsanstalt, 1969.

Henry, Leigh. *John Bull.* London: H. Joseph, 1937.

Historical Manuscripts Commission. *Report of the Marquess of Downshire.* Vol. 4. London: H. M. Stationary Office, 1940.

Hoppe, H. R. "John Bull in the Archduke Albert's Service." *Music and Letters* 35 (1954), pp. 114–15.

Hubbard, Frank. *Three Centuries of Harpsichord Making.* Cambridge, Mass.: Harvard University Press, 1965.

Hughes-Hughes, Augustus. *Catalogue of Manuscript Music in the British Museum.* 3 vols. London: Trustees of the British Museum, 1906–9.

Huntley, H. E. *The Divine Proportion: A Study in Mathematical Beauty.* New York: Dover, 1970.

Hymn-Melodies for the Whole Year from the Sarum Antiphonal and Other English Sources. 3d ed. London: The Plainsong and Mediaeval Music Society, 1914.

Jacquot, Jean. "Sur quelques formes de la musique de clavier élisabéthaine (d'après des oeuvres inédites de John Bull)." In *La musique instrumentale dans la Renaissance,* edited by Jean Jacquot. Paris: Editions du Centre National de la Recherche Scientifique, 1955.

Jeans, Susi. "John Bull." *Grove's Dictionary of Music and Musicians.* 6th ed.

Kastner, Santiago. "Parallels and Discrepancies between English and Spanish Keyboard Music of the 16th and 17th Century." *Anuario musical* 7 (1952), pp. 77–115.

Kelton, Raymond Harrison. *Christ Church Music Ms. no. 89: A Seventeenth-Century Organ Book.* 2 vols. Ph.D. dissertation, Boston University Graduate School, 1974. Ann Arbor: University Microfilms.

Key, Donald Rochester. *Two Manuscripts of Instrumental Ensemble Music from the Elizabethan Period.* Ph.D. dissertation, Boston University Graduate School, 1960. Ann Arbor: University Microfilms.

King, Alec Hyatt. "Fragments of Early Printed Music in the Bagford Collection." *Music and Letters* 40 (1959), pp. 269–73.

————. *Some British Collectors of Music, c. 1600–1960.* Cambridge: At the University Press, 1963.

Kirkendale, Ursula. "The Source for Bach's *Musical Offering:* The *Institutio Oratoria* of Quintilian." *Journal of the American Musicological Society* 33 (1980), pp. 88–141.

Kirkendale, Warren. *L'Aria di fiorenza, id est, Il ballo del granduca.* Florence: Olschki, 1972.

————. "Ciceronians versus Aristotelians on the Ricercar as *Exordium* from Bembo to Bach." *Journal of the American Musicological Society* 32 (1979), pp. 1–44.

Kitchiner, William. *The Loyal and National Songs of England.* London, 1823.

Klabansky, Raymond; Panofsky, Erwin; and Saxle, Fritz. *Saturn and Melancholy.* London: Nelson, 1964.

Knight, A. H. J. *Heinrich Julius, Duke of Brunswick.* Oxford: Basil Blackwell, 1948.

Le Huray, Peter. *Music and the Reformation in England 1549–1660.* New York: Oxford University Press, 1967.

Lenaerts, René Bernard. "Messaus." *Die Musik in Geschichte und Gegenwart.*

Lendvai, Ernö. *Bartók and Kodály.* 3 vols. Rev. ed. Budapest: Institute for Culture, 1979.

————. *Béla Bartók: An Analysis of His Music.* London: Kahn and Averill, 1971.

Linley, Mark. "Instructions for the Clavier Diversely Tempered." *Early Music* 5 (1977), pp. 18–23.

Lowinsky, Edward. "Echoes of Willaert's Chromatic 'Duo' in Sixteenth- and Seventeenth-Century Compositions." In *Studies in Music History: Essays for Oliver Strunk,* edited by Harold Powers. Princeton: Princeton University Press, 1968.

————. "English Organ Music of the Renaissance." *Musical Quarterly* 39 (1953), pp. 373–95 and 528–53.

Maas, Martha. *Seventeenth-Century English Keyboard Music: A Study of Manuscripts Rés. 1185, 1187 and 1186 bis of the Paris Conservatory Library.* Ph.D. dissertation, Yale University, 1968. Ann Arbor: University Microfilms.

Marpurg, Friedrich Wilhelm. *Historisch-kritische Beyträge zur Aufnahme der Musik.* Vol. 4. Berlin, 1758.

Mattheson, Johann. "Beytrag zu des Hrn. Professor Delrichs historischen Nachricht von den academischen Würden in der Musik." In *Beitrag zu die Hamburgischen Nachrichten aus dem Reiche der Gelehrsamkeit.* Hamburg, 1759–63.

Meer, J. H. van der. "The Keyboard Works in the Vienna Bull Manuscript." *Tijdschrift van de Vereniging voor Nederlandse Muziekgeschiedenis* 18 (1957), pp. 72–105.

Mellers, Wilfred. "John Bull and English Keyboard Music." *Musical Quarterly* 40 (1954), pp. 364–83 and 548–71.

Mersenne, Marin. *Correspondance du P. Marin Mersenne.* Vol. 1, edited by Carnelis de Waard. Paris: G. Beanchesne, 1932.

————, *Harmonie universelle.* 1636. Facsimile. Paris: Editions du Centre National de la Recherche Scientifique, 1963.

Miller, Hugh. "John Bull's Organ Works." *Music and Letters* 28 (1947), pp. 25–35.

————. "Sixteenth-Century English Faburden Compositions for Keyboard." *Musical Quarterly* 26 (1940), pp. 50–64.

Morley, Thomas. *A Plain and Easy Introduction to Practical Music.* Edited by R. Alec Harman. London: J. M. Dent, 1952.

Naylor, E. W. *An Elizabethan Virginal Book.* London: J. M. Dent, 1905.

Neighbour, Oliver. *The Consort and Keyboard Music of William Byrd.* London: Faber; Berkeley and Los Angeles: University of California Press, 1978.

————. "New Music: John Bull." *Musical Times* 104 (1963), p. 647.

Nichols, John. *The Progresses, Processions, and Magnificent Festivities of King James the First.* Vol. 2. London, 1828.

Niessen, W. "Das Liederbuch des Studenten Clodius." *Vierteljahresschrift für Musikwissenschaft* 8 (1891), pp. 656–57.

Noske, Frits. "Een apocrief en een dubieus werk van Sweelinck." *Mededelingenblad van de Vereniging voor Nederlandse Muziekgeschiedenis* 20 (1966), pp. 27–30.

————. "John Bull's Dutch Carol." *Music and Letters* 44 (1963), pp. 326–33.

————. Review of *Sweelinck: Werken voor orgel of clavecimbel. Music Library Association Notes* 24 (1967), pp. 134–35.

Ornithoparcus, Andreas. *Andreas Ornithoparcus his Micrologus, or Introduction: Containing the Art of Singing.* Translated by John Dowland. London, 1609.

Palisca, Claude. "*Ut oratoria musica*: The Rhetorical Basis of Musical Mannerism." In *The Meaning of Mannerism,* edited by Franklin W. Robinson and Stephen G. Nichols, Jr. Hanover, N. H.: University Press of New England, 1972.

Peacham, Henry. *Garden of Eloquence.* Facsimile. Edited by William Crane. Gainesville, Fla.: Scholars' Facsimiles and Reprints, 1954.

Pereyra, M.-L. "Les Livres de virginal de la Bibliothèque du Conservatoire." *Revue de musicologie* 10 (1926), pp. 204–9; 11 (1927), pp. 36–39, 205–13; 12 (1928), pp. 235–42; 13 (1929), pp. 32–39; 15 (1931), pp. 22–32; 16 (1932), pp. 86–90; 17 (1933), pp. 24–27.

Persons, Jerry C. "The Sambrooke Book: Drexel 4302." M.Mus. thesis, Wichita State University, 1969.

Persoons, Guido. "John Bull, organist te Antwerpen, 1614–1628." *Musica Sacra "Sancte Sancte"* 64 (1963), pp. 40–43.

————. "De Organisten van de O. L. Vrouwenkerk te Antwerpen van de Beeldenstorm tot de dood van John Bull (1566–1628)." Dissertation, Louvain, 1959.

Philipps, G. A. "Crown Musical Patronage from Elizabeth I to Charles I." *Music and Letters* 58 (1977), pp. 29–42.

Poulton, Diana. *John Dowland: His Life and Works.* Berkeley and Los Angeles: University of California Press, 1972.

————. "Notes on the Spanish Pavan." *Lute Society Journal* 3 (1961), pp. 5–16.

Puttenham, George. *The Arte of English Poesie.* 1589. Reprint. Edited by Edward Arber. London, 1869.

Reese, Gustave. *Music in the Renaissance.* Rev. ed. New York: Norton, 1959.

Riedel, Friedrich Wilhelm. *Quellenkundliche Beiträge zur Geschichte der Musik für Tasteninstrumente in der zweiten Hälfte des 17. Jahrhunderts.* Kassel: Bärenreiter, 1960.

Rimbault, Edward F., ed. *The Old Cheque-Book.* 1872. Reprint. New York: Da Capo, 1966.

Ruhnke, Martin. *Beiträge zu einer Geschichte der deutschen Hofmusikkollegen im 16. Jahrhundert.* Berlin: Merseburger, 1963.

Schierning, Lydia. *Die Ueberlieferung der deutschen Orgel- und Klaviermusik aus der ersten Hälfte des 17. Jahrhunderts.* Kassel: Bärenreiter, 1961.

Schlager, Karlheinz, ed. *Alleluia-Melodien I.* Monumenta Monodica Medii Aevi, vol. 7. Kassel: Bärenreiter, 1968.

Schmidt, Jost Harro, "Eine unbenkannte Quelle zur Klaviermusik des 17. Jahrhunderts." *Archiv für Musikwissenschaft* 22 (1965), pp. 1–11.

Seiffert, Max. *Die Geschichte der Klaviermusik.* 2d ed. Leipzig: Breitkopf und Härtel, 1899.

Shannon, John. *Organ Literature of the Seventeenth Century.* Raleigh: Sunbury, 1978.

Silbiger, Alexander. "The Roman Frescobaldi Tradition." *Journal of the American Musicological Society* 33 (1980), pp. 42–87.

Simpson, Claude M. *The British Broadside Ballad and Its Music.* New Brunswick, N.J.: Rutgers University Press, 1966.

Squire, Barclay. "John Bull." *Dictionary of National Biography.*

Stäblein, Bruno, ed. *Hymnen (I).* Monumenta Monodica Medii Aevi, vol. 1. Kassel: Bärenreiter, 1956.

Steele, John. "English Organs and Organ Music from 1500 to 1650." Ph.D. dissertation, Cambridge University, 1959.

Sternfeld, Frederick W. *Music in Shakespearean Tragedy.* London: Routledge and Kegan Paul, 1963.

Stevens, Denis. "Musicological Musings." *Musical Times* 101 (1960), pp. 554–55.

_____. "Les Sources de *l'In nomine.*" In *La Musique instrumentale dans la Renaissance,* edited by Jean Jacquot. Paris: Editions du Centre National de la Recherche Scientifique, 1955.

_____. "Thomas Preston." *Die Musik in Geschichte und Gegenwart.*

Straeten, Edmond van der. *La Musique aux Pays-Bas avant le XIXe siècle.* 8 vols. 1867–88. Reprint. New York: Dover, 1969.

Tokunaga, Takao. "A Survey of Paris Conservatoire Rés. 1185: A Data on its Peculiarities and Its Contents." *Journal of Japanese Musicological Society* 24 (1978), pp. 27–39.

Tuttle, Stephen Davidson. "William Byrd: A Study of the History of English Keyboard Music to 1623." Ph.D. dissertation, Harvard University, 1941.

Walker, Ernest. "An Oxford Book of Fancies." *Musical Antiquary* 3 (1912), pp. 70–73.

Walther, Johann Gottfried. *Musicalisches Lexikon oder musicalisches Bibliothec.* Leipzig, 1732.

Ward, John. *The Lives of the Professors of Gresham College.* London, 1740.

Ward, John M. "Apropos 'The British Broadside Ballad and Its Music'." *Journal of the American Musicological Society* 20 (1967), pp. 28–86.

_____. "Les Sources de la musique pour clavier en Angleterre." In *La Musique instrumentale dans la Renaissance,* edited by Jean Jacquot. Paris: Editions du Centre National de la Recherche Scientifique, 1955.

Webster, J. H. Douglas. "Golden-Mean Form in Music." *Music and Letters* 31 (1950), pp. 238–48.

Wilson, Thomas. *The Arte of Rhetorique.* 1553. Facsimile. Gainesville, Fla.: Scholars' Facsimiles and Reprints, 1962.

———. *The Rule of Reason, Conteinying the Arte of Logique by Thomas Wilson.* Edited by Richard S. Sprague. Northridge, Ca.: San Fernando Valley State College, 1972.

Winogron, Blanche. Review of *John Bull: Keyboard Music I. Music Library Association Notes* 2d ser., 18 (1961), pp. 642–43.

Wood, Anthony à. *Athenae Oxoniensis.* London, 1691.

———. *Historia et antiquitates Universitatis Oxoniensis.* London, 1674.

Wythorne, Thomas. *The Autobiography of Thomas Wythorne.* Edited by James M. Osborn. Oxford: Clarendon Press, 1961.

Yates, Frances. *The Occult Philosophy in the Elizabethan Age.* London: Routledge and Kegan Paul, 1979.

———. *The Rosicrucian Enlightenment.* London: Routledge and Kegan Paul, 1972; Boulder: Shambhala, 1978.

Zacher, Gerd. "Frescobaldi und die instrumentale Redekunst." *Musik und Kirche* 45 (1975), pp. 54–64.

General Index

Index of Bull's Keyboard Works
(Including Unauthenticated Pieces)